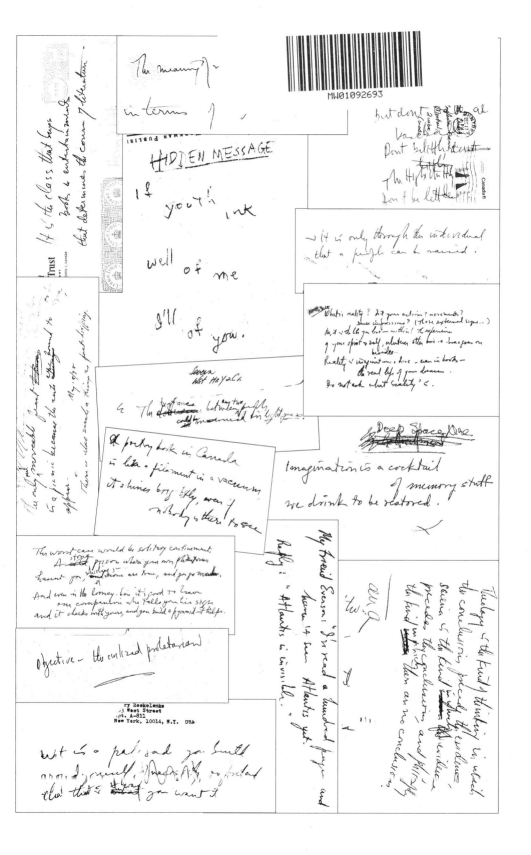

The meaning?—
in terms?

but don't... at
Var...
Don't belittle the doubt
The light...
Don't belittle...

HIDDEN MESSAGE

If
you'll ink
well of me
I'll of you.

~ It is only through the individual
that a puzzle can be raised.

What is reality? Is it your actions? movements?
Since impressions? (those external signs...)
No, it is the you lived — within! The experience
of your spirit & self, whatever else may happen on
the outside.
Reality & imagination — alive — even in books —
the real life of your dreams.
Do not ask what 'reality' is.

Seven
West Hoyaca

← The distance between any two ...
cold ... measured in light years ...

Deep Space Nine

A poetry book in Canada
is like a filament in a vacuum
it shines brightly, even if
nobody is there to see

Imagination is a cocktail
of memory stuff
we drink to be restored.

The worst case would be solitary confinement.
A ... prison where your own phantoms
haunt you, ... are true, and you go mad.
And even in the looney-bin it's good to have
one companion who tells you his signs
and it checks with yours, and you build a pyramid of helps.

My friend Eversa: "I've read a hundred pages and
know it's been Atlantis yet."
Reply: "Atlantis is invisible."

Objective — the civilized proletarian

ry Roskolenko
93 West Street
pt. A-811
New York, 10014, N.Y. USA

What is a palisade you build
around yourself, ... or palace
that that is ... you want ...

Theology is the kind of thinking in which
the conclusion precedes the evidence,
Science is the kind of thinking in which
precedes the conclusion, and philosophy
the kind in which ... then are no conclusions.

"Poetry activist and polemicist, anthologist and publisher, Louis Dudek inspired a generation of Canadian poets to explore the possibilities of the modernist form."

Douglas Barbour, *The Globe and Mail,* Monday March 26, 2001

Making it, we do not fret
whether the man-made heaven is the real heaven;

forget, for once, that the heaven we make
is all the heaven we'll ever get.

from the "Jeux & Divertissements" section, *Collected Poetry*

E T E R N A L
CONVERSATIONS

remembering
Louis Dudek

EDITED BY

Aileen Collins

Michael Gnarowski

Sonja A. Skarstedt

LIVRES
DC
BOOKS

Eternal Conversations: Remembering Louis Dudek
© 2003 All Contributing Authors.

Photographs © Bernhard Beutler, Aileen Collins, Stephanie Zuperko Dudek, Betty Gustafson, Geof Isherwood, Lionel Kearns, Stephen Morrissey, Sonja Skarstedt. Photograph ("Portrait of Louis Dudek: 1950") on the title page courtesy of Stephanie Zuperko Dudek. Laurence Hutchman's "Interview With Louis Dudek" appeared in *The River Review* No. 1 (University of Maine, 1995). Endpapers courtesy of Aileen Collins, who selected and assisted in the composition of two montages of notes Louis Dudek wrote on envelopes and other miscellaneous scraps throughout his life. These "scribblings" served as a rich source for Dudek's poems, essays and epigrams.

DC Books   950 rue Decarie, Box 662   Montreal, Quebec H4L 4V9

Editorial Board: Aileen Collins, Michael Gnarowski, Sonja A. Skarstedt.
Cover design and layout by Geof Isherwood.
Book designed and typeset by *Sasigraphix*: main text in 10-pt ITC Garamond, with titles in 14-pt ITC Garamond and 14-pt Ocean Sans.
Printed in Canada by AGMV Marquis.

DC Books acknowledges the support of the Canada Council for the Arts and SODEC for our publishing program.

0-919688-75-6 paperback   0-919688-77-2 bound

Dépôt légal, Bibliothèque Nationale du Québec and The National Library of Canada, third trimester, 2003.

First Printing.

National Library of Canada Cataloguing in Publication

Eternal conversations : remembering Louis Dudek / Michael Gnarowski ... [et al.].

Includes bibliographical references.
ISBN 0-919688-77-2 (bound).--ISBN 0-919688-75-6 (pbk.)

1. Dudek, Louis, 1918-2001. I. Dudek, Louis, 1918-2001. II. Gnarowski, Michael, 1934-

PS8507.U43Z64 2003   C811'.54   C2003-905146-3

ETERNAL
CONVERSATIONS

remembering
Louis Dudek

To see it falling past my eyes
        from now into the non-existent,
a world that I have loved, and had,
        beyond my power to hold it

from "To the Reader", *Zembla's Rocks*

Photo by SAS

Gregory & Louis Dudek with Bernhard Beutler, on Louis' 80th birthday, Montreal, February 1998.

Contents

Photo Courtesy of Betty Gustafson

Gathering of the Canada Council-sponsored Poets' Conference,
May 1964, Stanley House, Gaspé. Front row: Earle Birney,
Michael Gnarowski, John Glassco, Louis Dudek, Ralph Gustafson,
Fred Cogswell & F.R. Scott. Back row: George Whalley, Al Purdy,
D.G. Jones. Seated: A.J.M. Smith.

MICHAEL GNAROWSKI

**Michael Gnarowski
& Louis Dudek,
circa 1960.**

Introduction As History

THIS GATHERING OF VOICES, intended as a more permanent and more widely held record of the deeply felt emotions that found expression at the service for Louis Dudek on March 26th, 2001, now presents itself as a memorial and a tribute to an individual whose singularly creative life moved all of us who speak here to better and higher things. The genesis of this collection lies with an idea voiced at the service by Peter Van Toorn and readily embraced by many others on that sad day. The carrying forward of the idea, for reasons of efficiency and logistics, fell to a small group that met twice a month for some two years, and was given the task by the publisher to assemble a fitting and manageable manuscript from a large number of poems and recollections that were sent in by friends, colleagues, past students, literary associates, artists and educators—all combining to offer generous testimony to a remarkable poet and friend. The not inconsiderable task of corresponding with potential contributors about the project, and then the 'dailiness' of pulling things together, sorting through photographs, and making sense of the sum total of some very disparate material, fell to Sonja Skarstedt and her editorial skills, aided by Geof Isherwood who lent his graphic sense to the project, and brought many an aging and faded photograph back to life. Others—Steve Luxton, John Asfour—drifted in and out of the picture, called upon to offer advice and expertise as the need arose. Aileen Collins not only worked as an active member of the editorial group putting the project together, but was an ever-present source of detail and information on Louis Dudek's life.

HOW THE NEWS WAS BROUGHT FROM MONTREAL TO LONDON

The sad news came to me in the middle of the night in London, and I must say that it came as a terrible surprise. I had known that Louis had had serious health problems, and even though he looked frail when I saw him at the Royal Victoria Hospital a few days before my departure for England, I had been buoyed up by the liveliness of his eyes and by how we fell so readily into what we privately called our conversation—a 'conversation' which had been ongoing between us for some forty years. Flying back to Canada for what seemed to be an interminable seven and a half hours, my mind went back, sometimes sweepingly, sometimes in detail, over the circumstances of an early association that had become a deep friendship of almost half a century. I had known Louis for forty-nine years and five months.

Our first encounter had, on my part, all the respectful distance that a seventeen year old freshman newly arrived at university could muster, and on Louis' part, and I can still see it, the amused curiosity of a lecturer trying to make sense of a bumbling late arrival arbitrarily assigned to his section of English 100c. I had finally made my way to McGill after a long and tortuous journey from what was then still referred to as the Far East, arriving well into October, very late for the beginning of term. The Registrar's office, and they were the ones who ran our lives in those structured days, worked out my first year course load which included the mandatory English 100, a survey of English literature taught by Professor Ian Duthie, a

Shakespearean scholar and Chairman of the Department who was manifestly less than thrilled to be teaching a mob of restless freshmen (women were also 'freshmen' then!) in the cavernous precincts of Moyse Hall. Since freshmen—then as now—registered different levels of illiteracy, we were assigned to sections of English 100c to undergo remedial torture, and to be trained in the fine skills of composition and essay writing. Thus, truly by the grace of God and that enlightened instrument of his will, the Registrar's office, I found myself explaining to Louis why I was almost two months late in arriving in his classroom. He was intrigued by my explanation and the tale of my long journey, particularly so, I would like to believe now, since I had come from the land the ideograms, poetry and flavour of which had so definitively entered the soul of Ezra Pound. The best, however was yet to be.

From the outset I was completely overcome by Louis' teaching. Drilled in the authoritarian environment of a Catholic boarding school, I found his friendly easy-going ways in the classroom, his encouragement of us to express our opinions, and his openness to what we had to say, refreshing beyond belief. While Professor Duthie lectured us with ill-concealed contempt for our puny intellectual attainments, Louis brought the best out in us. He listened to us, marked our scratchy essays and, best of all, slipped into a discussion of contemporary poetry and Canadian writing whenever an opportunity presented itself. In late March of 1952 he let us in on a secret. He distributed a mimeographed one-page flyer announcing the forthcoming titles of the soon to be launched Contact Press. I was totally impressed. A real live poet was among us, talking to us about plans to publish books, treating us as equals!

The next fall marked my sophomore year and, being a student in the B.Sc. programme, I had precious few arts electives. I studied the calendar and found that Dudek was teaching a half course on Canadian poetry. I signed up for it and, more auspicious happenstance, found that the other half was Canadian fiction which was taught by Hugh MacLennan. Now, in retrospect, I realize that this was the all-defining moment for me. Not only did Dudek and MacLennan fling wide the doors of Canadian Literature, but the enjoyment I derived from their teaching meant that my days as a chemist-in-training were definitely numbered. I should note that I had had a bit of exposure to Canadian writing at the tail end of

English 100, the English Literature survey. In that course Professor Duthie brought in Arthur Phelps, professor and something of a poet himself, for a brief stint of four weeks or so to give us a tiny taste of Canadian Literature. Phelps was elderly and cranky, but a believer in the writers of Canada. Canadian Literature was not considered to be serious stuff at McGill then, and it is Dudek, MacLennan and Phelps, aided and abetted by Professor Harold Files, an open-minded and generous-hearted American academic, who were instrumental in pushing the study of Canadian writing onto the curriculum of the English department, a department in a university which could then boast of Stephen Leacock, A.M. Klein, Frank Scott and A.J.M. Smith, and to whose illustrious roll call would soon be added Hugh MacLennan, Irving Layton, Louis Dudek and Leonard Cohen.

In my third year, by now thoroughly captivated by the teaching of Louis and Hugh MacLennan, and with no other offerings in Canadian literature to turn to, I registered for Louis' Great Writings of Europe course and MacLennan's magisterial sweep through the best of English prose. In Louis' course our eyes were opened to what were truly the great writers of the western European tradition: Goethe, Heine, Leopardi, Stendahl, Flaubert, Schiller, the great Russians. In MacLennan's it was a study of finely crafted prose with a special emphasis on the consummate art of the essay, beginning with Francis Bacon and carrying us through to the glorious sprawl of Waugh's *Brideshead Revisited.* And over all of this, in the 'quiet still air of delightful studies', hung the desire to write, and we started to try to write our own poems, taking them to Louis for criticism, reading them at meetings of "LitSoc" (the McGill Literary Society), and sending them to *The McGill Daily* the student paper, or to *Forge,* the campus literary magazine.

Late in l955, Glen Siebrasse, John Lachs and I, all students of Louis', hatched a plan to start our own little mag. Louis listened to us over a plate of delicious Hungarian salami and french bread laid on by John's mother, and offered cautious encouragement. He was just coming off a two-year stint godfathering the little mag *CIV/n,* and was a year and a half away from starting his own little mag *Delta.* We were grateful for his support and launched *Yes* in April of l956, promptly mis-quoting on our cover Molly Bloom's utterance, that epiphany of affirmation and sexual nuance that so suited our mood: "Yes and I said yes I will yes".

Almost instantly we were reproached by a prominent Toronto newspaper reviewer (I believe it was William Arthur Deacon) who berated us for offending against the Joycean ethos. Louis was good to us, sending poems and steering others to our door, but before too long he was chiding us for not going quite the way he wanted us to go. We fought back with a cocky editorial and tried to stand our own ground, continuing to edit *Yes* as we graduated and moved on in our lives. Louis, of course, was busy with his own *Delta,* and while we were no longer students with quite the frequent access to him that we had enjoyed during our undergraduate years, we stayed in touch, meeting occasionally and exchanging poems. I had moved into the world of business, working in the financial district of Montreal just off St. James Street—my office was on St. Nicholas Street in old Montreal, and I took some pleasure in seeing the sign of John Lovell, an important early Canadian publisher, still visible on the opposite wall. Once in a while, when in the vicinity of McGill, I would drop in on Louis' or MacLennan's class and sit happily at the back of the room.

It was during the 1960's though when, having taken time to complete an M.A., I drifted back more firmly into poetry, writing and a new career as a just-appointed lecturer at the Université de Sherbrooke, stepping into a role which had been filled by Ronald Sutherland. I was also enrolled in the doctoral programme at the Université de Montréal, a shift which enabled me to continue with another fine teacher, Thomas Greenwood, afforded me a modest friendship with Hugh Hood and, most importantly, reconnected me with Louis. Newly married and unhappy with the nationalist racism at the Université de Sherbrooke, I had accepted a position at Lakehead College in what is now Thunder Bay (then Port Arthur). But the pull of Montreal continued to work upon me, and no sooner was the term completed in the Spring of 1963, than I packed my young family and headed back to what had imprinted itself upon my sensibility as my literary roots. On the 1st of May, Diana and I went to

**Louis Dudek,
Earle Birney &
Michael Gnarowski,
circa 1964.**

visit Louis on Vendome Avenue. We sat in the living room, Louis playing idly with his guitar, talking about Canadian writing in a way that would become the hallmark of what we came to know as our ongoing eternal conversation. I wanted a copy of *En Mexico* and Louis kindly dug it out. When I proffered the requisite dollar for it, Louis signed the dollar, wrote on it "paid for poems" inscribed the book, and gave the whole lot back to me. The dollar is pasted into that sun-faded copy of the book to this day.

But the larger significance of that visit was that I had come back to Montreal to work on little magazines, and having settled in, I began to see Louis on a fairly regular basis. As I was working in the McGill library, it was a simple matter for us to arrange to have lunch. We would usually find our way to Murray's, then an institution in Montreal located on St. Catherine Street almost opposite Eaton's Department Store, where you could be assured of indifferent food served by elderly waitresses who called you 'dear' and clucked like anguished hens when you turned down one of two desserts that came with the meal: rice pudding or custard. Louis was more accepting of the desserts, although in spite of frequent visits to this eatery he would always ask if the dessert came with the meal. This business of lunches became a mainstay of our friendship, and now in retrospect, it seems to me that what we had was an ongoing process of eternal lunches with eternal conversations. We moved on to what I liked to think was better eating at better restaurants, although Louis stuck with frequenting the Westmount 'branch' of Murray's (which was located on Sherbrooke Street on the corner of Victoria Avenue), mainly because Ron Everson seemed to favour it.

DELTA DAYS—BEER AND KNUCKLES AND OTHER THINGS

Early in 1964 I received a letter from John Glassco telling me that there would be a gathering of poets at what, I believe, had been the Vice Regal fishing lodge on the Baie des Chaleurs, and which had come into the purview of The Canada Council, a benign agency that was underwriting what Ron Everson described (surely with considerable irony since he had not been invited!) as a "gathering of the bards." The assembly has been immortalized in a photograph that appears on page 8 of this book. Louis and I decided to travel in my car, and we were joined almost immediately by Al Purdy. Glen Siebrasse, who could not get away for any length of time, rode with us as far as Quebec City and then had to return to Montreal. I drove my great big blue boat of a Mercury, Louis sat in the passenger seat strumming his guitar (Al remembers, in his memoir *No Other Country,* not a guitar but a mouth organ, and recalls Louis wearing a beret and looking like a giant mosquito, although the reliability of this recollection, as of everything in that book, is doubtful since, in this instance, he is off by six years!). Al and Glen were in the back seat.

It was beautiful weather and Al had seized the opportunity to stock up on beer, being greatly taken with the fact that in Quebec you could get beer in large quart bottles; a delightful practice that was taboo in an Ontario where you had to fill out forms with name and address in Liquor Control (note the word "control") Board outlets when you wanted to purchase alcoholic beverages. To add insult to injury, these outlets were usually located in gloomy premises painted in a bilious mortician's green. Well Al sipped on his beer and got progressively more argumentative and truculent until Louis finally snapped at him "Shut up Al, you're stupid". I was startled by Louis' vehemence. I had never known Louis to be nasty, but clearly Al had caught him at a dyspeptic moment, one in which Louis chóse not to suffer fools gladly. I think that Al's studied 'yokelism' irritated and provoked Louis. Years later he sent me a review that Al had written of Pierre Berton's *Starting Out.* To it Louis attached a poem in which Al is styled a "boondocks intellectual." But to get back to that incident during our trip, an abashed Purdy settled into an injured silence from which he recovered soon enough and we were back on friendly terms again. Our conversation turned to E.J. Pratt who had just died, and Louis suggested that we compose a dirge for "old Ned" which we would then deliver to the assembled 'bards' upon our arrival at Stanley House.

We set to the task, Louis doing double duty with words and music (the tune, Al recalled correctly was "The Bonnie Earl of Moray"). Louis scribbled on the back of a road map as we rehearsed the verses of the newly-composed dirge, singing loudly as a ragged chorus of three until we thought we had it right—more or less. We pulled up to Stanley House that evening and, unloading ourselves, we burst upon the large lounge with much comfortable furniture in which sat, sprawled and reclining various unsuspecting poet types. We delivered ourselves of the dirge in what was obviously a sufficiently stirring rendition so that the startled assembly invited us to make it an encore the next evening which we duly did, and which I have somewhere, captured on my Philips tape recorder for an equally unsuspecting posterity.

Later that summer, Louis and I walked one day after lunch in leisurely fashion on Sherbrooke Street, and on the corner of Sherbrooke and McTavish I broached the possibility of starting a new small press. Louis was still part of Contact Press, although a somewhat disaffected part and, I believe was readily persuaded to try a new venture. This was a time when we were entering upon what I now describe as the literary wars in Montreal, an outbreak of open hostilities between Louis and Irving Layton that had been simmering below the surface for a long time; occasioned initially by a letter that Layton had written to Louis while the latter was still living in New York, accusing Louis of having 'sold out'. It had been Layton at his worst, giving vent in a truculent and radical mood. Later, the affair was patched up after Louis' return to Montreal in 1951, mainly through the good offices of Betty Sutherland. The pair went on to join Ray Souster in founding Contact Press, an interesting collaboration that produced their ground-breaking *Canadian Poems 1850-1952* (1952). This anthology was intended to see Canadian poetry in a new way, and to serve as a challenge to Arthur Smith's *The Book of Canadian Poetry* (1948). This was the anthology that Louis and Arthur Phelps both used in teaching Canadian poetry for a couple of years after its publication. At this point Louis championed the poetry of Souster and Layton, and their uniting between the covers of *Cerberus* (1952) was a significant moment in the all-important beginnings of Contact Press.

That was to change a few years later as Louis watched Layton move off in the search for popularity and a public persona. Louis, always suspicious of commercialism and the publicity that inevitably served it, saw Layton's poetry becoming a creature of the imperatives of commercial publishing, and said so in the reviews (he accused Layton of, among many things, "popular buffoonery") he would write for *The Montreal Star*. A furious Layton lashed back with vitriol and abuse, and soon the lines were drawn. Layton, it should be noted, had attracted to himself a small group of acolytes who were anxious to imitate and serve Layton's cause: Henry Moscovitch, Seymour Mayne and the late K.V. Hertz, come to mind. Louis had his defenders, of course, prominent among whom was a colleague, Brian Robinson, who gave as good as he got, and waded into a battle with Layton that played out in the "Letters to the Editor" section of *The Montreal Star* and *The McGill Daily*. But Robinson was a doughtier campaigner than most of the other protagonists who took up the public cudgels in the Dudek/Layton affair. Robinson not only spoofed Layton in a collection of poems called *Laytonic Love*, but also winged Seymour Mayne, who had just published two slim collections of verse. One of these, *Tiptoeing on the Mount*, appeared (oddly?) as Number 9 in the McGill Poetry Series and was described thusly by Paul Stacey in the "Literary Section" of *The McGill Daily:* "The first half of this slim volume contains 17 spastic poems, the second half is a series of eight navel scrutinies constituting the title poem." Such was the tone of the sniping that characterized what in today's parlance would be described as collateral wounding. The exchanges between Louis and Dudek involved verbal weaponry of a heavier calibre.

Late in December of 1964 I returned to Montreal to be with family for the Christmas holidays. Louis and I had been writing back and forth during the fall term, and a decision had been reached to start a small poetry press. Ron Everson, Colin Haworth, a business partner of Ron's and a fine graphic artist, Louis, Glen Siebrasse and myself gathered for lunch at the Troika, a Russian restaurant on Crescent Street. There we agreed to create a press to be called Delta Canada and to have Louis assume a leadership role in the undertaking. We also decided that Ron's *Wrestle With an Angel* including graphics by Colin Haworth would be our first title, slated to appear early in 1965. It duly appeared, a modest, saddlestitched book which went out to reviewers containing a folded-in note that read:

> Hoping that this book, the first from a
> new publishing venture, merits your
> attention and review.
>
> > Louis Dudek, editor
> > Delta Canada Δ

Colin drew back out of all participation almost immediately after that first meeting, and Ron became an all but sleeping partner in the venture—his contribution being to take us out for roast beef at the Montreal Press Club then located in the now defunct Mount Royal Hotel. He would pick us up in his Cadillac convertible, and, with the top down (weather permitting), we would sail down Metcalfe Street to the Club's entrance. Frank Scott never forgave Ron for this overt display of success—he, Frank, his socialist soul greatly exercised, having told us on many occasions that he could never afford a new car until he was well into his fifties—and just a middle of the road Dodge at that.

Delta Canada began its life in 1965. We used Louis' address on our stationery, and featured his name as a kind of grand, overall editor. This coincided with my own return to eastern Canada on leave from Lakehead College, and deep into work for the Royal Commission on Bilingualism and Biculturalism. We settled in Ottawa, and Neil Compton offered me a course in Canadian Literature at Sir George Williams University, which I accepted gladly since it made it possible for me to come to Montreal every week. We developed a wonderful routine. Louis was doing a kind of bachelor thing in digs on the corner of what was then Dorchester Boulevard and Atwater Avenue. He was writing those poems which became *Atlantis,* and had seemingly graduated to the violin as a new musical interest. Bits and pieces of the *Atlantis* poems were stuck up on his walls, and he would amble around the room, violin in hand, reading parts of the poems out loud, punctuating this procedure with a flourish of the bow on the strings.

On days when we had Delta business, Glen would join us and we would go to the Sun Kuo Min, a Chinese eatery on the corner of Clark Street and Lagauchetière, and each one of us would order his favourite dish. For Glen it was garlic spare ribs and pineapple chicken; for me a large Won Ton soup and some other dish. For Louis it was—unswervingly—an egg foo yung, although I nagged him mercilessly that what he was having was not a true Chinese dish but an omelette. Inevitably when the bill arrived and we did our mathematics in figuring out who owed what, Louis would always complain that I had had the best and largest amount of food and was paying the least. Sun Kuo Min remained a Delta Canada ritual for almost the entire six years that we operated the press. But Delta Canada was not only convivial meals and occasional effort. Louis had become seriously estranged from Contact Press. He felt sidelined, and with Peter Miller having joined Ray Souster in running that press in Toronto, Louis saw his influence wane materially. He had been mightily annoyed when Layton, without much (if any) consultation with Louis and Souster, had given Henry Moscovitch the go-ahead to publish his, *The Serpent Ink* (1956), under the Contact Press imprint. Then, almost ten years later Margaret Atwood's *The Circle Game* (1966), would come up as a source of discord. Louis never favoured its publication and, irony of ironies, it would go on to win the Governor General's Award.

But by then Contact Press was in its last year of existence, and Louis' interest had shifted totally to Delta Canada. Here we sought to define and crystallize our objectives, knowing full well that we were not simply doing the 'little poetry press' thing. Louis, Glen and I were very much aware that a profound change had overtaken Anglophone life in Montreal, and that the city itself was no longer quite the center it had been in the glory days of what should have been, but never was, described as the Anglo Ascendancy. What we sensed (Louis was most resistant to it) was that the center of literary gravity in Canada had shifted to Toronto, and that somehow, our task now was to preserve and maintain the work of those anglophone poets on the Montreal scene whose chances of gaining recognition in Toronto were growing slimmer by the day. One of the things we joked about over our Chinese food was what we termed Layton's defection when he decided to uproot himself and move to York University.

Clearly it could be taken as a kind of bellwether of the decline and retreat of the Anglophone presence in Montreal. Ours was becoming a rear guard action, but we were also deeply concerned with trying to determine where the new poetry was headed. Things seemed to be so rosy. The Canada Council was lavish with its grants—although we didn't get much of this largesse. Actually in an impolitic but principled move we became embroiled in a quarrel with the Council over the right to send more than one participant to a conference/seminar the Council was holding in Montreal. We were told by a Council bureaucrat that only one of us could attend the conference. Louis was deeply angered by this, and we held a quick caucus in the lobby of the then Windsor Hotel and decided to walk out. The anxious bureaucrat called Ottawa and Louis received a late night telephone call from Ottawa telling him that we were all welcome at the conference. It was a Pyrrhic victory, due partly, I like to think, to the diplomatic intervention of Peter Dwyer who seemed to be running the Council but whose real, mysterious and greater claim to fame lay with the fact that, as a member of the British Security Intelligence Service he had helped to sniff out the treasonous activities of Kim Philby and his associates Burgess and MacLean. Dwyer entered our lives one more time, but more about that, later.

After I had accepted an appointment to the faculty at Sir George, and had moved to Montreal, we developed a routine of looking after the business of the press by weekly meetings on Saturdays at Louis' new home at 5 Ingleside Avenue. There we packed books for shipment, discussed newly-received manuscripts, dealt with production problems and helped Glen with accounts. Neither Ron nor Colin ever joined us, simply confirming that Delta Canada was Louis, Glen and myself. We spent a lot of time and energy discussing the needs and the direction that poetry should be taking, with our primary function defining itself almost imperceptibly as that of the only small poetry press in Montreal serving local writers. We were particularly concerned with being open to new and young poets, and came up with the idea of smallish chapbooks to be sold for a dollar. We called these our Buckbook series, and Glen invented an even more modest series of pamphlets to be sold for twenty-five cents which he called Quarterbacks. At the other end of our publishing spectrum, we produced significant collections of poetry such as Eldon Grier's *Pictures on the* Skin (1967), Frank Scott's *Trouvailles* (1967), Louis' own *Collected Poetry* (1971) and, reaching beyond Montreal, more modest books by Douglas Barbour and Stephen Scobie.

The books by Grier and Louis were substantially produced, almost uncharacteristic of our normal production process. Louis was a firm believer in simple, straightforward production values: it wasn't the packaging or the wrapping that mattered but the contents. Glen and I, to different degrees, subscribed to that philosophy as well. I had always been taken with French book design, and was happy with simple typographical cover designs and simple layouts of the contents. Louis' *Collected Poetry* was undoubtedly our major project. It was carried forward by Glen and printed in Belfast. Almost too stark in its simplicity, it tested Louis' penchant for the unadorned. Delta embraced one other activity that was not something that avant-garde little presses normally took to heart, that was my own interest in exploring early Canadian poetry, and in making it available under the Delta imprint. Glen and Louis were encouraging, although Louis mocked my inclination to what he teasingly called literary archaeology. Not inappropriately I felt, we published the first modern edition of Oliver Goldsmith's *The Rising Village* (1965). Later, prompted by my enthusiasm for early Canadian writing that I had dug up, Louis wrote the poem which is reproduced here, fittingly, as a Louis ' artifact' (pp. 24-25). I had started my own little press after the break-up of Delta Canada (as did Louis who launched DC Books, and Glen, who also created his own little press), which I called The Golden Dog. I had published some late eighteenth century 'Canadian' verse under the auspices of the Lande Foundation at McGill University, all of which served handily to feed Louis' exercise in satire.

Looking back now, one sees that the 1960's, especially the middle of the decade, were a time of wonderful activity and variety of experience. Phyllis Webb had moved away from Montreal and was working for the CBC. She had been given the task of creating a series of television programmes under the title *Extension: Modern Canadian Poetry*. Phyllis hosted some thirteen 'episodes' in which she interviewed a remarkable range of individuals. Louis and I, together with George Johnston, appeared on Programme # 2—The Fifties." We were flown to Toronto and rehearsed in a free-wheeling fashion, before our appearance. Combining Johnston with Louis and myself was a bit of an odd arrangement since George, avuncularly bearded, intensely blue-eyed, kindly but very dogged in his notion of verse was immediately at odds with how we saw the role and function of poetry. I believe that for George poetry was a matter of wit and craft and literary intelligence, while for Louis it was a larger concern with society, ideas and the philosophical order that nature suggested to us. There was some pre-programme skirmishing which Phyllis guided productively into our on-camera discussion, so much so that, differences notwithstanding, we all came away satisfied with our 'performance'. It was on this occasion, as well, that I had an evening at the bar of the hotel with author Hugh Garner. Gruff, gravelly-voiced and chain smoking, he was every bit the rough diamond that I had always imagined him to be. Late in the summer of 1966, I was teaching in the Summer School at Carleton University in Ottawa when Ray Souster telephoned to say that he and Lia were in town, and on their way to Montreal to meet with Ron Everson and Louis. The Sousters had an 'expedition' planned to meet some writers in Montreal and then travel on to Vermont and points east with the Eversons and, presumably, Louis. The Sousters and I met briefly in Ottawa and then set out for Montreal. Here my recollection of events differs from what Ray has recalled in his little monograph, *Making the Damn Thing Work* (2001). I recall our drive to Montreal in a convoy of two cars, I remember landing at our house in Pierrefonds, and I remember phoning Louis and Ron Everson to say that Ray and Lia had arrived and were with me. It was then decided that we would all travel the next day to North Hatley to the Gustafsons.

The idea of the League of Canadian Poets was already in the air, and the trip to see Ralph and Betty was also intended to give us a chance to assemble as many poets as possible to discuss this idea that Ray had brought with him. North Hatley—the Athens of the Eastern Townships—as it was jokingly styled by Buffy Glassco, was chosen because Frank Scott, Ralph Gustafson and Doug Jones (this being a week-end) would likely be there. Ray has told the rest of the story pretty much as I recall it as well. Both Louis and Frank Scott were sceptical about the idea. Louis thought that if anything were to be created it would have to be something of an 'academy' of established and proven poets, and that membership in such a body would be strictly controlled and decided by a small committee of 'senior' poets. Frank, who as Ray recalls it had had a martini or two, asked dramatically how this new body would be different from the Canadian Authors' Association which he had lampooned so savagely in his much-anthologized poem "The Canadian Authors' Meet".

I, feeling neither senior nor junior nor anything else, didn't say very much until Ralph's deck chair in which I was sitting collapsed under me. Shaken and with a gash in my leg I wouild go on to say that I was the only one who had shed his blood at the founding of the League of Canadian Poets. It is interesting to reflect now that while Louis and I joined the League at this founding occasion, neither one of us remained a member for very long, although it was pleasant and flattering to be fussed over a bit when the League celebrated its twenty-fifth anniversary at a banquet and self-congratulating 'do' at which, if memory serves, it was announced proudly that the League now boasted better than seven hundred members. Walking back to our hotel that evening Louis muttered glumly ". . . seven hundred poets . . . imagine that."

During my stay in Montreal in the summer of 1964, and when I was working on foundation-funded research on Canadian little magazines, I had thought of extracting the most important material from this research and of making it available for discussion and classroom use. I had mentioned the idea to Louis and he responded in a very encouraging way, so much so that I copied a few key articles and began to use them in my Canadian poetry class that fall at the Lakehead. The idea for an "essential articles" quickly established itself in our correspondence in 1965, and I began to mention it to publishers representatives who called with offers of new texts.

There were nibbles of interest from the likes of Prentice Hall and what was then McGill University Press, but it was not until I had moved back from Lakehead and had settled again in Montreal in the spring of 1966, that Louis and I began serious work on the collection for which the working title was "Essential Articles for the Study of Modern Canadian Writing". Here too we quickly fell into a routine: Louis coming to our house in Pierrefonds on Sunday, and we would sit in the back yard under the trees reading material, evaluating its importance, sketching out our introductory remarks, and gradually teasing a large volume of potential content into what would become *The Making of Modern Poetry in Canada* (1967). This would be published by Ryerson Press/ McGraw Hill Canada, and would go into two hard cover and one paperback edition, selling some six thousand plus copies in its lifetime.

An aside here. Ryerson had asked us to explore funding possibilities for the book, and we naturally thought of our friends at The Canada Council. I travelled to Ottawa to present our case, and was ushered into the office of Peter Dwyer, who listened to what I had to say. Right there and then he told me that the Council would be forthcoming with a grant.

The Making of Modern Poetry in Canada was published late in 1967 and after its release, coinciding with a poetry reading at Sir George, Frank Scott invited us to his house to do a bit of celebrating. He had placed his copy face forward on the mantlepiece, and with an ironic flourish asked the assembled group, which included Arthur Smith, what should be done about this book which contained no small heresy since it was taking away the primacy of the role in launching modernism in Canadian poetry from Smith and himself. He was kindly and generous

YE GOLDEN DOG

I have brought out, in this current *series*

a collection of

Early Canadian Valentines,

these being a document

too rarely considered

in our literary histories

in fact one might say almost neglected.

Now made available

in this *Deluxe* Edition

with Notes & Appendices

(including two signed notes & copies)

chosen from items

these being

the best

so close to have been rarely collected

of long neglected Canadiana

deposited at McGill University, in the Archives

of the Canadian Room

GOLDEN DOG

I have brought out, in the current series

if Inedited Canadiana,

a selection of

Three Early Canadian Valentines,

these being

authentic documents

too rarely considered

in our literary histories--

in fact, one might say, almost neglected--

now made available

in this Variorum Edition

with notes and appendices

including two signed holograph copies

(senders unidentified)

these items

being chosen from

the Laundry Collection

of Rare Canadiana

deposited at McGill University

in the archives of

The Canadiana Room.

[signature]

January 6, 1971

about it all, but Smith, I suspect, took it less happily, and I always felt afterwards that Smith's friendship towards me had cooled somewhat, although Louis weathered it all very well.

The relative success of the publication of *The Making* (as we called it) was overshadowed by the general unrest that had begun to sweep the Universities and their student population. The student revolt in France had its echoes in Montreal, fueled, undoubtedly by the rise of nationalist sentiment in Quebec. In addition, the United States were swept by much unease over the war in Vietnam, most of it finding expression through the often violent demonstrations of a disenchanted and threatened youth.

There were 'manifestations' and sit-ins on university campuses, with McGill coming in for more than its fair share of disruption. Sir George Williams, where I was teaching, was not immune to any of this. Essentially an 'open' university it had a substantial element of radically disposed students, proof of which would come down upon our heads in 1970 when a serious riot *cum* sit-in and hostage-taking in the Principal's office erupted on an already restless campus. Louis was deeply disturbed by these events, and in his quietly outspoken way expressed his disaffection with what he saw as a chaotic and destructive tendency in the youth of the day. This earned him strong criticism on the McGill campus, as well as the reputation of a conservative who stood in the way of true democracy and social activism.

While all of this swirled around us, Louis and I had fallen into the wonderful habit of lunching together, usually twice a week. We would connect by phone and then always meet half way, spending valuable minutes arguing about which restaurant we wanted to go to. That section of Montreal between Guy and University Streets, especially Mountain and Crescent, had become vibrant with newly-opened pubs and bistros and Italian restaurants. For a while we would go to Le Moustache, a bistro on Mountain Street (later relocated to Closse Street) where the speciality was a sandwich on a crusty half of a baguette and a generous glass of red wine.

Our favourite, though, was the Rymark Tavern, then a genuine Quebec tavern, by which I mean a segregated male preserve, to which Louis and I repaired regularly for pig's knuckles and, in my case, several drafts of whatever was on tap. Louis was not (certainly not in my experience) someone who drank alcoholic beverages, although there was a time when taverns served porter, and Louis would order a bottle, believing in the restorative power of whatever it was that went into its brewing. Later, when the Rymark became a 'brasserie', and still later morphed into a fast food outlet, we found our way back to the Peel Pub which to this day still serves a mean knuckle. The Peel Pub has had a checkered history, at various times being a student hang out, a gay pub, and latterly a noisy sports tavern where one can eat well at reasonable cost, but where audible conversation is all but impossible. By the way, it has literary credentials of a kind since in its earlier life it was a place favoured by Patrick Anderson. Many McGill types passed through its doors.

At this time, which is to say during most of the sixties, Louis was deeply engaged in a near incredible range of activities. Not only was he writing his own poetry, teaching a full load in a department which treated him shabbily—running, first Contact Press and then Delta Canada—but also doing a lot of writing for the popular press in the form of reviews and short articles on literature, film and ideas. He believed profoundly in the need to educate, and by educate he certainly meant reaching out beyond the university to the intelligent and interested public at all levels. This latter sense had led him to assemble an anthology, *Poetry of our Time* (1965), the intention of which was to address a readership at the schools. This missionary zeal of his also made him a willing and frequent participant at conferences of teachers involved in the teaching of language and literature.

He drew me into this activity, and I spoke on a couple of such occasions, the most memorable one being when we travelled to Vancouver for a conference of the Council of Canadian Teachers of English. There, in addition to the conference, we had dinner with Earle Birney one evening at his flat where the conversation ranged widely with Earle exhibiting his usual nervous, argumentative and irascible energy. He had written to Louis shortly after the publication of *The Making of Modern Poetry in Canada,* to complain about the 'eastern bias' in our book. Louis and I had discussed this and felt that there was nothing wrong with our approach, and that if anyone felt otherwise they should assemble their own collection of relevant material to make a different case for Canadian modernism.

But Earle, in spite of Louis' placating reply, would not let matters rest, and that spring in 1968 he came to Montreal to meet with us. Louis and I took him to lunch which, as I recall it, saw much heated debate but no resolution of Earle's grievance. Earle was an intense man, not easily swayed and holding fast to his opinions. I had got to know him as a result of my work on indexing little magazines when we corresponded about the possibility of an index for *Prism*. Nothing came of it, but I now knew Earle and in 1965 he drove up our driveway in Port Arthur with Ikuko with whom he was travelling in a sports car to Toronto. They had dinner, stayed the night and were on their way. Ikuko left an inscribed copy of her poems as a memento of the visit and Earle signed my copy of *Turvey* upside down or topsy-turvey as 'Turvey'. Louis and I also spent a delightful afternoon with Dorothy Livesay, drinking tea in her garden and, again, catching up on what was happening in poetry on the Vancouver scene, a scene which Louis had made known in the East when he published a selection of the Tish poets in his own magazine *Delta*.

Towards the end of 1971, and knowing that I had accepted an appointment at Carleton University in Ottawa, Delta Canada began to pull apart. We all knew that it was only a matter of time before we would have to close shop. Louis was not in favour of my move (one of the rarest such moments when he ventured to influence me in my private life) arguing that Ottawa lacked vitality as a literary scene, and that my place was really in Montreal in which I had, so to speak, grown up. But I had become apprehensive of the stridency of Quebec nationalism (for which Louis had no patience), and the events at Sir George Williams when, for months on end, we had endured student activism in the form of class invasions and haranguing. This culminated in the sacking of the University's computers, which finally convinced me to put that turmoil behind me.

Besides, the offer from Carleton was particularly attractive since it meant assuming the General Editorship of the Carleton Library Series, a distinguished list of books dedicated to the reprinting of important works relating to Canada in a number of disciplines in the social sciences. More grist for my 'archaeological' mill. Naturally, the move to Ottawa in 1972 meant that Louis and I would have to maintain our friendship and our 'connectedness' in a somewhat different way. Gone were the weekly lunches and the telephone conversations, to be replaced by my visits to Montreal which I strove to manage on a fairly frequent basis. These would center on an extended lunch (although we sometimes had great breakfasts at the hotel when I stayed overnight, or on other occasions when I made a quick visit we would have late afternoon tea and cookies at Louis' and Aileen's house) at which we would do intense 'catching up'. Quite remarkably, we always picked up seamlessly from where we had left off the previous time.

We had a repertoire of things we talked about, and we fed on these topics, consistently building and developing the ideas which had first suggested themselves to us—hence the notion of 'eternal conversations'. But in their own inexorable way certain themes and topics became the essential stuff of all and any of our conversations. We rarely strayed into international politics. Louis abhorred any kind of totalitarianism, and Communism was, obviously, anathema to him. On that we had no disagreement, although I felt a tiny bit superior in that I had actually experienced it, first the incipient excesses of Maoism in China, and later, the European variety when I taught at the University of Leningrad and the University of Warsaw. I told Louis a great deal about the nature of that beast.

He listened attentively and, I believe, was grateful for what I shared with him. I wrote to Louis during my stays overseas, infrequently and less openly from behind the iron curtain, but much more elaborately when I went to teach in a German university and when I lived for a term in Villefranche on the French Riviera. As I browse through my file of correspondence with Louis, packed as it is with his letters and enclosures of things that he had read in the press and wanted to share, I am surprised at the volume and intensity of what flowed back and forth between us.

Our ongoing conversations carried over into our letters, and the same matters that cropped up over the breakfast table would find their way into the letters. Louis' was the kind of sensibility that engaged its time with passion and deep concern. From the days of his doctoral work at Columbia, and influenced to some small extent by Pound's attitude towards the corruption of values, Louis raised the alarm, time and again, at what he saw as further deterioration in the media, the review press, and the commercialism of publishing. He was also seriously at odds with Northrop Frye's sense of literature, and rarely missed an opportunity to try and draw Frye into a public debate. McLuhanism was another bugbear, and here again Louis saw the too ready, easy corruption of knowledge and ideas by the utterances of someone who had become the adopted guru of the advertising age. The letters I have also reveal a Louis who could be testy and unyielding. I had been at work for a long time on what I saw as an unravelling of the complex weave that was John Glassco's *Memoirs of Montparnasse* (1970). The business of authorial mischief in autobiographical writing became a major topic for us. Louis was not much of a believer in auto-biography, but he took my point (and my obsessive insistence on historical accuracy), and made what he called 'prevarication' in literature a lively item of debate for us. When I published my edition of the *Memoirs* (1995), Louis complimented me on the annotations but also took issue with me, feeling, especially that I had not really given him full credit for 'discovering' Glassco's deception. And since I claimed that I had known about it from the time when Glassco was writing his reminiscence (actually the summer of 1964) Louis waded into me in no uncertain fashion, saying that I had colluded in the deception.

Another example of his testiness came up on an earlier occasion when he wrote commenting on the just-published *The Canadian Encyclopedia* (1985). Of one contributor he said: "[He is] A carrier of AIDS—Artistic and Intellectual Deterioration Syndrome." It was also in that year that, one breakfast morning when I brought up the need for a new 'Selected Dudek' (we, Glen Clever, Frank Tierney and I in a new publishing partnership in Ottawa called The Tecumseh Press, had published a compact selection of Louis' critical writing, *Selected Essays and Criticism* (1978)) that Louis in agreeing with me created another one of his instant artifacts on a napkin, reproduced here, of the hotel's restaurant. But the biggest challenge that arose with time, and something from which no amount of debate and argument on my part could move Louis, was his growing conviction that, some-how, modernism had lost its way. Inklings of his disillusionment cropped up in his letters, and even though he continued to write well into his retirement, always seeking to point society in the direction of the search for beauty and the rational, he left me with the stark memory of the indictment of modernism he worked into what was to be his personal statement by way of introductory essay for a new edition of *The Making of Modern Poetry in Canada*. In l990 Louis had scribbled a brief note to me that he opened with "I hope you are at least *thinking* of modernism. All I've got so far is the word 'avant-gardebage'". On July 28, 1992, Louis sent me his introduction for the new edition of *The Making*. In part it said:

> In any case, by now it must be clear that poetry has not found a public, as it also must be clear that modernism has not been a fully evolved literary movement—we now suspect that it may rather have collapsed, or be in danger of being obliterated altogether. But modernism is secondary to what is even a greater issue. This is the collapse of the literary tradition, both classical and modern, which stood behind modernism and gave it its great possibilities of intensity and tension—the tension between contemporary vulgarity, or triviality, and past glory, or dignity, or artistic power.

It is worth remembering that, in spite of his courageous stand in the face of the overwhelming sweep of popular culture and its vulgarisms, for which Louis paid a price in the coin of wide recognition, he was, nevertheless, a much respected figure in the world of Canadian letters. His Department—its envious, obstructive and infinitely less accomplished members silenced by Louis' manifest standing—honoured him with distinctions, including the Greenshields Chair; he was inducted into the Order of Canada; honorary degrees came his way; and cohort after cohort of students he had taught paid tribute to his teaching and his immeasurable influence on their lives. But best of all, as I liked to remind him, he had penned some of the most noble and reassuring lines when he wrote:

> Beauty is ordered in nature
> as the wind and sea
> shape each other for pleasure; as the just
> know, who learn of happiness
> from the report of their own actions.

> *Europe*

How can I not miss the Man?

It must be from an invisible source

present among these molecules

present in all these letters

from "Continuation III [fragment]", *The Caged Tiger*

Photo Courtesy of Aileen Collins

**Louis Dudek at home,
Montreal, 1980.**

**Louis Dudek with apple harvest,
Way's Mills, 1990.**

An Extra-Thick Slice of Raisin Bread

in memoriam Louis Dudek

I SUPPOSE all insomniacs
have their own special hour.
Mine's 3 to 4 a.m.,
at which time I'm usually seated
at my table in this brightly-lit
second kitchen turned study,
an extra-thick slice of my favourite
cinnamon-and-raisin loaf
on a bread plate in front of me.
It was only this late afternoon I learned
of the sudden (at least for me),

totally unexpected death
of one of my oldest, most treasured friends,
Louis Dudek, honoured citizen of Montreal,
poet first, then scholar, teacher,
no slouch either on the flute, the recorder,
leaving me still scarcely comprehending
such a loss, not wanting to believe a word of it.

Can this be the same man I stood beside
in that Ste. Catherine Street East food store,
listening amazed as he talked swift *joual*
with a grocery clerk? The same lovable, irritating man
always ready to suspect some underhanded plot
being hatched by those two traitor poets
in devious Toronto, Ray Souster and Peter Miller?
The same man I remember as a poet
seeming to change in a few short years
from one world-loving lyricist
to a flippant, know-it-all philosopher
of sad, cynical one-liners? (But true enough to his art,
turning much of this bitterness, desperate uncertainty
upon himself). And I still ask
is this the same man I waited three hours for
while he talked his way through Canada Customs
at the Vermont border? The same one who watched with his friends
the unspoiled spill-over wonder of Split Rock falls
leaping down that gorge
from light into darkness?

Other questions, so many still unanswered.
Who really knew this man? Questions I'm sure
I'll not answer tonight,
with only the crumbs of my extra-thick slice of raisin bread
still on my plate in front of me,
so many questions for another old man to save
for his next sleepless night and the next. . .

You're really dead, my friend,
right now that's all I know for sure
as I turn off our kitchen light,
begin to walk slowly toward my bed
through the early morning darkness,
that and the knowledge that you've made your final move at last,
leaving all of us still left behind
with the unsettling job of coming to terms with,
coming to grips with your ultimate triumphs, final victories,
so very plain now for everyone to see.

Louis, dear friend, goodbye for now;
no doubt I'll soon talk with you
on one of my future long, sleepless nights. . .

(From left) Louis Dudek, Ken McRobbie, Aileen Collins, Raymond Souster and Genevieve McRobbie at Dudek's Montreal apartment, August 1965.

Men live for famous deeds
and leave their deeds behind.

from "Shakespeare", *The Caged Tiger*

Photo Courtesy of Betty Gustafson

**Louis Dudek, Ron Everson
& Ralph Gustafson,
Way's Mills,
June 15th, 1984.**

Photo Courtesy of Aileen Collins

Louis Dudek picking apples at Way's Mills, the Eastern Townships, Quebec, circa 1990.

Quiet Hero

I MET LOUIS in the summer of 1997 when he agreed to let me interview him for research I was doing on the role of the little presses in Montreal during the 1940's, 50's and 60's. He suggested we have our first meeting in the cafeteria at Concordia University and when, after introductions had been made and we had settled down to talk, I asked him why he had chosen that particular location, he told me how much he missed being around students. He said he missed their energy and enthusiasm; he missed the intellectual stimulation and challenge they offered him; and he missed the simple hustle and bustle of being in their midst.

I was taken by Louis' response. Here was a man who had travelled extensively—who had known, befriended and published some of the greatest modernist writers in Europe, the United States and Canada. Here was an academic, whose intellect was towering, whose education was vast, and whose breadth of knowledge was formidable. Yet, it was to his students that he longed to return—to those who were the least knowledgeable, least experienced and most naive. I was touched by his humanity and inspired by his loyalty—a loyalty that I grew to understand was deep and profound.

The first part of my research involved a study of *First Statement* magazine and press. And so Louis and I met several times in the following months to talk about his association and friendships with Frank Scott, Arthur Smith, P.K. Page, Patrick Anderson, A.M. Klein, and other *Preview* members, and then to consider his relationships with John Sutherland and Irving Layton and their joint commitment to "open the windows and doors and let the sun and the wind in—when it came to writing." He told me how he had met these various people, as well as anecdotes about parties and literary gatherings; and on several occasions recalled the story of how he and Layton had walked home one evening from McGill University after a literary society meeting and, feeling like they had found a kindred spirit in each other, stopped in the middle of the Jacques Cartier Bridge to proclaim to the world that they would change the course of Canadian literature—which they did.

He talked of his admiration for Layton's "spunk," and his concern for Sutherland's health. He also worried about Sutherland and Layton's changing perception of him as he continued to pursue an academic career at a time when they were unable to. But most of all he reflected on the enthusiasm and hard work and the fun of the *First Statement* days when they met to select the poems and essays they wanted to publish, as they typed the stencils, and ran the Gestetner and collated the pages for stapling. He had many stories to tell about the purchase of the press, and how because Layton seemed unable to touch it without it breaking, that he—Louis—became the primary typesetter in the group. And he spoke longingly of the smell of the press—of the oil and ink that permeated his clothes when he was working on it.

Louis also told me of the tensions that were sparked as *First Statement* merged with *Preview* to form *Northern Review* and the change that took place in Sutherland as his health continued to decline. He spoke of the conflict that he, himself, felt when, while wanting to be loyal to Sutherland as a friend, he could no longer align himself with Sutherland's literary vision and so felt compelled to agree to work with Ray Souster, who was ready to begin a new little magazine—*Contact*.

And so, the first major part of my dissertation came to be. As Louis talked to me, he "made it new" and, even more, he made it *real*. John Sutherland's early vision for *First Statement* was Louis' vision, as well. Layton's initial triumphs were his, too. The important events he recounted were from his own memories. The people of whom he spoke were his friends and colleagues. They were ordinary human beings, with personalities that both gelled and clashed, who worked together to do something extraordinary. But that was just the beginning...

Ever supportive and encouraging, Louis agreed to continue meeting with me to discuss the next magazine and press that he was involved in—*Contact*. Both Louis and Ray Souster had come up with the name independently of each other, because both shared a belief in the need to provide a means by which writers could make contact with one another—in the U.S. and Canada. And because Souster lived in Toronto, while Louis and Layton resided in Montreal, the majority of their early activities was centered at Louis' house in Verdun. It was there, for example, that the press was installed. And once again, Louis did the majority of the typesetting and printing.

Louis recalled the exhilaration of those early days with *Contact*. As he, himself, has pointed out in various essays, Montreal was a particularly energetic venue in the middle part of the century, filled with young and ambitious artists, musicians and writers. And so the time and the place were lively, and the magazine did not lack for submissions. In fact, in addition to launching their own careers as poets, Louis, Souster and Layton helped provide a base from which all of Canada's major writers sprang. In the sixteen years of its existence, Contact Press published most of Canada's most important modernist poets of mid-century, including Al Purdy, George Bowering, Louis Dudek, D.G. Jones, Daryl Hine, Henry Moscovitch, W.W.E. Ross, R.G. Everson, Milton Acorn, Gwendolyn MacEwen, Alden Nowlan, Irving Layton, Raymond Souster, Leonard Cohen and Margaret Atwood.

Interestingly enough, these names are now known to us because Louis, Layton and Souster promoted them through Contact Press when no other publisher would. Then, after Contact Press had proven them commercially viable to the larger, more established presses, these writers moved on, leaving the little presses—and Louis—behind. Here, again, then, is where Louis' integrity and loyalty can be found.

As first Layton then Souster pulled away from Louis, attracted by the attention of American writers and publishers, particularly Robert Creeley, Cid Corman and Charles Olson, Louis remained loyal to Canadian writers, continually attempting to redirect his colleagues' energies on their behalf. And while his colleagues found recognition—even fame—through the larger publishing houses, Louis remained true to the spirit of the little press—a spirit that demands liberation from the constraints of the establishment which, in turn, requires and promotes intellectual and artistic freedom. But he did so at personal cost.

In so many of our conversations Louis became wistful, concerned that while he had devoted his life to the promotion of Canadian poets and poetry, his work would be forgotten when he was gone. That most people did not understand the power in Canadian literature and in its poetry in particular, and were therefore unwilling to advocate for it, frustrated him. He told me that when he was particularly depressed he wondered if all his effort had been worthwhile.

This also informed his concern about the advent of the Canada Council, and its influence over the freedom by which poets might write. In a letter to Peter Miller, for example, he writes,

as soon as you submit to gov't subsidy you've got civil service mentality to deal with: the MS has to be immaculate, with starched shirt and full-dress suit and before long the poetry too will toe the mark. They are bound to help poetry that has nothing to say and that is perfectly finished as a new-laid corpse.

Considering Contact Press in retrospect, Louis recalled that as it became more successful, it also became more establishment-like. Consequently, Louis recalled being less and less committed to the enterprise. So, in 1964, when his former student, Michael Gnarowski approached him about starting another little press, he was ready to begin again. In this way, then, Delta Canada was born and a new generation of Canadian poets—the last Canadian modernist poets—was given a place to sound their voices.

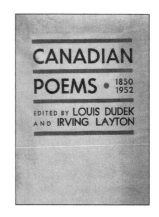

First Statement, Contact and Delta Canada were only three of the little presses and many literary activities in which Louis participated. These three, however, gave rise and place to modernist poetry in Canada. Through them Louis directly influenced the shape of our national literature. For this he needs to be remembered and celebrated. But that is not enough.

Those of us who knew Louis and of his selfless devotion to promoting Canadian poets and poetry are changed because of him. And as he changed us he can change others—as long as we continue to bring *him* forward and tell those who will listen of his work. Furthermore, if we value the work that Louis did, then we must continue it.

Now that I am a teacher, myself, my initial surprise at Louis' need and desire to be with students is replaced with understanding. Now I can see that it is in those who are seeking knowledge that there is hope for change—hope for a better world. On our own it is too hard to maintain the energy and the enthusiasm to get the work done; above everything else, Louis taught me this.

In terms of Canadian literature, there is so much work to be done. And we *must* do it, for, as Louis reminds us,

The way to freedom and order in the future will lie through art and poetry. Only imagination, discovering man's self and his relation to the world and to other men, can save him from complete enslavement to the state, to machinery, the base dehumanized life which is already spreading around us.

(Cerberus 13)

Now, where do we begin?

In a free spirit, play with the truth,

and love beauty.

Listen to the inner voice.

from "The Open", *The Surface of Time*

Photo Courtesy of Aileen Collins

Louis Dudek, circa 1968.

Photo Courtesy of Aileen Collins

Wanda Rozynski, Louis Dudek, Aileen Collins and
Stanley ("Buddy") Rozynski, at Way's Mills, 1979.

Remembering Louis

I ARRIVED IN FLORIDA in the winter of 2002, with this old typewriter,
a bunch of paper and a new ribbon, intending to write a remembrance of Louis Dudek. Despite three weeks of miserable weather,
I couldn't seem to get started. It isn't as if I didn't know what to
say, having known Louis for more than sixty years. He was a profound friend.

Louis and I were cousins. His mother and my father were
brother and sister. The family—three boys and four girls, their
spouses and children—all lived together in three triplexes built
by my grandfather on Bercy Street, in east-end Montreal. Every
summer, we would all head off to a farm in Lachenaie, off the far-
thest tip of the island. Grandmother kept her brood close at hand.

Louis' mother died when he was quite young. My father died when I was eight. It was perhaps for this reason that he took an interest in me, and this interest, along with his friendship and generosity, was to have an enormous and positive influence on my life.

From the very beginning, Louis always had time for me, listening to my concerns and encouraging my explorations. He illuminated, opened the world to me. We built a crystal radio set together. He explained the physics behind the bubbles that rose in the porridge he cooked. We spent time fishing during our summers on the farm. He sculpted a portrait of me, a bas-relief in clay, followed by a mould, which he cast in plaster. I listened as he played his music, while he in turn enthusiastically admired the model airplanes I built. Mostly though, he talked and I listened. I was a good listener.

There was very little of the personal—gossip or trivia—in his talks. Once the hello's and how-are-you's were done with, he was soon into the world of abstract ideas. I listened and asked a few questions, which I now think might have provided him with the space to develop and articulate his own thoughts and ideas— bounce them off an enthusiastic audience of one.

There was the sense that Louis was constantly there for me, and I for him. All of this while he was a student at McGill, writing his poems, being involved in *First Statement,* and so much more. There was a twelve-year difference in our ages: he was devoting a large portion of his time to a kid! As I think back on those years, I am amazed by the extent of his patience and generosity. Louis' first gift to me was a pair of boxing gloves: there must have been some logic for this choice, although it turned out that my friends beat me up!

There were books, tons of books. Louis grew up with his two sisters and an aunt. The Chinese ideogram for trouble depicts a man and two women under one roof. I, on the other hand, was a lone child. Following my father's death, my mother went to work in a sweatshop, and her mother moved in with us in order to look after me. There was also the flurry of female cousins who lived close by—the boys were off at war.

When Louis married Stephanie—who taught me how to dance at their wedding—and they moved to New York to pursue graduate studies, we started a correspondence. His letters often ran to four and five pages. He would send me books—and lists of books for me to find at the library. Whenever he came back to Montreal, which was several times a year, we would go for very long evening walks: down to Ontario Street, west to Delormier or Amherst, up to Sherbrooke and back east to Bercy Street. Ideas dominated our discussions. I remember one walk during which the talk revolved around the various levels of meaning in Dante's *Divine Comedy.*

Each selection of books he sent or recommended was carefully balanced: Romain Rolland's *Jean Christophe* teamed with Somerset Maugham's *Of Human Bondage;* Neitzsche's *Thus Spake Zarathustra* alongside the essays of Montaigne. Literature. Art. Philosophy. Music. He outlined a study of philosophy that started with entries from the *Encyclopedia Britannica,* Bertrand Russell's *History of Western Philosophy,* some of the *Dialogues of Plato* (Jowett translation) and so on. He indulged my love of the Romantic but stressed the Rational. I explored Eastern thought on my own: with the exception of Ezra Pound's *Confucius,* Louis had little patience for the East with its "Buddha contemplating his navel." During these formative years, there was a strong moral tone to the ideas I digested—and sometimes even choked on.

The recollections to follow cover events that took place over fifty years ago. At the beginning of 1955, I began a diary whose main purpose was to keep notes on my painting. What angst! What is remarkable is the amount of contact—visits, phone calls—I had with Louis at that time. In retrospect, it seems to have been a difficult, even chaotic period for all of us.

When Louis returned to Montreal to teach at McGill, I had already been painting for a number of years. I considered myself an artist and worked hard at creating enough spare time in which to work at my art. My paintings were realistic, surrealistic and teeming with social commentary—that "Cerberus" spirit of the 1950s. Around the beginning of 1952 I met my wife Wanda, and it was through us that Louis met Aileen Collins—and *CIV/n* was born.

Wanda and I were married in June of 1953. Louis was touring Europe at the time. Aileen and Jackie, another close friend and classmate from Montreal's Marianapolis College, were the bridesmaids. At the wedding reception that followed, Irving Layton's bacchanalian polka dancing with Wanda terrified my grandmother. The early 1950s were a period during which we saw quite a bit of each other. There were countless parties at Irving's where we reviewed submissions to *CIV/n,* read poetry and railed against the world.

Wanda and I moved to New York City in March of 1959. Wanda began making pottery and I gave up painting to make sculpture. Michael Lekakis was our guide to the art world of New York: he found us a loft on Broadway and 28th Street, and introduced us to the artists in that community. It was Louis who had introduced me to Michael: we visited his studio in New York, he visited us in Montreal, saw my work and encouraged us to move to New York. Louis, in turn, had looked up Michael at the suggestion of Ezra Pound, who considered Michael the only "worthwhile" artist around.

There was respect, but no real affinity between Michael and Louis. Pound had written of Michael: "How much mist can a mystic stick if a mystic could stick mist". They were both dedicated to Art. Michael, however, was immersed in his Greek heritage, and Louis was rather put off by his forays into grandiose poetry thick with the retelling of ancient myths. We all agreed, however, that Michael was a tremendously gifted sculptor.

This was also a period of release for both of us, a coming-of-age filled with courage and vibrancy. My work became abstract and the ideas were of the medium, rather than literal ones. I produced a great many sculptures working with Wanda's materials. There was minimal contact with Louis during this period, as we didn't have the money for trips to Montreal and he didn't care for New York. There were letters, to be sure, but what we discussed I cannot recall.

Louis and then Michael were powerful egos and formidable influences on my life. I chose them, needed them—and they chose me. We were very close. Without them, I sometimes wonder how differently things might have turned out.

Wanda and I had exhibitions in New York before returning to Montreal in April of 1960, in order to establish our Studio/Gallery on Mansfield Street. We had an opening exhibition in our gallery and later I exhibited at Galerie Libre on Crescent Street. Wanda's pottery sold well, her work was exhibited across Canada, the US and Europe, and her pottery classes were full. As a founding member of the Quebec Sculptors' Association, I sometimes exhibited with them, but did not have much interest in exhibiting or selling my work.

Art for me is a personal exploration whereby one attempts to come to terms with and accept the forces in nature and in change, to make forms that move in a space that reflects this energy, and both the horror and the beauty within the process. It is all very necessary to make the attempt—even if one fails, because without art life would be intolerable and stupid. Michael referred to Art as a religious practice. But that was then, the Holy Grail has become tarnished. Years before it happened, Louis had warned us to prepare for the coming of the Dark Ages.

In 1965, we moved to Way's Mills in the Eastern Townships, where we converted the town's abandoned school into our home, studio and a summer resident school of pottery. Louis and Aileen often visited, before renting and eventually buying a house of their own. We saw each other on weekends, spending our Saturday nights playing games and reading plays.

As always, we talked a great deal. However, I felt a change coming over my relationship with Louis: I became more wary, more careful not to allow myself to be overwhelmed. Perhaps this was due to some mid-life insecurity. In retrospect, it always puzzled me that Louis did not have a larger following of disciples, hangers-on. He had so much to offer. The reason for this may lie in the fact that he was not an easy person to be with: he was serious and uncompromising, challenging and difficult.

One strong image I have of Louis goes back to a certain summer day when I visited him in Montreal. I rang the bell and waited a long time for him to appear, slowly coming to the door, a book in his hand. The house was dark and quiet. He had obviously been reading. This was his world, sedentary and solitary, engrossed in ideas.

I think it was Thomas Mann who wrote of Dostoevsky that we must be grateful to him for going so far, so deep, and for bringing us so much, saving us from this profound trip.

The weather has changed here in Florida. We spend our mornings on the beach. This is what we come for—the incredibly clear skies, the warmth, the sun and the sound of the sea. We were here in the winter of 2001, at the time that Louis died. I had talked with him on the phone before we left Quebec: a few words, a few choked-up silences. When he entered the hospital and remained there over a week, I knew the situation was ominous. Louis had always been "dying." When he was born his grandmother had said that he would not live, due to his extremely feeble physical condition. Her "prophesy" would haunt him for the rest of his days. We had always kidded him that he would be the one left to write our obituaries when the rest of us died. This wasn't to be, after all.

We heard of Louis' death when we returned to Canada. It was all over. Done. I wouldn't have to face it, to look into the grave.

A few years ago a cat adopted us. This stray appeared out of nowhere, watched us gardening and followed us into the house that evening, hoping to be fed. A handsome animal, smart and ingratiating, he had probably been abandoned by summer visitors returning to the city. It seemed he had been mistreated, maybe kicked, because he walked slowly, gingerly. One evening some months later, he died without warning. I placed his body in a box in a cold room, planning to bury him the next day. Suddenly the tears came in a flood, a wrenching, unstoppable outpouring. I couldn't hold back. It was ridiculous. I then realized that this was the grief I had held back, the grief that had not come out eight years ago, when my mother died. This same, full realization of my loss in connection with Louis' death has yet to happen.

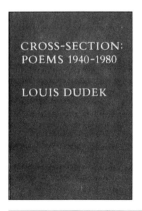

CROSS-SECTION:
POEMS 1940-1980

LOUIS DUDEK

JOHN ROBERT COLOMBO

Louis Dudek, circa 1980.

Lunchtime Conversation With Louis Dudek:

Montreal, 8 September 2000

IT IS A BRIGHT sunny day, the kind I associate with Montreal's Westmount (the Empire over which the sun has yet to set). What with his cane, Louis is a little wobbly, but otherwise in great form as he steps from the dark house into the bright daylight. The sun shines down upon him, as if to cause him to part with his shadow; but as it is near high noon, the strong-willed poet takes precedence over his own darkness. He proceeds to inform us that Jacques Barzun's latest book, the one about the progress of civilization, is the finest that the scholar has ever written. "And he wrote it in his nineties," Louis adds wickedly, reminding everyone but himself that he is now enjoying his early eighties. At lunch, the poet's gusto for ideas extends well beyond the pasta on his plate and flowers into conversation's ionosphere.

"Is science a technique or is it a body of knowledge?" The question is as mouth-watering as the delicious *gnocchi*. "Because Barzun is a realist and not an idealist, he holds no brief for the independent existence of concepts."

I rise to the bait. "Science is a technique."

He retorts, "But it's not a technique if you admit that ideas exist in their own right."

Toronto's Aristotle and Westmount's Plato battle it out for a while; the two ladies who are present smile and enter the debate with the occasional jibe or interjection. With the arrival of coffee and dessert, the conversation digresses, descending from the empyrean of ideas to the morass of book-publishing. "I have just completed a new collection of poems. It is a long meditation and I call it *The Surface of Time*."

The twin flushes of pride and pleasure play over his distinctive features; he looks as pleased as punch, rather like the cat that swallowed the canary, or Monstro the Whale who gulped down Jonah—or was it Pinocchio? I pun, "Is it 'the time of surfaces,' Louis? Or perhaps it's that you are merely 'scratching the surface of time'?"

Louis is amused. "You know," he says, with a wan smile, "it's a dangerous adventure for someone to enter his eighties."

We concur. I am not sure whether it is a technique or a concept, but I do know that if Louis writes about time, eternity will never, ever be the same again.

⟨ 21 September 2000

Source: John Robert Colombo's collection *Far Star: Poems and Effects* (Toronto: Colombo & Company, 2001).

Poet Raymond Filip, Louis Dudek and poet
Antonio D'Alfonso, Montreal, circa 1992.

The Verdun Years

WHEN I WAS GROWING UP in Verdun, I often sat beside the St. Lawrence river, hidden inside an abandoned thicket, my "reading bush." Instead of going to school, I would spend whole days there, devouring cheese and crackers and books. Boyhood ran into adolescence. Mark Twain's *Life On the Mississippi* flowed into Hemingway's *Old Man and the Sea* which disgorged into James Joyce's *Ulysses*. Within my solitary bush, I happened upon a poem entitled "Pomegranate" by a certain Louis Dudek. He was supposed be a great Canadian poet (my favorite oxymoron). And that poem in particular was supposed to be a memorable classic. I wasn't so sure, guided by unseen attachments: life and meaning, books and burrs.

I had arrived at Louis Dudek through Ezra Pound. I trusted Pound's cryptic wisdom. He wasn't a "madman" but a Modernist.

Years later in 1970, during the War Measures Act, I distinctly remember sitting on a bench in Cabot Park trying to decipher *The Cantos,* (the English as well as the Chinese), while a military tank rumbled up Atwater Street. I then parked myself on the steps of the Church of St. James the Apostle to puzzle through Pound's fulminations against "usura," while personnel carriers shook St. Catherine Street. And I ended up laying my body down on McGill's campus, gazing up at the highrises, totally bewildered by Pound's repentant fascist allusions to the heavenly city of Dioce in the Pisan Cantos, while Canadian armed forces infiltrated Montreal. Pound was too *recherché,* too much going on in his texts, definitely not a one-man job. So I decided to study with the man who had faced the sage himself.

In 1971, I enrolled in Louis Dudek's Canadian Literature course. A glum hyphen linked my lost Lithuanian roots to a country that was still searching for its own identity. I carried physical scars from the insanity of war, having been born and mutilated in a DP camp as a sixteen-month-old infant, compounded by traumas from domestic violence, my parents' divorce, and family disintegration into dirt and nothingness. Corporal punishment had been smacked into the back of my head at Verdun Catholic High. And in addition to these chalkdust memories, I had been kicked out of the McGill School of Social Work. Formal institutions of learning slowed me down, to say the least. So what did this tall literary figure Louis Dudek have to say to someone like me? I sat inert and mute by the window seat in his classroom, ready to fly.

Dudek fired the deadly CanLit canon at us, starting with Lucy Maude Montgomery's novel *Anne of Green Gables.* I had already swallowed that sweet potato ages ago! Not to mention the other required readings on his list. Dudek's course offered nothing decapitating, nothing to meet my requirements. An idea for an essay about ethnic writers in Canada motivated me to finally come forward and broach the subject to the distinguished professor. His encyclopedic memory recommended that I look up a certain writer bearing a Lithuanian name whose two poems he had spotted recently in *The Queen's Quarterly.*

"Raymond Filipavicius?" I asked, declaratively.

"Yes. That name sounds familiar."

"He's me," I pointed to my chest.

Dudek paused for a second, smiled, and then brushed the corner of his eye, as if wiping away a tear. After that moment, I knew we would be friends for life: "Louis" and me. A special connection between the two of us had clicked, I felt, as I peddled uphill and downhill, in and out of the Atwater tunnel on my 3-speed CCM bicycle, back and forth from McGill to Verdun, Verdun to McGill.

Aware of my publishing history, which had begun at the age of 16 in small magazines such as *Fiddlehead* and *The Canadian Forum,* Louis invited me to teach that very same class in which I had enrolled as a student a few months earlier. It was the winter of 1972, the year that Ezra Pound died. Louis himself was slated to undergo a difficult operation that would keep him away from his pedagogical duties for two weeks. During his hospitalization, I team-taught with David Chenowith. David was also a registered student in Louis' class that year. Chenowith had personally financed a small anthology of poetry entitled *Snowmobiles Forbidden* while employed as a reporter for *The Montreal Star.*

Chenowith and I were not really that well-versed in the legalities of student substitution for teachers. But! Fie on scholarity! Shelley dictated that poets should serve as the unacknowledged legislators of the world. And being chosen as replacements, for and by our illustrious accreditor, boosted our confidence higher than any grade Louis could have ever bestowed upon us. During our two-week tenure, I attempted to explain the puns of A.M. Klein. But almost every male and female student desired to "get into" the love poems of Leonard Cohen. Chenowith and I managed to hold the poetry fort, staving off any student uprisings, until Louis returned in his usual healthy state of good humor.

The Great Encourager continued to nurture this budding young poet through the thorns of post-graduation unemployment. The hungry years did not stop. Louis fed me sandwiches and abstractions. My ties to Verdun seemed to touch off unsettling memories. His first marriage had been an unhappy one. He had lived in Verdun during those troubled years. And furthermore, his former mother-in-law, Mrs. Sagaitis, also happened to be Lithuanian, artistic, and a resident of Verdun. Louis, the poet of ideas, slowly opened up his emotions to me: the confessional poet. But most of the time, we found ourselves engaged in convivial duels, exchanging counter-arguments about art, aesthetics, metaphysics, or politics, with the joyous air of musicians trading fours. Such meetings became a friendly tradition, usually at Ben's. We whined and dined, reminiscing about the advertisement in the window that had once beckoned: "After the Riot, Eat at Ben's."

The language debate that Louis and I grappled over tenaciously concerned poetic diction: the demotic versus the hieratic. After insuring that Louis would pick up the tab for our smoked-meat sandwiches, pickles, fries, and cole slaw, I would then begin our lunchtime face-off by tossing a few provocative words onto the table.

"Bluh! The age no longer demands Ezra Pound!"

"That's because Ezra Pound demands a civilized reader!"

And off we would go into more delicious dialogue that even Plato would have relished. Louis appeared to be most himself during these gabfests in restaurants, coffee houses, or outdoor cafes outside the strangling tassels and trappings of the university environment. Paradoxically, Louis often referred to the off-campus crowd, the masses, the collective individuals out there, as the "hoi polloi." While we stuck to our positions like horns to a bull, Louis' East End/Verdun origins would occasionally pop up in his vernacular usage: "Look, man, you should read Robert Graves' translation of 'The Golden Ass' by Apuleius!"

And it was a greater treat to be invited to Louis' house in Westmount. Tea and crackers and meaty topics satiated us: two gentlemen from a working-class background. We nursed no insecure need to boast about beer intake. Both Louis and I had a low tolerance for alcoholic writers. The serious thinker must *not* be a serious drinker. I was a milk-and-cookies man myself. And Louis seemed to enjoy consuming biscuits off shelves as much as he did books.

Our afternoon teas often took on a religious fervour: conversion not conversation. I could never convince Louis to acknowledge Duke Ellington as one of the greatest composers of the 20th century. And Louis could never swing me over to his side of poet's paradise. Yeats, Zembla, Bach, Segovia. . . we dropped immortal names like crumbs. And who were the most beautiful and truthful poets in Québec? The English or the French? Louis had the answer.

He went upstairs. He came back down. He gleefully revealed an enlarged photograph of himself. The picture had been taken in his country garden at Way's Mills. His impish smile couldn't hide the center of attention: a humongous zucchini cradled between his legs. This photo had given Louis an idea. Poets needed "decent exposure." Where? According to his poetic vision, the Montreal landmark most commensurate in grandeur with the transepts and censing angels of Westminster Abbey was Ben's! The owners of the historic delicatessen, those two Litvak *mensches* the Kravitz brothers, had agreed to display Louis' picture along with others in a proposed Poet's Corner. Louis suggested that I solicit publicity pix from the French poets who were reciting their verses beside English poets in the multicultural reading series that I was then organizing called "Pluriel" (Canada's finest hour!). We sent out our call for submissions. *Grace à la connection* Verdun-Westmount, twenty photos of Montreal's best-looking bards now hang high in Ben's Poets' Corner—rivaling for attention nearby celebrity glossies of Richard Chamberlain and Michael Jackson.

A serious feeder, and a serious reader, Louis' laughter came from his belly. This is what I loved about him. His genial chuckles emerged from a hearty depth, while his clasped hands smiled across his stomach. He combined levity with profound insights. Literary types are the worst offenders when it comes to judging a book by its cover. But Louis' sensitivity went beneath surface impressions. He understood stigmatization (as in my case). He

The Poet's Corner at Ben's: carbon copy of the original application form (including Dudek's handwritten postscript).

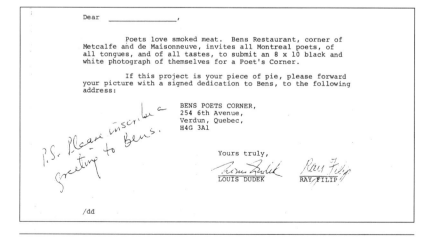

Poet's Corner, Ben's Delicatessen, Montreal, Quebec, March 2003.

saw me zoom through thirty years of radical changes. Yet, not once did I ever have to cater to some false image Louis may have preconceived of me. And I, in return, accorded him the deference due a truly enlightened human being.

This did not make him my 'mentor.' As a wandering scholar, I rode on motorcycles, but never traveled on anybody's coattails. Or to phrase it another way, I shuddered at the thought of being labelled a 'Dudekian.' Unlike Louis who proudly jumped into the stack of 'Poundians.' Verdun was our common ground. I felt privileged to engage in mortal dialectics with an intellectual from the same part of town; someone ahead of me schooled in the hazards of the Atwater tunnel, class struggle, and the caprices of Paganini.

Arguably, we were sparring partners. We clashed over the cartography of Reality. Where was it? How could meaning be reached? The life lived must come first, I maintained; the words are secondary. The stereotype of the 'literary bore' exists because the majority of authors are teachers. The majority of teachers with literary pretensions are excellent students who plod their way through the safe corridors of academe to become excellent instructors (or bad burnouts). Dull, but correct bores. Louis had followed this pattern. But he was different. He livened up the atmosphere with his artillery of ideas about art and civilization, whether he spoke in a sandwich shop or in a lecture hall jam-packed with students listening to his every word. The voice in his writings seldom imitated his spontaneous 'live' voice. And this discrepancy may be the reason why critics dismissed the literature he created as dry or 'didactic.'

"It's a mug's game," Louis was wont to complain. Good sportsmanship definitely did not prevail within the Canadian Literary Arena. Despite our polemical quibbles, Louis and I supported each other. I was living in poverty for my craft and sullied art. I had quit the League of Canadian Poets in tears in 1985, after having arranged the first English/French poetry *rencontre* for the League, starring Louis Dudek, Ron Everson, Claudine Bertrand and Francois Charron. I had received no thank you's or *merci's,* no basic civility. No-talent hustlers were flooding the gates, pursuing "a career in poetry." (Would Rimbaud have joined any League?) Slush puppies on committees lived for awards. Awards = Fame. Fifteen minutes in America. Fifteen seconds in Canada. If success is to be measured by literary awards, then Louis Dudek failed to achieve the same level of recognition as some of the peers he had published and promoted. This caused recurring rancor within him. Good poets make bad politicians.

So in 1988, as part of our Polish-Lithuanian coalition, I called up Louis when I was freelancing as a contributing editor for *Books in Canada*. I wanted to write a feature story about the little-known side of Louis Dudek: his Verdun years. Louis volunteered to brave the winter weather and visit me for the first time in Verdun. I was freezing inside a brick garret located over the storage room of a textile shop on 6th avenue. Something seemed to bother him—apart from the cold floors.

Louis and his first wife Stephanie had begun their married life together on this very same street in 1944. Their first dwelling, a four-room flat within a brownstone row at 1143, had been situated beside the aqueduct in front of the Lithuanian church *Ausros Vartos*. Louis' association with Verdun was deeply rooted in family entanglements and early poetic ideals, "searching for the meaning of existence." His poems had been written "at random," but not as jottings-in-passing. Louis was never one of the phoney *literati,* merely slumming, or renting temporarily to gather material for a book.

He dug into his briefcase and removed a sheaf of papers. He had photocopied them from his various works. They were poems that Verdun had inspired, a long 20-year period between 1942-1962. As he sipped on a cup of Red Rose tea to stay warm, his feet snuggled inside my slippers, his thoughts stretched back to the past. He and Stephanie had bicycled along the boardwalk together, and nestled beside bonfires at night watching the St. Lawrence flow onward throughout the 1940's into the '50's. They couldn't afford to eat steak in those days. Instead, they enjoyed picnic outings down by the riverside with friends such as John and Betty Sutherland, or Audrey and Irving Layton. (The inspiration for Layton's poem "Boardwalk at Verdun" had come from one of those fond repasts.)

Stephanie's parents owned a modest brownstone at 1202 Foch St. in Crawford Park, a Verdun annex. In 1945, the place became a *pied à terre* for Louis and Stephanie during the summer months. They spent the rest of the year in New York while Louis studied at Columbia University for his MA in History, and then later his Ph.d in Literature. This waterfront property on Foch St. involved a move upward, westward, since it afforded a lawn with flowers, plus a handy garage. Louis had learned how to drive a rusty red

Pontiac in order to commute back and forth to New York. On one trip, just as Louis was approaching the US border, the old Pontiac "rotted right under me." He had to push the scrap-heap all the way across to the American side for assistance. However, instead of offering help, the border guard detected some disparities in his documents, and accused Louis of driving with the wrong license. Louis considered selling the lemon for $25.00 at a used-car lot, but then changed his mind. Ironically, the judge hammered him with a fine of $25.00 American!

After landing a teaching post at McGill University in 1951, Louis and Stephanie remained on Foch St. until 1955. From there, they moved eastward along the river to 739 Allard St. A cement victory arch adorned their front door. Louis introduced the high ceilings of his new domain to the lofty music of Bach, which he played on violin, as well as on the recorder. Peter Dale Scott would show up at Christmas parties, "amused by the Christmas lights" that illuminated almost every porch and every window on every block, creating a carnival atmosphere. In 1958, an increasingly complex home situation necessitated yet another move. This time Louis selected a "fancy" two-storey house with a fieldstone exterior, metal railings, and a basement carport as his next haven in Verdun. His son, Gregory, born that year, took his first baby steps upon the sidewalks leading to 781 Beatty Avenue.

Leonard Cohen had also climbed the cement steps winding toward that same address. He would ring the doorbell, and personally deliver poems fresh off his typewriter for Louis to appraise. He and "Leonard" would stroll along the north side of the aqueduct since Cohen was "favorable toward it." Louis sifted through Cohen's latest outpourings, turning the pages with a gentle hand, pursing his mouth, assessing the originality of the lines like a gem cutter assaying a diamond. Louis was a man of letters possessed of a priestly reverence for the word, be it inside a sacred tome, or a work in progress. If only he and Cohen had strayed from their path to walk beside the river instead. They probably would have bumped into me reading inside my bush, avoiding discovery, leafing through *The Invisible Man* by Ralph Ellison. Regardless! What was the name of the manuscript that Louis Dudek and Leonard Cohen had discussed while lingering along the Verdun aqueduct? *The Spice Box of Earth*.

Louis was a universalist. This may have worked against him

when the trend toward regionalism arrived in the 1960's. The trend became entrenched, splitting into neighborhoodism. Neighborhoodism eventually deteriorated into streetism: territorial battles over which author owned which crack in which sidewalk at what end of the street? St. Urbain belonged to Mordecai Richler. No trespassing. The Plateau belonged to Michel Tremblay. No trespassing. And Reality belonged to?

Louis wrote about the streets of Verdun while seeking larger verities, similar to Plato exploring the alleys of Syracuse, disinterested in spurious local claims.

> I walk in the echoing streets searching
> the opposites that meet, or trap the constellations
> and the beautiful dark, in my net, as I lean
> over the edge of night.
>
> "A Warm Night" (*Zembla's Rocks,* 1986)

Beauty preoccupied Louis' thoughts. Verdun awakened the "pastoral imagination" within him. The ever-present river, the aqueduct, the verdant fields, all offered small wonders for an inquisitive mind to decode.

> What *you* want is not luck,
> nature's jackpot,
> but an intellectual seal of order and approval.
> But pleasure overflows, and love
> overflows, and beauty overflows!
>
> "The Jackpot" (*The Transparent Sea,* 1956)

And the winds of March blew over and under, cold and sensuous, as in this excerpt:

> But when you sweep the ivory canes
> and the stiff shirt from the house corner
> and smash the monocle on the backyard puddle,
> you'll still have the people, chilled in propriety,
> to prod with some up-the-petticoat obscenity
> before we can go on
> to meet the lascivious summer.
>
> "March Wind" (*The Transparent Sea,* 1956)

Even in the 1950's, Verdun community standards flaunted carnal knowledge in public, as evidenced by this sneak peek:

A teenager sitting on the bars
near the High School, her legs spread,
a thin slip of pants
covering her crotch,
smiles at me—
"as innocent as they come.

"Early Spring Emotions" *(Laughing Stalks,* 1958)

Louis did not exclude cheap or popular entertainment from his observations. One poem dealt with various stage acts at the Odeon theatre. Uncharacteristically, he even mentioned a specific location: Point St. Charles.

After 'Helen' the tapdancer of fourteen,
after 'The Snake' who farted to the delight of all,
came 'Stentor' the man with a voice,
Cyclops with an electric guitar;
and when he had toured the world with Hymnbook No. 1
he came to Point St. Charles
with 'The Irish Washerwoman' to raise the Holy Ghost
off his backside.

"On the Stage" *(Cross-Section: Poems 1940-1980)*

A Louis Dudek concordance would reveal words such as 'beauty,' 'delight' and 'love' as most representative of the poet and the man. His mother-in-law was a refined lady who likewise enjoyed music, and could not resist the temptation to spread the news about beauty in the world.

What a delight it is to hear
mother humming a Mozart aria
when the Magic Flute is on
as, when The Messiah began,
she called her two friends
to tell them to listen.

"Reply to a Critic" *(Laughing Stalks,* 1958)

Did Social Realism lend itself to beauty treatments? Betty

Sutherland attempted to capture in a charcoal sketch "the mob" that lived on 6th avenue, back in the 1940's when this street marked the outer limits of Verdun. Louis wrote a poetic sketch to 'parallel' her graphic vision.

> Beer, and perhaps cards,
> in the sun porch, on a Sunday afternoon,
> with the dumpy wives, the red-faced
> infants on the stairs, of cheap "new" frame houses
> at the edge of the city, paint
> parched by the sun, on the porches,
> locks rusty, grass gone grey:
> they look out of inflamed eyes
> at the blistering street, someone passing
> who is not a friend.

"A Charcoal Sketch" *(Laughing Stalks,* 1958)

And death, the great discourager, prompted Louis to compose these elegiac comments about the unexpected passing of Walter Zuperko, Stephanie's father, a worker at Ramsay Paints.

> He wouldn't have wanted to know how it happened;
> would have looked angry, stubborn as he was,
> at the cheap trick death played on him; also because
> his dead body was helpless to answer or resent it.

"On Sudden Death" *(The Transparent Sea,* 1956)

The poetry, the tea, and the stories suddenly ended there—with death. Charmed by Louis' presence, I urged him to continue. But it was getting late. And as he put on his boots within the bleak interior of my "icebox" living quarters, his heart rankled to prove something, to erase some misconception of himself. He had been a "maverick academic," he averred. His teaching job had functioned as a "cover" for his writing. John Lachs, the philosopher at Vanderbilt University, had even mentioned one of his essays in the Marxist magazine *Yes.* And Ezra Pound himself had singled out Louis as a rare "solid man."

If Louis Dudek had passed the Ezra Pound test, he had certainly also passed the Verdun test. I escorted him down the dingy stairway. As he stepped onto the pavement of 6th avenue, Louis looked back at me and smiled that chipper smile of his. I could tell he was satisfied about something. Verdun redux. Fragmented selves reclaimed. The circle was complete. As if by fate, shortly after Louis' visit, I managed to obtain a teaching job at John Abbott College. I also moved out of Verdun. Finally! To Ste. Anne-de-Bellevue. Mean streets to green streets!

Louis Dudek had laid the foundation for Modern Canadian Poetry while living in Verdun. From his basement printing press, he had established *Delta* in 1957, before the era of Canada Council coddling. Louis had also joined forces with Irving Layton and Raymond Souster to steer Contact press and Canadian literature in a new direction. Louis would journey back to Verdun after his voyages around the world. He would gush forth such voluble and valuable texts as *Europe* (1954), *The Transparent Sea* (1956), *En Mexico* (1958), as well as parts of *Atlantis* (1967). These works which unveiled the magnificence of civilizations, lost, found, or imagined, were written while living on the lowly streets of 6th avenue, Allard, Beatty and Foch. (You can almost hear Irving Layton, during one of their kitchen disputes, salaciously mispronouncing the word 'Foch.') Mapping Verdun in all its vulgar and beautiful anger would be left to another generation of writers. And Louis Dudek would play a role in that transition too. Within the living room of his Westmount *maison de la culture,* during a book launch for Marc Plourde in June, 1973, I met a certain David Wyper. This character with a 'Verdun accent' would go on to become David Fennario, and help to lay the foundation for Modern Canadian Theatre with plays such as *On the Job* and his blockbuster hit *Balconville.* While sitting on Dave's balcony at 3987 Ethel St.—the actual setting that would one day inspire the play—Dave and I shared many a twilight conversation about revolution. And we witnessed many a sunrise together also, singing beside the St. Lawrence river, our Stratford-on-Avon, dubbing ourselves the 'Verdun Renaissance.'

Lous Dudek & Stella Sagaitis circa the 1940s.

Re-birth or ruins, Verdun survives. Louis' former residence at 739 Allard is now a parking lot. My condemned hole at 242 6th avenue also has been torn down. And my secret "reading bush" beside the river has disappeared to make room for a bicycle path. I now live within a model hideaway, off the island of Montreal, close to the Outouais river. Thoughts always need a river. . . .

Every day of being alive is a bonus. Lining my book shelf, I read the poems and essays of Louis Dudek. I remember our laughs over funny epitaphs that he would collect and read out loud. But on his deathbed, when I quoted Dylan Thomas' exhortation to "rage, rage, against the dying of the light," Louis snapped back in outrage: "Oh, that drunk didn't know what he was talking about!" Louis believed that this Reality was all a dream, an illusion. I hope, beyond every way that Louis sought to understand the mystery of life and death, that he is now at peace in the Reality of God.

This winter, on New Year's Day, I ate a pomegranate. I selected it from a basket of fruits that were part of a ceremony my Filipino wife and I still honor called *Palihi-lihi*. The Visayan term means 'abundance and openness.' To welcome in a new year of prosperity filled with all the sweetness of life, a festive basket must include more than twelve fruits for each month of the year, plus a pouch containing more than twelve coins of the same denomination. This year, our basket brimmed over with sixteen different fruits! As I feasted on the "jewelled mine of the pomegranate," I thought of a beautiful man, Louis Dudek, his life, his openness, and his abundant accomplishments: a celebration.

BERNHARD BEUTLER

Louis Dudek with Bernhard Beutler,
Montreal, February 1998.

Louis Dudek, Poet and Humanist:

"—whatever soul is!"

THERE *ARE* NO COINCIDENCES. Louis Dudek, promoter of the modern age in poetry, died on the same day as one of his greatest humanistic *Vorbilder,* the 'classic' Johann Wolfgang von Goethe (1832). As Louis' son Gregory put it when I mentioned this fact: "Louis Dudek would have loved that".

The editors of this tribute volume have generously asked those who knew Louis to submit original poems dedicated to him and, of course, scholarly criticism on aspects of his rich poetical and critical writings. Also welcome are contributions discussing aspects of the *man,* Louis Dudek. In trying to do so—as imperfect as it can be after all these years of both physical and geographical distance—I would like to give thanks to a man who has, after my Catholic-Protestant upbringing, influenced my adult life, as well as my intellectual and 'philosophical' quest for the *Sinnfrage im Leben,* more than any other individual. He achieved this through his poetry, through his associative thinking in going back to the roots of humankind, and through his *anima.*

Louis Dudek displayed both reason and soul. He therefore bypasses a good number of Catholic priest-friends, Moslem students, and professors of high caliber (Romano Guardini, Professor *für Christliche Weltanschauung* of Munich, whom he admired, Carl-Friedrich von Weizsaecker, Marshall McLuhan et al.). As we would discuss deeply only in later years—the last occasion being my visit to his and Aileen's Westmount home on February 6, 1998, in honour of his eightieth birthday—both of us had had a Catholic upbringing. He partially defined his as being 'illegal', because as a Catholic, he had nevertheless attended some religious instruction classes at the United Church[1]. My own religious upbringing was perhaps equally "illegal." Yet it was intended to be ecumenical: my parents, having converted to Catholicism, still permitted me to sing all the Bach cantatas and oratorios during Lutheran Sunday services in our Hamburg suburb of Bergedorf. However, I was still expected to attend the "real" service, the Catholic high mass afterwards. Our lengthy discussion in Dudek's Ingleside Avenue study was full of aphorisms and associations, from the importance of sacred music to the understanding of what might be behind our existence. This dialogue would mark my last direct personal encounter with Louis Dudek.

1. THE POET

While starting a professional career with Montreal's Goethe Institut (Montreal's German Cultural Centre was located first on Drummond Street, and later in Place Bonaventure during the 1970s), I simultaneously attempted to undertake a thesis towards a German Ph.D. for the University of Hamburg. In June of 1971, during a meeting in Cape Cod with my German official *Doktorvater* Rudolf Haas, the topic we agreed upon was "The Influence of

Imagism in Anglo-Canadian Literature"[2]. Doing a doctoral thesis abroad for a German university constituted one challenge. Researching imagism in Canada was a second obstacle; part-time writing and researching during weekends was a third. Prior to a visit back to Europe, when I made a transatlantic phone call to my Hamburg supervisor to discuss the possibility of a rendezvous, he coolly replied: "You know my office hours. Thursdays from 14-16 o'clock". When somebody—it might have been James Reaney—gave me Louis Dudek's name and I dared to call him at the office, he asked: "Where are you, at Drummond?" And immediately: "Well, let's meet right now at the corner of Stanley and de Maisonneuve!" So much for the differences between academic hierarchies in Europe and North America.

During our first conversations, Dudek had already touched upon the essentials that lay beyond the formal aspects of poetry in general and imagism in particular: what would induce a young German to write a thesis on Canadian poetry? What was the relationship between modernism in literature and arts and modern war? But also: why had Europe been haunted by such tragedies as the wars and the *holocaust*, apart from the German contribution to this fact? With a sweeping motion of his hand he put aside any talk of "collective guilt" by Germans or others, and was empathetic and noble enough to discuss the eternal *"why?"* which lay behind the crucial atrocities of the holocaust. This direction in our discussions would take place only after our literary relationship had turned into a deep, profound and mutual friendship—during the 1990s.

Thus Louis Dudek had given me his first "private lecture"—on imagism—sometime during the fall of 1971, in some downtown Montreal cafeteria. In fact, almost all of our conversations took place away from the campus and home, except for our very last conversations in 1997 and 1998. At that time, we drove to east end Montreal, where he showed me the area where he had grown up; and it was a greater treat to be invited to Louis' home in Westmount. As has been well-documented, even in some of his poems, he preferred to talk about literature and philosophy in a location where everyday life was taking place: in some simple cafeteria like Ben's Delicatessen, a Chinese restaurant, or a snack-bar in the Alexis Nihon Plaza—for him, modern locales for such *symposia* of ancient origin. As I recall, I took many notes on that first occasion; these

The Imagists

(1948)

In the great summer of '39
   they came like dawn
and in their midst a man.
War made no noise
as yet, but in the world of poems
                    light and silence —
a dawn, where things came into place
as the sun warmed.

O heart, you tumbled
turning, inside out
          — whatever soul is!
One day, sat in the park and wept
it was war
            the end of summer
and the lines falling
out of shape, as it would never be again
in our world.

were unfortunately lost in the course of several moves, but their essence remains clear: Dudek regarded his beginnings as being rooted in the footsteps of Imagists like Ezra Pound or William Carlos Williams: "...the specific influence of both Pound and Williams is clearer in my own writing than either in Layton or Souster, or in any other of the 40's poets"[3].

It was Dudek who sent me on the trails of Raymond Knister, W.W.E. Ross, Dorothy Livesay, A.J.M. Smith, F.R. Scott and others. It was Dudek who handed me his and Michael Gnarowski's *The Making of Modern Poetry in Canada* (Toronto, 1967). To this day, I consider this volume to have been my indispensable 'bible' throughout these studies. Dudek also initiated my first visit to the National Library of Canada, that marvellous, hospitable and generous institution where I, supported by my wife Hildegard, would work on weekends for the next several years, trying to decipher *microfiches* (I would sometimes doze off on a couch facing the elevators, due to my full-time teaching position in Montreal—something which, at that time, would have been unthinkable in a German National Library!). There, I was to stumble across two quotations which Dudek perhaps liked best out of my otherwise-limited discoveries in that thesis. Both quotations lucidly encapsulate the attitudes of that time.

Rev. B. Dollard, the Toronto *Globe and Mail*'s literary critic, attacked free verse: "On this continent of late, fame and pelf have been showered on many sham bards who could give the public nothing better than reams of 'shredded prose', miscalled poetry"[4]. Louis Dudek, in retrospect, found the fusion of literary criticism for political purposes in the following quotation by J. Lewis Milligan, both intolerable and hilarious: "Nietzsche has been blamed for the war in Europe. He ought also to be held accountable for *vers libre* and other Hun-like liberties that have been taken with thoughts and morals in these latter days ... The *vers librist* has started on a road which will lead to mental disintegration. He will shortly find himself in company with those who try to convince themselves that the devastation of Belgium was a sublime epic of action, and that Krupp is a modern Homer, whose *vers libre* thunders through the world"[5].

Having graduated from both Hamburg University and the University of Western Ontario, where I started my Canadian teaching career and earned my Canadian M.A., it was in Montreal where my professional life began. For a long time, my intended thesis became the procrastinated-against victim of my professional duties at the cultural institute. Louis Dudek, with his very human concern, was full of understanding for this difficult task of my combining research with a full-time job. On the other hand, he regularly enlivened my comfortable conscience by sending me a consistent trickle of notices on forthcoming literary events (poetry readings, publications et al.). He did everything to motivate, to stir up, and to provoke questions and reflections, always associated with the recurrent theme: "What is behind it all?" "What is essential in life?" And so forth.

During those years in the mid-1970s he also generously made available to me an impressive number of documents, poems and correspondence, some of which were unpublished. Included were some Pound documents which are now, I understand, in the possession of the National Library of Canada. Of the original manuscripts, I kept the poem (page 68) which was typed by Dudek in 1948. He had written "The Imagists"[6] as an allusion to William Carlos Williams' poem "Aux Imagistes". Because its content summed up the basis for our first encounters, Dudek handed this original to me, accompanied by a dedication, on May 11, 1978, during the presentation of the thesis—finally!—at Montreal's Double Hook Book Shop.

Bernhard & Hildegard Beutler with Louis Dudek at The Double Hook Book Store, Montreal, May 1978.

He had asked Hélène Holden, Judy Mappin and the staff to sponsor a little *'lancement'* under the auspices of the German Consul Schmidt-Schlegel. This fine reception concluded our seven years' stay in Canada; for professional reasons we had to return to Germany.

My next and last personal encounters with Louis Dudek took place in Westmount during the summers of 1992 and 1997, and again, on the occasion of the celebration of his 80th birthday, in February 1998. What had impressed me during our prior meeting in 1992, was his wish to buy me a mini-cassette-recorder, or Dictaphone. He had recalled the problems I'd had with my first little machine in the seventies (this syndrome continues to the present, as I battle my computer). We did eventually get a taped session on Imagism and poetry in his retrospective. I asked Dudek how, in looking back upon his early observations of the 1970s, he regarded the importance of this literary movement. He now qualified his earlier remarks:

"Throughout my life I always thought to try this theory of imagism in order to strengthen the poetry and I think it is good for the poem to have an imagistic quality in it. I came with time to realize that Pound's theory .... actually leads to chaos, disintegration of the poem...because it has no intellectual order of underlying images."[7]

An image without meaning now seemed useless to Dudek. While Imagism contained an "aesthetic" value, poetry needed an "intellectual" expression as well. Dudek, in this conversation, even went back to the roots of creation, in citing St. John's (in Greek!):

"ευ αρχη ευ ο λογοσ... that is, there is some intellectual order in the universe. The same would be true for poetry. Imagism has had its time, which it reflected, but reality was shown without any real coherence, a kind of phenomenology without any religious implications. But now things have changed. The real question nowadays should be: 'what is behind the actual?'"[8]

After many associative allusions to the early imagists, to Flaubert, Husserl, the medieval scholastics, Thomas Aquinas and others, Dudek ended pronouncing the key and lasting phrase: "I am a seeker"[9].

2. THE HUMANIST

Throughout my years of contact with him, Dudek has struck me as being a man of universal knowledge. Despite the fact that this term seems only to exist as an adjective, he was in every sense a 'universalist'. I am sure, however, that he would have loved to be perceived as being at the origin of such a term—being the ingenious, active *penseur* and mirror of things that happened centuries ago on this planet, right up to the present day; through his poetry, essays, interviews and correspondence. He spoke or at least read several languages beyond English and French. He adhered to a classical horizon (Latin, Greek, Hebrew) and was in this aspect close to Goethe, who has stipulated that the study of Greek and Roman Literatures should serve as the basis of all higher education[10].

He also had a working knowledge of Eastern European languages (how often did he quote from Dostoevsky, Nabokov, in his earlier years?) and was translating Goethe, Heine, Thomas Mann and Stifter from German into English. During some vacations in Way's Mills in the late seventies he even studied writing in Chinese, once asking me—in that language!—to give his love to my wife Hildegard, "whom you must treasure more and more, as 'woman with broomstick' ...or 'good wife'". His last correspondence contains evidence of his thorough study of an anthology of poems I had sent him[11]—"The world is large, but human beings are all one."[12]

Dudek adhered to the European roots of his ancestors as well as the settlers of North America and Québec, well demonstrated in his famous long poem *Europe* of 1955. In his new preface to "Europe" he clearly states his *credo:* "Democracy, yes, humanity and justice" (p. 9). Or in the poem itself (no.83):

> Democracy is this freedom, this light
> shining on the human mind,
>   light
> in faces, actions —
> as the Greeks once carved it in these stones.[13]

It is thus perfectly appropriate to call him a 'humanist' although he would have shunned such labels. Yet in times of widespread *Selbstreferenz* (auto-references) Dudek tried to be human, humorous, smiling on himself, teaching both modesty and empathy through his living example. In later years we discussed the impact of acquired, universal knowledge in relation to autobiographical experience. Dudek abhorred any sort of self-reference, yet admitted that in much of his poetry he used the first person ("I") when speaking about his own personal observations. This tendency is reminiscent of Pound's in the *Cantos,* but, of course, without wanting to generalize on this, it is exactly this personal touch that reaches the reader. Some of the most revealing lines in his long poem "Europe" can be found in his conclusion: what count most—apart from all elements of the old continent—are *people* (no 72):

> Having come to find in old Europe
> The cities and temples plural (according to Pound)
> and the statuary, and the living dead, their places
> remarkable in memory
> (preserved by unimportant people, inhabited by tenement dwellers),
>
> we have found little, soon almost forgotten,
> and the images that live, continually in the mind,
> are not of the arts at all,
> but of people:
> ...[14]

I may omit here any criticism on *Europe,* except for the fact that since I myself have travelled the same classical routes as Dudek had during the fifties, some of his observations are now obviously outdated. Yet most will remain valid indefinitely.

We did not discuss any details of this epic poem, but he was a bit unhappy about the minor geographical error of having placed Frankfurt, the city of Goethe's birthplace, on the *Rhein* rather than on the Main (corrected in the 1991 edition of *Europe),* which flows into the Rhine twenty five kilometers west of Frankfurt. We agreed on the well-known love of the northerners to head south:

> I knew what Goethe
>
> was glad to get away from ...[15]

But we disagreed on the skies, where he felt, "looking at the sky, in Germany, 'this is already home'". Apart from the cloudiness we often have in common, the vastness of North American skies is regarded as unsurpassed by each European who crosses the ocean.

Having returned from Canada to Germany in June 1978, I survived—following a head-on car collision on Route 13 in Germany—a clinical death in the fall of that year. Belatedly informed of this accident, Dudek wrote a consoling letter to me on his McGill University stationary with its famous red letterhead, on December 15, 1978: "...Here is a May Day poem I was typing out this morning. It might strike you fancy, as you also return to life—...It's entitled 'As May Flowers'—I dedicate it to you, and it will appear in a new anthology soon to appear"[16]. I was deeply moved—and felt greatly honoured. Oddly enough, we only had a detailed discussion

about this poem, which is full of alliterations and in part comparable to Gerard Manley Hopkins, whom we both loved, only fourteen
years later, during my 1992 summer-visit to Montreal. I remember us
sitting in the Alexis Nihon Plaza cafeteria and seeing his totally surprised expression when I ventured to begin an interpretation, stating that my own immediate response to the first three words (and
title) of the poem, had been an association with the Mayflower ship,
an idea which had not crossed his mind at all. [N.B.: The tapes of
this long conversation, were lost during a move, but they have
recently turned up again and are waiting to be transcribed].

My near-fatal accident "intrigued" Dudek as it did others: the
vision of a "tunnel" while "dying", the light that followed this tunnel, then re-entry into the body... "...we go down to oblivion and
feed the earth for a new season", as stated in the last line of this
poem. Is there something after death? In 1998, during my last visit
to him, he had just published *The Caged Tiger* and handed me a
draft of the "definitive edition" of his poetry: once again, a mirror of
Louis Dudek's cosmos. At the time (1998) he was resolved not to
publish anything again. He suggested that my small book on
Imagism should be translated into and published in English—the
accident of 1978, followed by the resumption of my professional
career back in Europe, had halt-
ed our negotiations at the time.
Now, in 1998, he pressed the
issue once again, even offering
to pay, if necessary, for this
endeavour. However, I managed
to convince him that time had
passed, the situation had
changed, and that a thorough
new study would have to be
undertaken. I would much prefer
to bring Dudek back to the old
continent by publishing a selection of his works in German. We
vowed to each other that we
would try to do this together—
beginning upon my retirement in

Under the patronage
of
the Consul General of
the Federal Republic of Germany
and Mrs. Philipp Schmidt-Schlegel

YOU ARE INVITED

to celebrate
the German publication of
IMAGISM IN CONTEMPORARY CANADIAN POETRY

Come and meet the author
BERNHARD BEUTLER

Thursday **at**   **O'clock** May 11th, 1978

Double Hook Bookshop
1235A Greene Avenue
Westmount, Quebec
Tel. 932-5093
(Regrets only)

May 2001. Thus his sudden death during my last week in the office struck me as a terrible, personal shock—and ensured a legacy.

Despite my misgivings for having abandoned such a noble project for such a long time (due to my professional obligations), I derived some consolation from his last letter to me. It serves as an excellent summary of Dudek's evaluation of poetry in general: "Don't worry, poetry is not in a hurry to conquer the world. For those who want it, it's already there."[17]

Dudek's inspiring, even caring, attitudes may be glimpsed throughout his correspondence. The greetings to my family were more than mere ritual: they were profuse in empathy, always brimming with useful hints for the pursuit of the subject. They were also accompanied by articles, his own recent books and personal memories. One of them concerns his great love of music. He liked Bach, and even listened to the Vienna Boys' Choir's interpretation of "Silent Night"—despite the fact that both of us felt it was somewhat on the kitschy side.

In a letter to my wife Hildegard, who had not been able to accompany me for his 80th birthday, he describes an emotional moment during our last meeting in Montreal:

"Bernhard will tell you of a strange coincidence: I wanted to play for him two or three pieces from my favourite Buxtehude records, which I have had for 50 years (acquired in New York), *Schaffe in mir, Gott, ein rein Herz* and *Herr, wenn ich nur Dich hab*—when Bernard stopped to tell me that the 'Instrumental Ensemble of the Bach Anniversary, Hamburg' was well-known to him, and that his aunt was actually playing the first violin in this record. Margot Guillaume, Soprano. Extraordinary. I loved this record long before I ever knew Bernard—but we were already connected!"[18]

Yes, Louis Dudek was a humanist: full of knowledge, wisdom, the gift of associative thinking, empathetic, meditative, humorous, with a great sense of self-irony, helpful to everybody in pursuit of intellectual or even spiritual search, a cosmopolitan teacher. He would not give rapid answers but rather, by posing questions, stir up the students, partners in discussion or his readers, to re-think and question what lay behind the given subject and the habitual interpretations—the eternal quest for both essence and existence. In pronouncing himself a 'seeker', for justice and truth behind life and the universe, he demonstrated both Socratic and 'Faustian' values.

In this lifelong quest as a human being inspiring students and friends alike he was probably lonely, apart from his love for his wife Aileen, his son and his family, but he knew that in this existential loneliness—before death—all individuals are united:

It is an art observing
   "the truth of human experience"

Directly or indirectly—does it matter?

So today, the individual

   Is at the heart of it

As in the past, some god
   some universal truth
   was the aim.
Today the individual is at the heart of it.
You yourself.
You are the subject of poetry.[19]

Having asked Louis Dudek in 1993 about the sources of his humanism, he wrote: "You are so right about my 'humanism'. It is directly descended from Goethe. The line is from Goethe to Carlyle and Matthew Arnold, then to T.S.Eliot and Ezra Pound as humanistic social critics, and finally to my actual teachers at Columbia University, Lionel Trilling and Emery Neff." [It is interesting to note that Dudek was amazed by the fact that as a pupil, I had attended a ceremony during which a Hamburg Goethe prize was given to T.S. Eliot, where the latter had spoken in the Rathaus on "Goethe as a sage."]

He went on to cite Goethe's "harmony," although without providing religious support. Yet he left wide open that question on the possibility of life after death that has haunted humankind since the beginning: "Who knows whom we shall meet in the hereafter, even we humanists?" And finished: "Actually I'm re-reading Goethe's Wilhelm Meister, the *Lehrjahre* and *Wanderjahre*. So good, and much more wholesome in style! Tell it to your students."[20]

Like his *Vorbild* Goethe, Louis Dudek continued in his search for the 'absolute' behind the universe, but he combined it always, it seems, with pedagogical advice; and thus confirmed by this attitude his 'Greek', classical roots. And he confessed: "We are, with Goethe 'citizens of the world.' "[21]

Yes, it is a 'strange coincidence' that Louis Dudek, poet and humanist, died on March 22nd, the same day as Goethe....

BONN, GERMANY, MAY 2002

NOTES

1) "Louis Dudek 1918—." *Contemporary Authors Autobiography Series.* Vol. 14. Ed. Joyce Nakamura. Detroit: Gale, 1991. 121-42.

2) Bernhard Beutler, *Der Einfluß des Imagismus auf die moderne kanadische Lyrik englischer Sprache,* Lang, Frankfurt/Bern/Las Vegas, 1978.

3) Louis Dudek, *The Tamarack Review,* Toronto, Summer 1965, p.59.

4) Rev. B. Dollard in *The Globe and Mail,* Toronto, January 21, 1916, p.16.

5) J. Lewis Milligan, "Is Vers Libre Poetry?", in *The Globe and Mail,* Toronto, November 24, 1917. p.18.

6) Louis Dudek: "The Imagists" (1948), privately-owned manuscript. Another version of this poem appears on page 54 of *Zembla's Rocks,* Véhicule Press, Montreal, 1986.

7) Transcribed from a privately-owned tape, Feb. 7, 1998.

8) *Ibid.*

9) *Ibid.*

10) Gert Mattenklott: *Wie bewährt sich Goethes Weltliteratur?* in: *Bernhard Beutler/Anke Bosse: Spuren, Signaturen, Spiegelungen—Zur Goethe-Rezeption in Europa,* Böhlau, Köln-Weimar-Wien, 2000.

11) Joachim Sartorius, *Atlas der neuen Poesie,* Rowohlt, Reinbek bei Hamburg, 1995. Note: Sartorius translated and published Dudek's "Blowing Your Own Horn" and "The Last Word" in Sueddeutsche Zeitung, München, Dec. 11, 2002 and Jan. 4/5/6, 2003.

12) Privately-owned letter, Sept. 22, 1997.

13) Louis Dudek, *Europe,* rev. edition, Erin, Ontario: The Porcupine's Quill, 1991. Afterword by Michael Gnarowski.

14) *Ibid.*

15) *Ibid.*

16) Privately-owned letter, Dec. 15, 1978. Cf. *Zembla's Rocks,* Montreal: Véhicule Press, 1986. p. 141.

17) Privately-owned letter, Jan. 13, 1999.

18) Privately-owned letter, Feb. 8, 1998.

19) *The Poetry of Louis Dudek.* Ottawa: Golden Dog Press, 1998. p. 245.

20) Privately-owned letter, June 23, 1993.

21) *Ibid.*

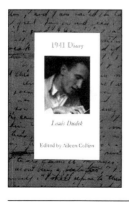

Louis Dudek, Ken Norris & Marc Coté,
Montreal, 1989.

A Dudek Alphabet

ATLANTIS.

DUDEK'S SYMBOL of the transcendent.

> "Here nothing is real, only a few
> actions, or words,
> bits of Atlantis, are real."

> —*Atlantis*

BARBARIAN.

Louis saw the barbarian as someone knowingly or unknowingly opposed to civilized values. He saw primitivism as sometimes unwittingly crossing the line into barbarism. What offended him most were the commercial barbarisms of popular culture. He was never a big fan of heavy metal music or hip hop.

BEN'S.

While teaching at McGill, his favorite lunchtime restaurant. Initiated The Poet's Corner.

CANADIAN.

Dudek worked long and hard to create a meaningful infrastructure for Canadian poetry, as opposed to poetry in Canada. What's very interesting to me is how Dudek combined an international artistic scope with a national cultural concern.

CIV/n.

"CIV/n not a one man job." —E.P.

A magazine, and also a mission. Louis believed strongly in civilized values, while always waiting and working for the civilization to come.

CONTACT.

A magazine (edited by Souster, with much assistance from Dudek). A press (editorial board: Dudek, Layton, Souster, and, later, Peter Miller). A philosophy of how to build Canadian culture from the ground up.

CONTINUATION.

The last of his long poems, in three parts, written over 30 years.

DELTA.

An extremely engaging personal little magazine of the 1950s. Later to expand into a press (Delta Canada), and offshoots (Delta Can, DudekCollins, The Golden Dog, New Delta, DC Books).

EUROPE.

And *En Mexico*. The two great long poems of the 1950s that moved the long poem away from the traditional narrative poem laid siege to by Pratt, and showed the way towards the long poem as it is currently practiced in Canada.

FRYE, NORTHROP.

Great cultural and critical antagonist. Louis saw Frye's structuralist literary theorizings as being quite harmful to poetry, particularly in Frye's justifying of turning a blind eye towards social realist poetry.

GREEKS, THE.

Dudek saw the Greeks as the starting point of Western Civilization, rationality, the birth of reason.

H.D.

Along with Marianne Moore, perhaps an unobvious influence.

IDEAS.

Ideas For Poetry. Ideas for living. Louis was a true intellectual, in the finest sense.

JUSTICE.

There is a perpetual search for justice in Dudek's poetry and critical writings.

> "Beauty is ordered in nature
>   as the wind and sea
>   shape each other for pleasure; as the just
>   know, who learn of happiness
>   from the report of their own actions."

—Europe 95

"KATZ IS KATZ".

Phrase from a Pound letter to Dudek that has always stuck with me. Prompted a long discussion between Louis and myself about Pound's further assertion that "leaf is a LEAF." Implication that the symbolic value is always inherent in the real object. And, in the first case, that a person is who he is.

LAYTON, IRVING.

Great friend, and great enemy.

MODERNISM.

In his teaching and critical writings, Dudek preached the doctrines of Modernism all his adult life. He was a poet of Modernist values, and always spoke highly of the Great Moderns: Pound, Eliot, Joyce.

MONTREAL.

He took great pride in his cosmopolitan city.

MUSIC.

His clear favourite of the sister arts.

NOTEBOOKS.

One of Louis' last publications was a selection from his notebooks, which he had been keeping since the early 1960's. A good place to stockpile poems and ideas. A writer's drawing board.

OPENNESS.

In *A Real Good Goosin': Talking Poetics,* Louis commended The Vehicule Poets for their openness. In point of fact, even although he was always subject to likes and dislikes, Louis was always open to at least entertaining the full spectrum of philosophies, ideas, and poetical approaches.

POUND, EZRA.

A great early influence. Pound sent Dudek heading in the direction of European Modernism. Only to come back to a Canadian concern, despite Pound's insistence that Dudek get his eye off what Pound considered local concerns, and onto international criteria. As a man and thinker, Pound comes in for a lot of criticism in Dudek's later critical writings. But Louis always had high praise for Pound's poetry.

QUÉBÉCOIS.

Dudek is very much a *Québécois* poet. I have always thought that he would have enjoyed much more critical success had he written in French rather than in English. The French are neither afraid of the intellect nor of abstract ideas.

REASON.

The great civilizing influence.

SOUSTER, RAYMOND.

His great collaborator in giving Canada an indigenous poetry and an indigenous publishing industry.

TRAVEL.

"'I hate travel' but all the poetry I've written seems to be about travel."

—*Atlantis*

UNDERSTANDING.

As a teacher, I never saw Dudek reject or undermine a student's opinion. He was always interested in creating the conditions for understanding.

VIOLIN.

A favored instrument.

WIT.

Louis valued wit (perhaps revealing a secret love for Pope and Swift?), and there is a lot of it on display in his poetry, critical writings, and epigrams.

X.

As in mathematical equations. I have never met another poet who was so interested in math. Also as in "x marks the spot":

> "Today we passed over Atlantis
>   which is our true home."
>
> —*Atlantis*

YES.

Gnarowski and Siebrasse's late Fifties Montreal magazine.

ZEMBLA'S ROCKS.

Perhaps another expression of the "Atlantis principle," this time in the form of lyric poems, and at the opposite end of the alphabet. From Nabokov, a favorite author: "blue inenubilable Zembla."

MARIANNE BLUGER

Photo Courtesy of Aileen Collins

In February

in memoriam, Louis Dudek

TENURED there a vaunted don
But never really one of them . . .

Clear-eyed cranky enervated thin
No gap-tooth sucking one white thumb
No honourary mystic with loins in pins and gauze

No Sam Johnson whom I much adored
No Wittgenstein noble in lucid confusion
No flame-hearted Simone Weil
Just a sallow dislocated wit
With a knack for richly random thought
In the crush of that first moderns class
I saw the guy was dangerous

When he declared intent to breed in us
A lust for *le mot juste*

With a bent-back book gripped to his face
swaying and rocking in near trance
he'd read aloud the choicest: Pound
H.D. Williams Housman Frost
Dickinson Cummings Moore
Yeats Hopkins Eliot and the rest
blissed as his free arm beat
the iambs trochees dactyls
and the stunning spondees out
With one at least he did succeed
side-tracked by poems
who never finished Meds
a high-strung woman—middle-aged

who on a winter Monday decades later
struck with an urgency to find
among the dusty thousands stored here
one slim volume—his late poems

settles now in cellar gloom
by a naked bulb on a bent lawn chair
to read by a lozenge window
beyond which silent snow-flakes drift

the rafters creak
the furnace drones

again the old beams groan
the furnace stops

the snow floats down
but I read on

glad this lonesome winter afternoon
for the *de profundis* of that honest man

Ode to Literature

A man wrote a book in which
a man wrote a book in which
a man wrote a book
or so I had thought
but now we debate—Louis and I
who like robust families
delight to disagree
whether the third author wrote that second book
which 'fact' would make the second author
fictional or whether the second author
wrote his own book
in which case he'd be 'real'
(given of course that Nabokov wrote the lot
: his beautiful joke *Pale Fire)*.

Louis Dudek

The **Caged Tiger**

So you and I, when these plant leaves appear
Like days unfolding in the calendar,
Will watch the flowers sent out in shoots
And love grow out of his mysterious roots.

from "Flower Bulbs", *The Poetry of Louis Dudek: Definitive Edition*

Photo Courtesy of Stephanie Zuperko Dudek

**Stephanie Zuperko
and Louis Dudek
with Stella Sagaitis, 1970.**

Photo by SAS

Louis Dudek with his son, Gregory, celebrating
Dudek's 80th birthday at home, February 1998.

Eulogy

T HE FOLLOWING IS about Louis Dudek, my father, my private vision
of him as opposed to his public persona. I think it is fair to say
that he felt today's social climate embraces a voyeuristic attitude in
relation to its public figures. Subsequently, the profound confusion
between poetry or other creative endeavours and the personal
habits of the artist, is quite inappropriate.

Throughout my life, my father consistently expressed the
desire to keep his private life separate and distinct from his role
as writer, critic and teacher. He impressed upon me the feeling
that one's contribution to the arts or to public discourse should
not become entangled with one's private affairs, or whatever you

happened to have had for breakfast. Writing this article thus troubles me, since it partially abrogates that intent. My motives are twofold: on one hand, both our academic and popular cultures have become so obsessed with the lives of public figures, I think such an examination is unavoidable. As such, I might as well try and contribute to making this portrayal an accurate one. Perhaps more importantly, I have a personal desire to comment on my father and who he was. This is probably not the place for modesty—which he normally preferred—and so I'll risk embarrassing him, should he happen to be listening somewhere.

Although I want to comment on my personal relationship with my father, I should note that, to paraphrase the poet John Asfour, Louis Dudek was "probably the most accomplished and multifaceted poet in the country" and that he greatly affected the course of poetry in Canada. While I myself would not presume to comment on the significance of his influence on the Canadian literary scene, he was certainly inundated by visitors, manuscripts and phone calls from both established and aspiring writers. The only real manifestation of this in his personal life, however, was an infrequent discussion regarding a review of one of his books.

By and large, my interactions with my father were characterized by discussions of the kinds of complex ideas that one usually associates more with philosophy lectures. He was a very deep and creative thinker, with an exceptional breadth that he communicated unpretentiously. While he was earning his reputation in poetry and literature, as I was growing up, our dinnertime conversations often centered around the meaning of randomness and indeterminacy, the nature of the number *pi,* or the manner in which the Ancient Greeks did or did not express democracy.

These subjects in particular served as themes for the discussions we carried on for weeks, even decades. These exchanges were epitomized by dialectic and passionate discourse. Yet I think to a large extent that this quite possibly may have been the result of my own doing, a typical Oedipal interaction. Irrespective of why we argued so passionately over these ideas, it was owing to my father's unique hallmark as a debater that he would constantly attempt to turn down the level of diatribe and gamesmanship, in order to return to the truth of the subject at hand.

Although my father loved, and lived in, the world of ideas, he was very sensitive, caring, and full of humor. A poet and former student once marveled at my father's ability to combine logic, analysis and rationality with whimsy and playfulness. This playfulness was manifested both intellectually and prosaically. He invented the electric toothbrush before the first commercial one ever existed, and he loved to play games and music. One of his epigrams, from the book of that title, reads: "The only thing I regret is the time I spent not playing chess and the violin."

I can remember sitting on his foot, back in the days of my childhood. My cousin John-Anthony would sit on his other foot, and my father would carry us around the house like a pair of impossibly heavy Ski-Doo boots. I remember him picking up five or six copies of some play and spending the evening with friends reading parts of, for example, "Much Ado About Nothing."

At family gatherings, he would usually serve as the primary cheerleader while engaging in some sort of game, whether it was *Charades, Dictionary* or the board game *Risk.* Paradoxically, despite the fact that he loved games, he was very non-competitive. (Similarly, in literature, he disdained promoting his own work.) For example, while playing *Risk,* the ferocity of which he abhorred, he would always set out to lose for the sake of having a more enjoyable game, no matter how lucky he might get.

Dictionary is a game in which players vie to make up the most credible definition for an unknown word. If he had chosen to, he could have trounced us with ease. Instead, he would consistently make up the most whimsical pseudo-definitions, once suggesting that a "fraken" was the term for the handle of an ice-cream machine.

A friend recently recalled to me how, during a game of *Scrabble,* the rest of us were struggling anxiously over a crammed board with competitive fervor. At one point my father remarked, "This is getting boring," and plopped down a huge word that liberated us as well as the board—demonstrating that one could play for the fun of it, rather than for the sake of competition. Such behaviour was typical of all aspects of his life.

His lack of competitive enthusiasm was consistent with an unparalleled sense of fairness and generosity of spirit. He frequently subjugated his personal gratification to his ideals, and sought the truth over any desire to simply win an argument. He would laud a student for making a good case that was completely antithetical to what he himself had said and believed. This was later corroborated by a story from Robbie Drummond regarding Tas Bey. This former student received an A+ for a paper idealizing aspects of Leonard Cohen's work that had been dismissed in earlier lectures.

In a world where poets are often portrayed as disheveled wild-eyed eccentrics, my father maintained a rare sense of modesty and propriety. During the 1970s, I'm not sure I ever saw him without his necktie. When I was a child he used to take me bowling along with my friends Jim and John, then for hamburgers (although we would coerce him by getting him to sing the A&W theme song with us—did he actually sing, or was it only us kids?)—and I seem to recall he wore a jacket and tie even then.

This element of formality was combined with his love of simple pleasures: campfires outdoors, playing guitar, a steamed hot dog at the market, lunch at Alexis-Nihon Plaza, accordion music with my uncles—as well as playing the *Chaconne* on the violin, and translating the poetry of Jean Narrache and Pierre DesRuisseaux. Or reading the original Ancient Greek version of Melissus, who said: "what exists has not come into being. Therefore, it has always existed. Nor will what exists be destroyed." At one point he taped the sheet music for the *Chaconne* up along the length of his hallway so that he could play it on the violin while walking the hall, and thus avoid having to turn any pages.

As I grew up, I gradually came to realize that my father was a writer of some reputation as well as a respected teacher. His course on the Great Writings of Europe (English 290) was vast in its scope; it was also apparently immensely popular with students, some of whom even sat in the aisles in order to be able to hear it. Or, as Gilbert Plaw told me, some of those who attended were not even students at McGill.

His former students have told me what an excellent lecturer my father was, or what an inspiring and supportive graduate supervisor he made. One of them mentioned to me that he considered my father to be one of the most influential figures of his formative years. He even added that: "Strange as it may sound, one of the greatest regrets of my life is that I turned down an invitation to play chess with him once."

I believe my father's devotion to and capacity for presentation and communication, carried over into his poetry and public speaking. During what might have been the first of his public readings I attended as an adult, at Harbourfront in Toronto, I couldn't help but be struck by how well he connected with his audience, combining both rapport and content with humor.

Despite his effectiveness and experience, each talk was a trial of nerves and stamina for him—perhaps his lectures were so good because he invested so much in them. On some days following his lectures, or more typically, departmental meetings, he would collapse with a migraine on the living room sofa. During other evenings, sometimes several times a week, he would play piano and perhaps sing to me. I can't recall the number of times, over many successive years, I heard him say: "This may be my last public lecture." Eventually this became something I would tease him about, "Oh, this is your NEXT last lecture!" I always knew there would be another one in the not-too-distant future . . . until now.

My father meant more to me than I can possibly express here—and I think other members of his circle similarly cherished him. I don't know how I will go on without having him around to discuss great ideas with: the meanings of things, and the birth of the atomic theory in Ancient Miletus, as well as how to live and what to worry about and how to cope with my own mundane worries and fears. His absence, and the absence of such talks, has left a painful hole in the fabric of my life. The personal impact of such an absence is obviously unique, but despite several rich and rewarding relationships with intellectually stimulating colleagues, students and family members, I have little hope of finding anybody with whom I can discuss these subjects in the same way.

However, I also reflect on the messages he strove to convey and would want us to remember: to be true to one another. Not to be overwhelmed or seduced by the barrage of barbarism in the world today. To remain in contact with truth in art and the richness of our culture, even when it is hard work to do so. And to play life in order to seek the truth, instead of merely trying to have our side win.

Photo Courtesy of Stephanie Zuperko Dudek

Louis & Gregory Dudek, circa 1967.

ATOMIC RACE

Keep slim or fat, descend or soar,
    You follow nature's plan:
The sequoia has outlived the dinosaur
    The maple will outlive man.

from the "Laughing Stalks" section of *Collected Poetry*

**Louis Dudek
& Ralph Gustafson,
Way's Mills, 1993.**

Photo Courtesy of Aileen Collins

**Robert Allen, Louis Dudek and Steve Luxton,
Way's Mills, 1990.**

Dudek's Uncertainty Principle:

Some Reflections on Physics, Outer Space, and the Poetry of Louis Dudek

There, somewhere, at the horizon
        you cannot tell the sea from the sky,
where the white cloud glimmers,

the only reality, in a sea of unreality,

out of that cloud come palaces, and domes,
                and marble capitals,
and carvings of ivory and gold—
                      Atlantis
shines invisible, in that eternal cloud.

                  Atlantis, "96"[1]

ON A LOVELY AFTERNOON last summer, canoe-tripping on Lake Superior with my good friend Ber Lazarus, I paddled from the lee of Simpson Island out towards the main. Daunting in worse weather, it was beautifully becalmed. Grand and blue, the sweet water ocean lay before our *Royalex* 'tripper'—while up on the horizon stretched a marvellous cloud. Spotless white, it screened a section of horizon while claiming its elegant and equivalent form from both sides of the line. Louis Dudek's famous verse passage drifted into my mind.

As did the poet's concern with "the affinity between the creative powers of the mind and the vital energy that produces beautiful things in nature."[2] The bisymmetricality of the airy, watery vision, like an artful tear along a paper fold, struck Ber and I deeply. Nervous in that huge water, we finally moved on, but still glanced sideways. During the minutes we spent turning into a bay, the wondrous cloud gradually dissipated, revealing not palaces and domes but a low, carbon-coloured smudge—likely Marquette, one hundred miles across the big lake, in Michigan. Bisymmetrical in more ways than one, the puff that had seemed both absolutely substantial and perfectly ethereal, was now a downright cloud, and likely toxic to boot! This lapse into the mundane might have disappointed some. But not Louis Dudek. He would have found the "proton decay" equally compelling.

This evening, crouched over my word-processor, I imagine that had Dudek been in our canoe (clad no doubt in his famous, plain white overcoat), he would have made light of any febrile or precious

melancholy. While appreciating the incandescent vision, he'd have celebrated its scarcity and the persistence of the mundane. As human being and artist, he was a realist-visionary who, rather than viewing the mostly "ordinary" nature of this world as testimony of its drabness and unworthiness, affirmed it, while at the same time treasuring its inspiration and transcendence. To seek meaning in the world—if not to necessarily find it—presented a conscious, no nonsense, yet higher challenge undertaken via the medium of poetry.

So the word of the wise is angry, it is against this world,
...
...Its work is slow.
It builds, not homes, but cities made of words:

"Meditation Over a Wintry City"[3]

In exploring Dudek's poems once again, the reader soon discerns that the object and very often the subject of Dudek's verse—especially within the long poems—is precisely this search for meaning within an quotidian world using lingo as plain, as nondescript, as that white overcoat. The poems' spirit shares a great deal with the scientific spirit. Science greatly interested Dudek: this I can confidently attest to, as the editor of his long essay *The Birth of Reason*, an examination of fifth century BC pre-Socratic Atomism and its links to quantum mechanics.

It (poetry) is a whirling
            spark in a vacuum,
And only scientists seem to
            enjoy the experiment.

"Pure Science"[4]

In fact, one need not squint very hard at the poet's shapely, seaborne vision of origin—nor for that matter at his treatment of the sea as a phenomenon—to view the passage quoted from the long poem "Atlantis" as a trope, not only for the artistic vision, but also for the mysterious microcosm described in modern quantum mechanics. It appears to be an analogue for the subatomic state with its quarks, bosons, fermions, gluons, etc.—all the increasingly numerous, restlessly creative subatomic particles—or are they "strings"? Or perhaps it's the Big Bang and original "singularity". In short, it presents a glimpse at the womb of matter.

Likewise, Dudek's vision suggests the big *cosmological* picture. Is that the "quantum sea" out there, or a nova—an exploding star enriching the interstellar medium with the heavy elements (carbon for example) that make life possible, including our own? Or could it even be a Black Hole, into whose own mighty and mysterious mixmaster of a spiral galaxy, we will one day be vacuumed to ultimate destruction-recreation? We are the offspring of this apparently unprecedented drama.

A quiver in Space-Time, they say
is the definition of man;
a quivering
Continuum, the definition of nature.

"Relativity"[5]

The paradox of destruction-recreation lies at the heart of Dudek's attempt to discern the "how" and the "why" of our—and the universe's—existence. This preoccupation is shared by the quantum theorists and the cosmologists. Equally significantly, these scientists are bent on developing a "GUT" or a General Unified Theory that will fuse the string-ends of the infinitesimal and the gargantuan together (at "Big Bang" heat!). This, I feel, is also true of the poet, with his goal of searching into the nature of being and reality: probing and weighing, like any twentieth century literary Modernist, the significance of microcosmic detail, the tell-tale particle, while also—less acceptable to Modernist doctrinaires—developing far-reaching, essentially ratiocinative, unifying statements. Linked to this general, unified approach, I'll later argue, is Dudek's very controversial style.

Our world and the universe, of course, operate according to "various hierarchies, or levels... For example at one end we have the fundamental laws of physics... Now, if we go higher up, from this, in another level we have properties of substances... On, up in the hierarchy. With the water we have waves, and we have a thing like a storm...."[6] (One is attempted to insert "sea" for "storm" in this professional physicist's exposition!) High in the "hierarchy", Dudek is primarily a literary and cultural physicist/cosmologist. His poems are the precise record and transcript of a powerful thinker and feeler writing about civilizing elements, and mostly cultural and aesthetic forces and values, in a manner he hopes will, as much as a man's thoughts may, survive and transcend the entropic forces of commercial and intellectual fashion.

And as for art, that's very long
—at least we used to think so,
yet Chaucer says
'al shal passe that men prose or ryme,
take every man his turn, as for his tyme...'

"A Short Speech"[7]

But there is the eternal in art

"Even Art Perishes"[8]

From the point of view of the poems' style, they eschew fine writing, overly elaborate imagery ("barren particularity"), and the classical concept of resolution or "closure". In this manner they embody the belief that the process of truth-searching is open-ended and processive.

At the same time, regarding their content, the poems are reflective, showing respect for literary tradition, and making no bones about advocating discrimination. When theoretical, they exhibit a bent that shuns totalism (the "exasperating megalomania of Hegelian theory"[9]), and is characteristically provisional. Though the poet is deeply persuaded of the value of art, his poems avoid becoming artifacts.

It is an almost unique combination: an apparent clash between form and content which puts many of our most ideological critics and poets at a cross-sea. Locked in battle, they agree only that Dudek's work is a bundle of contradictions and, grudgingly, paradoxes. The work in technique and content is deemed simultaneously radical *and* reactionary, though for different reasons: reflecting, in short, an exasperating mutual exclusivity.

A wave and a particle, Dudek's work resembles a Heisenbergian uncertainty. Bespeaking submerged aesthetic insecurity, each faction nevertheless tries to seat the poet in its own boat.

The late Modernists as well as those who consider themselves to be primarily lyricists, embrace his *content:* his concern with conscious art ("more consciousness not less"), and his passionate advocacy of the worthiness of the western intellectual and artistic tradition. His denotative *style* they throw overboard, dismissing Dudek's use of direct language, his often abstract expositions on culture and society, and so forth.

On the other hand, their unruly aesthetic opposition, The Black Mountain-L-A-N-G-U-A-G-E-Post-Modernist-e-t-c. faction, laud that plain style with its linked "phenomenological" open-ended form, and admire his status as perhaps *the* originator of the Canadian, long "culture-poem". It's Dudek's Classic outlook and *content:* with its embracing of a cosmopolitan literary tradition (Dudek, of course, admired the Greeks—see his poem "Kosmos: The Greek World"), with its advocacy of polite discrimination, its rejection of icon Charles Olsen's subjective hieroglyphics, its criticism of McLuhan and related communications and media theorists, that is unacceptable!

For both of these schools, Dudek's heart is in the right place, but his muse has somehow set herself adrift. Each believes Dudek's innovative practice should, more correctly and consistently applied, have given birth to their particular marriage of style and content, their "standard model" as the nuclear physicists say. The poet is somewhat like that elegant, curvaceous cloud, obscuring a straight (Newtonian) line. While removed from that white haze, temples and domes, his Atlantis of imaginative creation emerges. His "GUT" (General Unification Theory) transcends the uncurved space-time of the doctrinaires.[10]

A tireless critic of his age, Louis Dudek deplored the moral disorder he felt was due to wrangling, intolerant "orders". Sympathetic to Socialist leanings as a young man (See *East of the City),* he came, under the influence of Columbia University's Lionel Trilling, to realize that, whatever his proletarian sympathies, working class cultural values were not necessarily superior. In a way, but not in the sense of Frank Davey's characterization, he became an "elitist", believing that unlike in the ideal political system, all communications should not be created and treated equal, despite the nobility of the Democratic Fiction. Following missteps, dire struggles and confusions, poetic discourse and man's civilized and civilizing heritage, had earned genuine privileges. Therefore any characterization of his work as reactionary is glib or superficial.

Tellingly, his unique synthesis of content and form (apparent asymmetricality?) owes something, I believe, to the dynamics of the twentieth century Canadian poetry scene he wrestled with. Commenting upon another "hierarchy" at another now diverging moment in Space-Time, Richard Charques writes in *The Twilight of Imperial Russia*:

The distinguishing features of Russian social and political thought has always been a remorseless habit of abstract reasoning, an addiction to the extremes of logic, an incapacity for intellectual compromise. ...In a society at once so undeveloped and so rigidly controlled, a society which provided its most thoughtful elements with so little opportunity to share in the conduct of public affairs and the problems of government, only speculation on social and political subjects was free. In the freedom it suffered none of the disabilities imposed by experience. Impotent in practice, the intelligentsia, ... compensated itself by an abundance of theory.... Or, more accurately, since there was no native tradition of philosophic thought, it borrowed political doctrines from abroad and carried them to Russian extremes. Hyperbole and extravagance have at all times stamped the Russian revolutionary ethos, and Russian revolutionaries have always inhabited a world of phantoms.[11]

Like the theorems of nuclear science, Charques' critique of the Tsarist scene casts light on the processes of recent Canadian culture. Replace the term "political intelligentsia" with "cultural intelligentsia", make the borrowed foreign doctrines borne to extremes, cultural; view the general impotence as the product of marginalization and colonization by the American-dominated mass media, etc., and watch the shoe fit. In this country, the intercourse between poetic schools is particularly acrimonious and intolerant. They have debated and often continue to debate with the acute sanctimony of those who have very little at stake. Rather than being effectively seditious, they are inclined to insulate their small portion with often baffling theory.

But civilization, Louis Dudek, the discriminator, might have asserted, is precisely the ability to distinguish between practice and theory. Or at least to remain sensitive to a theory's provisionality, while keeping the windows ajar. Dudek's assertion echoes that of Stephen W. Hawking:

Any physical theory is always provisional, in the sense that it is only a hypothesis: you can never prove it. ...You can disprove a theory by finding a single observation that disagrees with the predictions of the theory. As philosopher of science Karl Popper has emphasized, a good theory is characterized by the fact that it makes a number of predictions that could in principle be disproved or falsified by observation.[12]

Popper believed that scientific theory, even when well-verified by results and capable of prediction, always remained conjectural. Of course this is physical theory. The application of principles derived from the natural sciences to the humanities and social sciences is termed *scientism*—perilous stuff; it was something Louis Dudek steered clear of. But shouldn't literary or aesthetic theories— if they are indeed viable theories or useful in any way, be even more attuned to their own tenuousness and provisionality? If perceived on a solely figurative level, the application of the concepts of theoretical provisionality and quantum indeterminacy to the evaluation of literary dogmas is very suggestive.

Harking back to nuclear physics and the explanatory writings of its practitioners, Dudek's work reminds me of the famous "thought experiments". With the aim of clarifying a complex issue or problem of physics, a "thought experiment" generates light by delving into and analyzing the operations of a simple but revealing analogue. I think of the small wheel and pawl mechanism with which, in his essay "The Distinction of Past and Future", the celebrated Richard P. Feynman explains to the non-mathematical lay reader the reasons for the irreversibility of Time.[13] Even the forthright, lucid style of Feynman brings to mind Dudek's own uncluttered transparency. Dudek's discourse stems from his position as human being and great teacher (as a teacher, he was a legend!) who openly thinks it through and presents, candidly and unpretentiously, the reasons and arguments that caught and persuaded him. There is no laying down of the Law here. ("The issue in modern culture calls for an entirely different treatment—disentanglement, clarification, plain good sense."[14])

There is an additional Dudek paradox, one that might have intrigued Popper, or Heisenberg: the best proof of Louis Dudek's open-mindedness may have resided in his inconsistency. I will leave for others to discuss the indisputable fact that although he was wary of Imagism, and, at the other end, extreme avant-gardism, he did everything to encourage and support the efforts of those sincere young Imagists and avant-gardists he knew, including this writer. More relevant to this argument is his rejection of Irrationalism and that which he deeply believed to be linked to it: mythopoeia. According to this highly-rational poet, the great bodies of water he observed—The Atlantic, e.g.—were, despite their thrilling effect on the observer, *material* seas—atomically-generated (though generative phenomena), and not deities deserving atavistic worship, for example. Yet any reader who delves into his great longer poems *Atlantis, Europe,* and *Continuation,* and experiences their seas' long, surging rhythms, somehow knows the poet's apparently positivist attitude doesn't tell the whole tale. The sea, as the poet dramatizes it, seems to represent Nature's mysterious creative origins (at its bottom lies the lost Atlantis—man's mysterious, unconscious imagination?) Here, surely, is not merely the reflection of a private perception. Such music, if not quite primitivist and mythopoeic, might well enthuse a Jungian!

At this point, with the poet in *my* imaginary canoe, I am reminded of the tale of Dr Johnson who, having "refute[d] Berkeley" by kicking a stone, some time later, sharing a boat in the Scottish isles with Boswell, tries to convince his companion that a wave has washed his iron spurs overboard!

Or maybe there is another explanation for Dudek's incipient proprioception. In an interview, John A. Wheeler, the father of the Black Hole, is asked by an interviewer:

A few years ago you asked the question: "Are life and mind relevant to the structure of the universe, or are they central to it?" Have you found an answer?

Wheeler: No. I'm one of the most baffled men in the world on this subject. There is a line of investigation involving the *anthropic (or man-related) principle* — the idea that the universe has to be much as it is or life would be impossible. Not only life as we know it, but any life at all would be impossible. On what else can a comprehensible universe be built but the demand for comprehensibility? My Princeton colleague, Robert Dicke, expressed it this way: What good is a universe without somebody around to look at... So why is the universe as big as it is? Because we're here![15]

The implication of such thinking is, of course, that we are products and participants in this universe, and the narrative of the Big Bang and the billion or more galaxies with their Black Holes are inscribed on our very genes. Trying with our hearts and brains to suss out the universe, we serve it and also realize the patterns of origin, deep within ourselves. While some physicists, like David Bohme, have taken this thinking into the realm of the explicitly ontological, one does not have to embrace traditional metaphysics to resonate to the incipient holistic view of the universe being presented here:

Individual theories may stand or fall but the unification approach is likely to persist, for aesthetic as well as rational reasons. ...Supersymmetry is particular depicts the universe as having begun in a state of sublime perfection, the contemplation of which elicits such enthusiasm in the minds of theoretical physicists that some have taken to calling the early universe "paradise lost." ...A cosmic fall from grace came during the first fraction of a second of the expansion of the infinite universe, when the symmetries of genesis fractured as the universe cooled. ...The fall from grace is seen as essential to existence as we know it. Absolute symmetry is beautiful, but it is also sterile. Life thrives on imperfection, and is full of examples of the cosmological principle that one has to break symmetries to get things done...[16]

Louis Dudek's poetry resonates profoundly to visions of perfect (earlier) universes, while celebrating and reworking the fertile asymmetries of the present one:

> Pressure of the suns
> buckles the atoms together,
> but man is a later structure
> who undoes the work of the sun.
>
> With a spark of the fire that burns in the stars
> smouldering in our ashes,
> we plan to try another earth, or finish this one.
>
> Atlantis, "51"[17]

Man is maybe a spike of order in the present thermodynamic inflation and thinning of matter.

> Every energy is an angel.
> But there is a great deal of waste in nature.
> Man is perhaps an attempt at economy.
>
> Atlantis, "41"[18]

Our cells wax nostalgic for the paradisal unities of the singularity (remember also Plato's *Symposium* in which Aristophanes identifies asymmetry with the fall from grace, asserting that human beings, once spherical, were separated in two by Zeus as punishment for committing the sin of pride). We are the observers of that curved cloud at the horizon, and that destructive-creative cloud. The primarily inductive, science-loving poet feels the mysterious swell of the ocean beneath his voyage!

Writing about his work on Atomism, in *The Birth of Reason*, Louis Dudek declared that "the ultimate reality is unknowable," —but he is "sure that if it were knowable it would satisfy both the materialist and the theist, and much more that we cannot imagine.[19]

NOTES:

1. Louis Dudek, poems from *Atlantis* (Ottawa: The Golden Dog Press, 1980), p. 96.

2. Northrop Fry, "Letters in Canada". *University of Toronto Quarterly,* Vol X XII, No 3, April 1953, reprinted in *Bush Garden, Essays in Canadian Imagination* (Toronto: Anansi, 1971), p. 20.

3. Louis Dudek, *Collected Poetry* (Montreal: Delta Canada, 1971), p. 29.

4. Ibid., p.151.

5. Ibid., p.66.

6. Richard P. Feynman, "Unified Theories of Physics," in *Physics, Astronomy, and Mathematics,* ed.Timothy Ferris, (New York, Little, Brown, and Company, 1991), pp. 160-161.

7. Louis Dudek, *Collected Poetry* (Montreal: Delta Canada, 1971), p. 153.

8. Louis Dudek, *The Surface of Time* (Montreal: Empyreal Press, 2000), p. 67.

9. Louis Dudek, in "H.A. Innis' *Empire and Communications,* H.A. Innis' *The Bias of Communication,* Marshall McCluhan's *The Mechanical Bride"* from *Selected Essays and Criticism* (Ottawa: The Tecumseh Press, 1978), p. 39.

10. Another way of looking at the apparent contradiction between Dudek's form and content is provided by psychoanalysis. This approach begins with the perception that Modernist poetry is fragmented, unwhole (Eliot in his essay "The Metaphysical Poets" arguing that "in the seventeenth century a dissociation of sensibility set in, from which we have never recovered.") The root of this splitting is (see Freud's *Civilization And Its Discontents)* the unbinding of Desire from the Intellect, the ego from the superego, content from form, etc. The two traditions within Modernism—the mainstream and purportedly establishment, and the Avant-Garde—embody incomplete selves. Both are fundamentalist and decadent, engaged in a Manichean conflict. Each denounces the other, Savanorola-like; each unwittingly or unwittingly ignores a symbiotic relation, and each enjoys a vested interest in preventing aesthetic homeostasis (i.e. this sharing of a mutual interest in being Tweedledum and Tweedledee is very productive of university jobs [i.e. successful capitalization], though with offices at the opposite ends of the hall!). The challenge, of course, is how to resolve this primal conflict at the core of the Modernist sensibility, in order to affect a new equilibrium. Dudek, by embracing the phenomenological present in his form and style—Desire—and the past, with its nourishing depths in his content—Reason and Meaning—attempts and I

believe in many ways gains a new fusion, thus articulating a unified, passionate poetic intellect. Of course, such theorizing smacks of the mythopoeia that deeply aggravated him, would have made his lips purse.)

11. Richard Charques, *The Twilight of Imperial Russia* (New York: Oxford University Press, 1965), p.40.

12. Stephen W. Hawking, *A Brief History of Time,* (New York: Bantam Books, 1988), P.10.

13. Richard P. Feynman, "The Distinction of Past and Future", from *Physics, Astronomy, And Mathematics,* ed.Timothy Ferris, (New York: Little, Brown, and Company, 1991), pp. 154 -156.

14. Ibid.

15. John A. Wheeler, interviewed by Mirjana R. Gearhart in Forum, *Cosmic Search* Vol. 1. No.4, p.4.

16. Timothy Ferris, "Unified Theories of Physics" in *Physics, Astronomy, and Mathematics,* ed.Timothy Ferris (New York: Little, Brown, and Company, 1991), p. 125.

17. Louis Dudek, poems from *Atlantis* (Montreal: The Golden Dog Press, 1980), p. 41.

18. Ibid., p. 51.

19. Louis Dudek, *The Birth of Reason,* (Montreal: DC Books,1994), Back Cover.

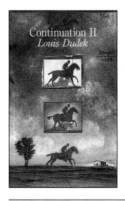

STEWART DONOVAN

Photo by Geof Isherwood

Brian Trehearne, Stewart Donovan, Michael Gnarowski & Louis Dudek at Dudek's home, Montreal, June 1996.

Down Home With Louis Dudek: An Interview

*I*N OCTOBER OF *1993 Louis Dudek agreed to do a reading tour of three Maritime universities. He was seventy-five at the time and had published a collection of essays the previous year. Two of the essays were on Rev. R.J. MacSween, a priest from Cape Breton who had founded* The Antigonish Review *and whose biography I was engaged in writing. Louis was eager to promote MacSween, as he regarded him as "Canada's great unknown poet."*

It was, on reflection, typical of Louis' generosity, humility and curiosity that he would spend time championing another poet when his own time, his remaining years, were so precious to him. This is not to say that he was an old man; he never became one. Consider

this: from the age of seventy-four until he died last March he pub-
lished no fewer than seven books and at least five of these were whol-
ly new compositions. His physical and intellectual resources seemed
boundless. He was, among many other things, our great intellectual
poet. Now he is gone, scattered, as Auden famously wrote of Yeats,
among a hundred cities and wholly given over to unfamiliar affec-
tions. It was a joy and an honour to have known him. When we
made our trip to St. Francis Xavier in Antigonish and the University
College of Cape Breton in Sydney, I recorded Louis' conversation.
What follows are some of the talk and some of the topics Louis med-
itated on while going up the road.

ON STUDENTS IN THE CLASSROOM

LD You see, I think it's become a general thing for young people
from the age of twelve or so on to respond very very emotionally to
the collective experiences of their own generation. The experience of
a classroom is almost irrelevant to their lives; it doesn't seem to
have any bearing or any meaning because they have a much higher
voltage experience with this other thing. And this other thing has
been generated by a number of mediums. The job is trying to iden-
tify it. There's a little defect there because one doesn't seem to be
able to put one's finger on where the collective aspect of the thing
is. It doesn't seem to require them to be altogether in a great big
bunch at one time. Although there are several examples of where
there have been a large bunch of young people listening to this
music—great big arenas in London, in New York. This group experience of listening is a crucial experience. This is like the early
Christians preparing an enthusiastic, joyful, celebration of this new
religion, activity actually. But what are they celebrating though?

ON CARMEN, ROBERTS, EARLY CANADIAN POETRY
AND THE AVANT-GARDE

LD It's pretty hard for them to imagine though to see where it
[Modern Poetry] is going. What is the frontier of poetry, what is its
most forward-looking direction? That such good poetry could be

written in Canada. We respond to that because an American had written that this was beautiful, beautiful. But what did he really recognize? He recognized that this poetry could not be much more advanced than it was, but there was something else. Now what was that something else happening around 1880? They couldn't know that in Canada. You and I would find it difficult now to say where they should have been looking in 1880-90. Who were the poets? Where could they look? In the 90s there is a thing that I have written about called the poets of transition, and it's the transition that's important. The transition doesn't really appear until the 90s and that's in Houseman, Edwin Arlington Robinson, the poetry of Thomas Hardy. And it was fine, but Hardy is very confusing because Hardy wrote a lot of sentimental, quiet poems and most people liked that very much. My sister likes the sentimental poems but she doesn't realize that what Hardy is good for is a bitter, hard,

(Left to right) Ray Drohan, Margaret Drohan, Stewart Donovan & brother Ken Donovan with Louis Dudek in October, 1993.

negative poem. Robinson also for his negative poem. So there was at that transition a very very pessimistic, unhealthy kind of poetry, but who the hell would realize that profound denial of life and negation—I mean, of all the assumptions it is really the truth that is wanted at the moment. It's not yet a renewal—it's simply a transition. Even in Ezra Pound you wouldn't see this early on because Pound himself had to go through the late Victorian poets and what he later called his own "cream puffs"—stale cream puffs. He had to write stale cream puffs first. And they are stale cream puffs—they're terrible! Full of idealistic nonsense. So it seems that the moment in which real talent and authentic Canadian poetry appeared in Canada was an unfortunate moment, because at that moment poetry was in an indefinable, fuzzy state; even to the best minds it would be hard to see just exactly where it should be. Ezra Pound and his stale cream puffs was all that you could find at that moment. And what is Carmen but stale cream puffs? But I also think Carmen was a very fine, fine, gifted poet.

On the Genuine Intellectual, the Importance of Humour and Play in Teaching and Learning

LD There's a definition Richard Hofstaedter has in a book called *The Intellectuals in America*. He defines what an intellectual is—it's someone who has this attitude to ideas, to new ideas, but he has a playful attitude towards them and at the same time a serious side. The two things go together. Now, just as when you were making this point about the rats, joking about these PhD's, [that "getting a Ph.D. is like a rat gnawing through a wall," I was quoting R.J. MacSween] you're quite serious and yet you're also joking. And what you really mean, well, Christ, you're not going to stop to paraphrase that with any serious meaning. You know, it's not worth doing. In fact, you shouldn't do that. It's not a necessity to do that. It's too difficult to do in any case because it's a very subtle situation.

SD It's like explaining your poems before you read them.

LD Yes, it's creative to put ideas in this slightly ambiguous challenging way. It's more provocative, it's more dynamic, it's moving somewhere. And that should be understood, you see. But this definition of the intellectual, I've never forgotten it.

SD *It's a good one.*

LD This playful attitude. You fool around with these and wonder why it is, whether it's religion or politics or anything else, whereas the other people are just somber. The true intellectual is amused by them. Oppenheimer was like that with physics and physics ideas. A true intellectual. When I think about intellectuals I've known, they're all like that. That's the characteristic of it. Playful but no less serious.

CROSSING THE NEW BRUNSWICK NOVA SCOTIA BORDER: THE TANTRAMAR MARSHES MADE FAMOUS BY CHARLES G.D. ROBERTS IN HIS POEMS

LD Now where are these marshes?

SD *Tantramar? They're all around here.*

LD Oh there they are. Yeah, I recognize them. Nothing on earth will change them because you can't build anything on them or do anything with them so they keep being the same. A bloody wet mess!

SD *Louis Dudek's* Tantramar Revisited, *a bloody wet mess! Of course it is, I agree!*

LD We should give it to the Chinese and they could grow rice—and feed millions.

SD *Give it to the Dutch.*

LD: This is very rich soil. You guys don't know how to use land of this sort. Drainage—or maybe you could use trays and lift a lot of this land and grow food on the raised plots which are dried up. And keep shoveling it from underneath—growing these huge tomatoes all the time. Maybe there's a way. You don't want that many crops—you couldn't use that much. Wandlyn—what's Wandlyn?

SD Wandlyn—it's the name of a motel.

LD Is that an English name or is that a Gaelic word?

On E.J. Pratt

SD Extraordinary to start out as a Methodist minister and end up an Agnostic. And then he got tied up in all that nineteenth century naturalistic thought.

LD He tried to reconcile it but he really wanted to believe it.

On Carmen, Roberts and Yeats

LD Anyhow your Carmen-Roberts people went to New York, don't forget, after years. And when they went to New York they were very much in the centre of things there. They edited papers and so on. When Roberts wrote some silly urban poems, I think they were no good actually. And then he went to England and was involved in public life, the First World War was on. And then he came back to Canada to discover that he was a famous poet here. Much surprise to him. The thing is that Carmen and Roberts were looking for the modern way, but they started a little too early. They are stuck in that transition period which is so ambiguous and difficult for anyone to get going in. 20 years later when they are past their prime real changes start happening in modern poetry. Ezra Pound and T.S. Eliot are in London and Yeats is undergoing great changes in his style. Yeats' poetry was of the same kind of stale cream puff variety. He found Carmen, you remember the phrase—"insufferably intelligent." A hell of a snobbish put-down. And then you say how is Yeats so unintelligent but so profound? But much of his poetry is all hooked on to this one love affair [Maude Gonne], insufferably obsessed with one subject matter.

So these boys Roberts, Carmen and Lampman, when they matured and Lampman was dead already (and he was the only one who had latched on to it properly) they were thoroughly dead set against the modern. Roberts and Carmen both set their backs against it. What did they see that they didn't like? It's quite easy to see. It wasn't that the romantic assumptions were gone, it was something too realistic, too factual, too lacking in illusion. The cream puffs were gone—all the cream must have been taken out. Somebody was serving cream puffs without cream anymore. And here these cream puffs were flattened; the new pastry was fine little biscuits. The reality biscuits.

What do you think? Is it because they would have seen what Pound was about, or is it simply that being born at another time they would have written at another time? At that time because history is what is different. It changes and you respond differently because you're in that time. It's consistent with a multitude of different things that make up this different response.

ON GERARD MANLEY HOPKINS

SD Of course we can argue this, but then we have a figure like Hopkins who makes a mess of everything we're saying.

LD Oh yeah, well, but Hopkins is not in the twentieth century. He belongs to his time even though you don't think so.

SD Yes, he belongs to his time, he's a Victorian poet in subject matter, but his language and style are modern.

LD He used Anglo-Saxon. Was it really modern? What is it?

SD The feel of the language, that rocking delivery, the rough verse makes it feel modern.

LD When Ezra Pound said, D.H. Lawrence discovered the modern voice before I did, he didn't mean that D.H. Lawrence found something like the bounce—bang, bang. Lawrence found the straightforward words. How easy the voice was, especially the male's speech. Straight forward, straight from the shoulder talk. This is more a sense of don't bullshit me. Give everything straight as it is. Have you ever played any of Hopkins' songs that he composed? *[Louis sings the first verse here]* I love my lady's eyes. . . Her lips, they be warm . . . that is really an Elizabethan song. When it comes to music, they were virgins.

SD Yes, but what about that concentrated and rough rhythm? You have to go back to Shakespeare to get that kind of rough rhythm.

LD You don't think of that as modern.

SD The rhythm was different.

LD Yeah. That's when we saw it for the first time. You know I must like you very much because I can't imagine that I sung that verse because I never did that to anybody in my life. Without an instrument—I've never done that. I started and didn't know I could do that whole verse.

SD You did a great job.

LD I haven't sung it for 20 years. It's a love poem.

On Reviewing

SD I just finished reading two biographies on Hopkins and I was going to do a review of them for George [Sanderson], but I was so disappointed with them, so tired of them, I decided not to.

LD: It's very good that you did that because I should have done that sometime in my life. There's no point in reviewing if you're going to pan somebody and hurt somebody terribly when they have worked hard at it. Let somebody review it who might say a kind thing about it.

SD I can't get past that rhythm, that concentration of language, the thing Pound had to struggle so hard to find. He'd gone back to the troubadours, to the Greeks, and to the Anglo-Saxon, The Seafarer

*and others. And then he finally roots out this balance between quan-
titative and qualitative verse and there's old Hopkins stuck away on
his own, digging it out himself.*

LD The Victorians were conventional and careful and they all liked
the same kind of rhythm as in Carmen. There would come a time
when a rhythm like that of Hopkins could be really enjoyed and
admired, it required a complete shift of taste. That is modern, therefore, we say it's modern because it's written for a taste that will say yes
to such experimental writing. It is experimental in the highest degree.

SD Eliot says that he overdoes it at times. There are stanzas in The
Wreck of the Deutschland *that are so intense that he loses the meaning. And he tries to use Latin syntax in English it doesn't have that
freedom, Milton and all that.*

LD He has about the same kind of eccentricities that Joyce had in
Finnegans Wake. You'd have to hear his own voice doing that to
understand what he was aiming at.

SD That's an excellent point. What would he have sounded like?

LD We certainly can't have his voice. But where are we now—
where's the Bay of Fundy?

*SD: Oh, the Bay of Fundy is way back. We're heading towards
Truro. Remember Stanfield? Robert Stanfield? That was his home
up here. Truro.*

LD: The landscape is beautiful.

A Partial Description of Nabokov's *Pale Fire*

LD: How does it go in *Pale Fire?* The professor goes up to the lectern
and lectures on why poetry is meaningful to us. It contains a reference to ultimate things. He seems to wander off but then he comes
back and he was dead—he was actually dead for a few minutes—
then came back. He had an intervening little while when he was

dead that he saw a fountain. A fountain! So he thinks that he has seen a key to the hereafter. His name is John Shane, the great poet. Now that he knows the key to the hereafter is this fountain, he thinks a lot about this. Some months later he reads in a newspaper that a certain woman was on the operating table and died. And then she was brought to and she had seen a vision of a white fountain. He's terribly moved and he decides to go and see this woman who had seen the same vision to check with her whether they had had this similar vision. So he travels all the way to see her and discovers this old biddy and oh yes, oh yes, she had had this vision—unfortunately the newspaper had a misprint—it was really a white mountain!

But you see that's what John Shane did, but that's the key. That's the game they play with us. There's a pattern of connections—that's what it is. Fountain into mountain. It's not a revelation. Not a texture. A number of interrelations and patterns of meanings that had come out of reality. That's what's important is the patterns and meanings—not any one meaning that means everything—not any one single meaning—but all the possible meanings that you can get. It's a wonderful thought. Now he suddenly understood it—he understood life and he will now write a great poem. He will write what no one else has written before. He will write this great revelation. That's the last chapter of this wonderful poem . . .

So you see it's a poem 'I will now write what no one has every written before.' The one who says 'I will now write' is actually the author of the book who has written both things, of whom John Shane is one projection. And he will write this wondrous thing. It's a wonderful idea. Very complicated. About two worlds.

ON SHAKESPEARE

LD So I would say that Shakespeare is committed because of this, really, what he believes in, not only by what he has conventionally accepted because he has to. It is also what he has to accept . . . The Tempest was an allegory of the wars and rebels.

SD I think your analysis of his acceptance of that world order is there—that he did accept it—or he seems to have.

LD It's not very surprising—that is what an intelligent, responsible person would do at that time. No less than someone like Francis Bacon would, or Edmund Spencer. Do you think Edmund Spencer...

SD *Well, he wanted to get out of Ireland because two of his kids were killed when he was there.*

LD Where he was stationed? I imagine him standing at that same window looking . . .

SD *I tore the ass out of a good pair of pants trying to get to it.*

LD Is that a fact?

SD *Yes, it's Kilcolman Castle you're talking about.*

LD That's right—Koleman Castle. I imagined Spencer there. But was Spenser committed that way also for purely personal advantage, or was he also honestly committed?

SD *Well, when he wrote that short history of Ireland where he attacks the Irish, he believed it. At least I believe he believed it, like Pound. But then he'd lost his kids.*

LD So I would see that Shakespeare was like Spenser and like Bacon, and like many others. Rebels who did not come out. . . Those that were had to be personal rebels against the Crown. It wasn't easy to be that. The principle of rebellion hadn't yet been organized into a consistent body of ideas. Thomas Moore is the one in Utopia who made certain ideas around which you might see real dissent. It isn't that Shakespeare is a terrible reactionary or conservative thinker, he was really in line with what today would be considered a good Liberal. A light thinker. Later on some would complain that that was the most stupid position you could hold. Well how could you know? Because today this is the thing to do if you want to be enlightened. Are we coming to the religious part of the voyage?

SD *I hope not.*

LD It's a long drive. It's a whole day's drive. It's not really exhausting, but. . . You know the problem with this region and the rest of Canada? It's the matter of communication. It's not a matter of anybody lacking anything or not having anything as good as somebody else, someone to look down on. It's a matter of a lack of communication. Communication needs to be set up. All the writers—they kept sending addresses to me. Correspondence. Some of them I have actually visited. . . It's also true that this will be a network next week, but it will be a network for the giants, with Toronto, with Vancouver. It costs postage—but that's not going to kill us. We should have a network. I established my poetry newsletter. Going to reach about twelve poets and I, say let's start with I send you my form and you read it, you write a comment on it, you put a form of your own and you take the two things and you send it to a friend. He comments on your form and my form and he sends it someone he knows. The guy comments on the three of us, puts in a form of his own or two, sends the whole package on to Montreal or wherever he wants. And the thing was around like that for twelve people. By the time it comes back to the first one, there was a package of about fifteen or twenty pieces in there—a lot of criticism. Take out your stuff and take out your last comments and put in a new one. It went through several circuits like that. The only trouble was there were several poems of William Carlos Williams, and some just wanted to get in touch with this poet. Nothing else. They weren't interested in other poets ...

SD: Fame, again, huh? They're concerned with fame.

LD: And that wasn't the point. The fact that Williams and Pound were there was simply they had an additional role to it. But it did help a little bit. Pound wasn't much for it but Williams commented and picked out some poetry by Souster he liked very much. In fact, Souster framed the letter and kept it for many years.

SD: You're thinking more of something along the lines of The London Review of Books *maybe?*

LD: The letters would be restricted primarily to contributors but not exclusively, because some people who are not contributors might add to this discussion on that level. But the editors would have to do that by strict selection, not just allowing in every letter submitted by contributors. Readership would discover what kind of letter sometimes has a chance, it joins with the party in the right spirit.

SD: Yes, it sounds like a very good idea. Creating a community.

LD: The format for most magazines is wrong—the format is too much of a museum piece. Dead.

SD: Terry ran The Atlantic Provinces Book Review singlehandedly for ten years. Then the funding got turned over to the book publishing industry. They wanted a trade magazine, nothing critical. He spent ten years building it up. It was wonderful for us, vital. Here's Antigonish. We're here.

LD: Where's Antigonish?

SD: Right here—billboard heaven.

LD: Don't be embarrassed.

SD: I'm not embarrassed—these are all new though—it's funny. All those stupid billboards. What have they got them up for?

LD: It's a small town.

SD: Father MacSween lived in this residence up here for most of his life—the part of his life that I knew him. I'll show you all those places later—where he lived.

LD: Tomorrow.

SD: I'll show them all to you tomorrow. The one over the other side there—that's the Coady Institute there.

LD: A beautiful campus. This whole notion of universities that have big names and big capitals. Doesn't mean a thing. It's who's teaching there as an individual that counts really. And there could be one person who you want to study, like Father MacSween, that counts more than the whole institution.

SD: This is the town proper—the Town Hall.

LD: We could take a walk along the streets.

SD: So you're going to want to eat and rest, huh?

LD: That's all we need.

SD: I'm going to stay with a friend in town.

LD: I won't visit tonight.

SD: Yeah, I think you should rest tonight—don't you? I mean I could take you out to see George and Gert [Sanderson] this evening.

LD: I'm not like Father MacSween, you know.

SD: There's your hotel right here. We'll have a bite to eat together.

**Stewart Donovan
with Louis Dudek,
October 1993.**

But land is delightful
After an interval of dreaming, of vertigo,
of suspension,
to walk again on soil, the sand
on which our cities and ephemeral homes are built.

from the "Atlantis" section of Collected Poetry

**(from right) Louis & Stephanie Dudek with friends
(Bill Ponman & unidentified), New York, 1946.**

In Honour of Louis Dudek

I LOOK AT my son Gregory,
His wife Krys,
their two children
Natasha and Nicholas,
And learn through their eyes
That life is a constant creation,
A never ending search for completion
Transcending through children, grandchildren,
The disappearance of self.

Life is a burgeoning joy,
Death, a semi-colon
In the ongoing stream.

I thank you, Louis
For the joy you brought me,
The gifts you left.

Your words made flesh,
And on paper,
Will honor you
In constant transcendence
As long as this world turns.

STEPHANIE ZUPERKO DUDEK

Photo Courtesy of Stephanie Zuperko Dudek

**Stephanie & Louis Dudek,
circa 1943.**

How We Met

L OUIS AND I MET at a McGill University Social which was organized for students who had already graduated—i.e., were "out in the world" and returning to catch up on their lives and share the fact that they had once had a home at McGill. I was there, trying to make conversation with all these strangers, and came upon Louis Dudek—and what a pleasure it was. We had something immediate in common, in that we had immigrant parents—his from Poland, mine from Lithuania. Both of us spoke Polish because my Lithuanian parents were of Polish origin. We were both advertising copy writers. I worked for J. Walker Thompson, the top advertising copywriters in town. We had a lovely time and he asked me for a date.

After an appropriate time he asked me to marry him and everyone was very happy about it. During our honeymoon in New York

City, we made sure to get accepted as students at Columbia University: I in Psychology, he in the Department of English. I was very ambitious and decided we should go back to school in New York. We received government permission to live in New York for the entire term of our studies, or until I received my MA in Psychology.

We went back to Montreal to pack our clothes, gather our money—and begin our life in New York City. We were living on the margin in cheap student five-floor walk-up apartments—and we loved it. It was great! He began work as an assistant at City College. We were always too poor to afford more than one room in an apartment building where the kitchens were shared. This worked out okay, as neither one of us was a passionate cook.

We studied during the school year but came home for the big holidays—Christmas, New Year's and the entire summer, spending these with family and friends. I must add that not too much has been said about the importance of his sister Lillian's influence on Louis' life. Because Lillian was thirteen or fourteen, about three years older than Louis, when Louis' mother passed away, she took on the 'mothering' role. This had its positive and negative sides, as Lillian was not only nurturing, but taking care of all the meals and house-cleaning, and was expected to be the disciplinarian, directing her siblings (Louis and Irene) to do their homework and other tasks. Louis always viewed Lillian as more of a mother than a sister.

Photo Courtesy of Stephanie Zuperko Dudek

Stephanie & Louis Dudek, September 16th, 1944.

In New York we went to all the museums, saw plays—among the things Louis and I shared was an intellectual curiosity and desire to "take it all in." I was passionate about opera and we did attend some together, but he had already seen most of them. The same went for plays. I was eager to see everything! He was selective however, so sometimes I would go to a play while he stayed home to read his books and write poetry. I admired him and we seldom fought. But when we did it was about ideas—and my desire for the excitement of new cultural experiences. He was four years older so he had already experienced some things I had not. He was also more intellectual, and he shared all those fascinating ideas with me.

I secured a job in the Psychology Department as soon as I had my MA, and Louis became an English instructor at City College of New York on the strength of his MA in English. We were both enrolled to continue for the PhD, and it was while Louis was studying for his PhD that he received an offer from McGill to replace one of the instructors for one year. He took the position at McGill but at the end of that year he was asked to stay for another. The position became permanent after a few years. During all this time, while Louis was at McGill, not yet a permanent professor, I was working and waiting tables in New York City. We still spent all our holidays together, but maintained our residence in NYC for when he would return. In Montreal, Louis lived in my mother's house, where my mother adored him and he appreciated her great cooking.

This back-and-forth life continued for five years—intense summers together, plus all the big holidays and small birthdays. I eventually left NYC and returned home. We took an apartment in a house my mother owned and I had my son. It was a very happy time. The child was a dream child. Louis was successful. He received a travel grant from The Canada Council and I encouraged him to tour Europe. We continued to share our intellectual and artistic passions, and were also very adventurous. We bought bicycles one year, and biked all the way to New York. It was not easy—but it was wonderful. I remember the time Louis caught a fish in a lake and us both feeling so sorry it had died, we cried. These early years were foolish and passionate.

Before Louis died, I showed him a group of poems I'd written. He read them and said: "They're astonishingly good. There's not a word to change." It was a gift and I thank him for that. I am still writing poetry and when I finish my book I will dedicate it to him.

Grains of sultry silence
grind in the eye. . .

The conscious mind knows nothing of art
That's why we forget our dreams

from the "Continuation I" section of *Collected Poetry*

**Louis Dudek and
Ralph Gustafson,
North Hatley, 1990.**

TONY TREMBLAY

Photo by Geof Isherwood

**Louis Dudek at Galerie Oboro,
Montreal, November 1988.**

Unrepentant Idealist:
Louis Dudek's Quarrels With Marshall McLuhan

"What matters is the emotion that carries the poem along . . ."
(Europe 15)

H ALF WAY THROUGH Ernest Buckler's masterful rural idyll *The Mountain and the Valley* (the purest coming-of-age story ever written in Canada), the young protagonist, David Canaan, makes an important discovery about himself and about vocation. Tired and frustrated from moving the immovable object on his property, the precocious David quarrels savagely with his father. What should be his moment of triumph registers, instead, as despair. David packs his bags, flees the house, and leaves, hitching a ride in a passing car.

His sensitivity, however, prevents his escape—David is more artist than farmer—and he cannot leave with the stain of hurt still spreading across his family. Buckler writes the scene beautifully:

He looked both ways up and down the road. Then he turned and began to walk toward home. . . . He came to the bridge. He could see the house again. The ash of the quarrel, of blows given and felt, was tampered down physically into his flesh. . . . Suddenly he put his head into the only place left to hide: the crook of his elbow along the rail of the bridge. He began to sob. He sobbed because he could neither leave nor stay. He sobbed because he was neither one thing nor the other. (171)

This is the formative episode of David's life, and his lack of choice—"he could neither leave nor stay. . . he was neither one thing nor the other"—renders the remainder of his life difficult, and his true vocation, writing, always slightly out of reach. David is what Northrop Frye terms a *pharmakos,* the befuddled agent of sufferance in classical Greek drama. He is expelled, because of giftedness, to suffer alone, his inability to fulfill the demands of his true vocation functioning as a constant reminder of a perverted and wasted life.

Part of what paralyzes David and deepens his suffering is the mocking presence of his *Gegenteil* in the novel, a city boy named Toby. (I use the German word *Gegenteil* to imply something more than opposite or counterpart; to imply, in opposition, a kind of symmetry, therefore a twinship of difference.) Toby is everything David is not: he is from the big city; he is unconsciously easy and urbane; he is unfettered to place; and he is a citizen of the wider world, not only free to experience that world but a recipient of its riches and opportunities. So attractive is Toby's world that David's twin sister Anna succumbs to it, fulfilling a desire that David shares but cannot realize.

The reason I use the example of Buckler's David is to illustrate the poignancy and consequence of the formative moment. In David's surrender to ambivalence and in his acceptance of inferiority to Toby, Buckler reminds us of the purpose of the formative moment: that it functions as a recognition scene, as an important psychological drama. It is meant to shock, liberate, and sometimes even humiliate the subject into some kind of action or attitude. In David's case it does none of the above, and so he must accept his life sentence as the buried artist, forever thwarted in his creative ambitions and forever inferior to city boys like Toby.

David has neither the strength nor the will to force his own moment to a crisis, and is defeated when he should be saved.

By contrast, Louis Dudek, though equally precocious at a young age, was an artist who never surrendered to ambivalence and never accepted the inferiority often conferred on those of heightened sensibility. Instead, he cultivated his difference from the Tobys of his world—figures such as John Sutherland, Irving Layton, Northrop Frye, and Marshall McLuhan—and built a career fighting for those values that Buckler's David was ill-equipped to battle. In Dudek, who intuitively embraced the vocation revealed to him by his own formative moment (regardless of how difficult and out-of-favour that vocation was), I find a model worthy of emulation in today's confused and equivocal world.

CS

Dudek's early career moved in parallel trajectory with Marshall McLuhan's. Both were of the same generation; both, feeling stifled by a post-war Canada that was colonial and parochial, went away to study (Dudek to Columbia, McLuhan to Cambridge); both were "bookish" in pre-1950s, pre-television parlance; both were culturally conservative, meaning they were conservers of the so-called "old values" (tradition, form, propriety, moderation, and custodianship); and both were, by training and inclination, literary modernists, striving in their early work to renew those old values and, in the process, revitalize what they saw as a decaying civilization. Both also sought out and became confidants of that most republican of cultural workers, Ezra Pound. I add this final similarity to show just how sympathetic Dudek and McLuhan were to what we would recognize today as Arnoldian or Leavisite values: they not only shared the fear of an apocalyptic demise of modern society, but they even sought out America's most infamous political prisoner of the twentieth century as a model of radical civilization building and re-construction through the arts. For their efforts to seek out and incorporate Pound's right-leaning state culturalism into their own critical and artistic programmes, Dudek and McLuhan became the key figures behind the emergence of what has been called the second-generation of Canadian modernism.

It is hardly surprising that Pound attempted on more than one occasion to bring his two Canadian prodigies together. In a January 1952 letter to Dudek, Pound associates McLuhan with the "live thought" of a new generation of academics, and passes along McLuhan's address, presumably to encourage a widening of the "northern coterie" (Pound to McLuhan, 20 June 1951). Dudek responded indifferently: "I did not communicate with McLuhan but kept in touch with his writing in Canada, and I ran into him at an academic conference very soon after" *(Dk/* 81). In another letter to Dudek of June 1953, Pound again associates McLuhan with the emerging "cohesion/ faintly appearing among profs," and suggests that Dudek "might even get McLuhan to lead a symposium on it [on encouraging, via a new "collective" and magazine, "maximum aware-ness" among the professoriate]" *(Dk/* 102).

But Dudek was cautious. Because he had read McLuhan (using the early work in his dissertation, *Literature and the Press),* Dudek detected beneath what appeared to be basic agreement the hints of a fundamental difference in approach. While, for example, the thought of the early McLuhan was unashamed of parroting Pound's high-modernist ideals—Poundian dicta such as "Let the critic or essay-writer disabuse himself of the idea that he has made anything. He is, if decent, fighting for certain ideas or attempting demarca-tions" *[Kulchur* 169])—McLuhan's thought was always tempered by a fascination with what he terms "clutter." The following lines from *The Mechanical Bride,* McLuhan's first book, will illustrate the point:

> One function of the critic is to keep the best work free from the surround-ing clutter. But, in order to free the mind from the debilitating confusion, it is not enough to claim priority for excellence without considering the bulk which is inferior. To win more and more attention for the best work it is necessary to demonstrate what constitutes the inevitably second-rate, third-rate, and so on.
>
> *(MB* 152)

While the first line above suggests McLuhan's simpatico to what Dudek considered "the right sort of values," the rest of the quota-tion anticipates what Dudek would later consider to be McLuhan's debilitating fetish for the inconsequential. Next to Dudek's insis-tence on uncompromising individual and civil order, the ethical con-duct of artists and critics to keep the language pure, and the Ciceronian pursuit of beauty, truth, and harmony, McLuhan's fetish for slumming amidst the clutter—the "second-rate, third-rate, and so on"—was, in Dudek's mind, a dangerous perversion. For Dudek, the clutter was nothing more than the rubble of barbarism:

> . . . only where you have afflatus—a touch of divine inspiration—do we get the ephemeral that is worth preserving. . . . it is the difference between a culture that knows nothing but rubbish and one that knows, or desires, the permanent lost in the scrabble of things. Those cultures that do, and that achieve it (in part) are called civilizations. The rest is barbarism.   ("Questions" 23)

For all the similarities in background, intention, and mentorship, then, Dudek would eventually break forcefully from McLuhan, a break that Dudek would remember as one his most significant formative moments, and a break from a thinker whom he would fashion as his *Gegenteil*. While David Canaan's formative moment incapacitates him, however, Dudek's drama does just the opposite, forcing a crisis that opens possibilities for Dudek that have monumental significance for us as well as for him. The following are the kinds of statements made by the older, "celebrity" McLuhan that Dudek would use to demarcate his difference:

> In 1936, when I arrived at Wisconsin, I confronted classes of freshmen and I suddenly realized that I was incapable of understanding them. I felt an urgent need to study their popular culture: advertising, games, movies. . . . To meet them on their grounds was my strategy in pedagogy: the world of pop culture.
> (Qtd. in *Letters of MM* 173)

> The METROPOLIS today is a classroom; the ads are its teachers. The classroom is an obsolete detention home, a feudal dungeon.
> *(Verbi-Voco-Visual Explorations* 38)

> When people have been accustomed for decades to perpetual emotions, a dispassionate view of anything at all is difficult to achieve. But surely our world, more than in any previous epoch, calls for detached appraisal.
> *(MB* 7 italics added)

> Value judgments have long been allowed to create a moral fog around technological change such as renders understanding impossible.
> *(GG* 213)

These statements—interpreted by Dudek as compromising the core modernist values of custodianship, Socratic mentoring, and impassioned resistance to detachment and populism—rendered McLuhan a tepid high modernist, one more interested in celebrity than in standing accountable against the erosion of literature and the arts. For Dudek, there was no compromising the high seriousness of literature, nor the poet-critic's role in building a better and more just civilization. The secular world, caught in the whirlpool of its corporate agendas, was deliberately reductionist, certainly no friend of the arts. And regardless of how careful might be one's attempt to study the action of that maelström in order to survive, such study was, in Dudek's mind, simply misdirected, for the intellect was worthy of higher, more noble reflections.

It was McLuhan's abandonment of the programme of high-cultural custodianship and his weakening commitment to the primacy of literature as an ethical firmament, that caused the rift between Dudek and McLuhan. For Dudek, McLuhan was a high-modernist on waivers, an opportunistic hybrid of his two principals, Thomas Nashe and James Joyce. As a result, the jokester was bred tragically in his bones. When Madison Avenue came calling after the success of *Understanding Media,* McLuhan relented, giving up his Poundism for exactly the commercial heresies that tested and eventually robbed Pound of his sanity. Though he, too, loved the popular amusements (music hall culture, film, the sights and personalities of the marketplace), Dudek never did relent, seeming, instead, to counter McLuhan's various positivist engagements. One example will suffice: As McLuhan abandoned the teaching of literature to become the prophet-guru of the "METROPOLIS," Dudek did just the opposite, fashioning his famous two-year course "Journey to the End of Night" (so-named after Céline's 1932 novel) to warn students of the misanthropy of existential detachment.

So incensed did Dudek become with McLuhan's drift from the old values—and the corresponding "disintegration of belief" *(Europe* 10) that was the inheritance of figures like Sartre and Beckett—that he started publishing anti-McLuhan propaganda in letters and literary magazines. In a comment on a 12 January 1955 letter from Pound in which Pound, too, laments the decline of a once-idealistic and right-thinking McLuhan—Pound asks Dudek, "'Why you spose anything can be got into McLuhan's occiputt don't / know" *(Dk/* 108)"—Dudek summarizes his feelings about McLuhan's embrace of the popular scrabble:

My various discussions of McLuhan in [Aileen Collins' literary magazine] *CIV/n* and elsewhere were highly critical because I saw him as compounding with Madison Avenue instead of making a radical criticism of illiterate culture; and also as turning away from the major arts to an exaggerated concern with the vaporous media, treating them, rather than the traditional arts, as the shaping forces of society. The Venerable Bede might as well have turned his attention to the dunghill in Anglo-Saxon England as begin the true education of his people with Latin and the Bible. *(Dk/* 110)

Dudek even went as far as accusing McLuhan in 1968 of being a fascist in his populist demagogy: "[McLuhan] has gone wildly astray. He is now someone to be warned against. . . . [his] 'message' is in many ways the same that Benito and Adolph spread abroad" ("McLuhanism in a Nutshell" 183). A final quotation from Dudek's work seals his case: "When McLuhan quotes John Cage—'give up illusions about ideas of order, expressions of sentiment, and all the rest of our inherited aesthetic claptrap'—I think he has forgotten everything that matters. I give him up" ("McLuhanism in a Nutshell" 185).

To his credit, McLuhan never responded publicly to these, nor other Dudek strikes, though he did quietly dismiss Dudek's study of media *(Literature and the Press)* in *The Gutenberg Galaxy* in 1962 *(GG* 217). The obvious questions that the association of Pound's two most significant Canadian prodigies raises are: why such vehemence on Dudek's part, and, conversely, why such indifference on McLuhan's?

It is to the latter of those questions that I would first like to turn, for McLuhan's indifference to Dudek's reprimands reveals an essential contrast between the two thinkers, which, says George Sanderson, goes some way toward illuminating Dudek's approach. According to Sanderson,

McLuhan was in many ways more tolerant of contradictory ideas, and that shows up in his awareness of the acoustic-visual counterplay. He was also more exploratory than Dudek and more playful with ideas. He was closer to being the Shaman [in Mircea Eliade's definition], making trips into the lands of the spirits and returning with stories and advice. Dudek had the personality of the Guardian. His was a fierceness and loyalty to the tribe. But at the same time he was playful in a different way. He was playful with people. McLuhan was playful with ideas but not with people. (15 February 2002)

McLuhan's fidelity to ideas and exploration—and to the cascading effects of media on the crowd rather than the individual (hence his attachment to historicists like Vico and Innis)—accounts for his corresponding indifference to people and, ironically, to the kind of practical catholic humanism that Dudek's "transcendental optimism" embraced ("Questions" 27). But while others, Sanderson included, read McLuhan's intention as being without malice or calculation, Dudek was not as forgiving.

The real cause of his exasperation with McLuhan is best revealed in a single line: "McLuhan's neutrality, on a subject where everything is at stake, where all we hold seems to be drowned in a flood of barbarity, has always puzzled me" ("Marshall McLuhan Defined" 181). As Dudek explains it, the absence of any apparent moral judgement on McLuhan's part is no real absence at all, but an elaborate Catholic hoax, a bit of the scholastics' sleight-of-hand meant to manipulate outcomes. So when McLuhan predicts a unified global sensorium, a populace re-tribalized by the action of new technology and media, he is not, according to Dudek, defining cosmic harmony in the Blakean sense, but seeding the idea of Catholic oneness and unity. Dudek's criticism of McLuhan's duplicity mustn't be misinterpreted as doctrinal difference, for Dudek, too, was ostensibly Catholic (lapsed, yes, but certainly catholic in sensibility). Rather, his critique is of McLuhan the rhetorician, of one who used secular miasma, the worthless "clutter" of the "METROPOLIS," to shroud and market his ecumenicalism. For Dudek, then, McLuhan was fraudulent on two counts: first, and most importantly, in misrepresenting the intentions of his "demagogic collectivism"—thus appearing as well-intentioned as Germany's newly appointed young chancellor in 1933 ("McLuhanism in a Nutshell" 183)—and, second, in conferring worth on, and thus elevating, low cultural "clutter" as populist bait to convert the masses.

Regardless of what might have been McLuhan's greater moral intention, Dudek thought both frauds were dangerous contagions, as he explained in a short description of his visit to the American Pavilion at Expo '67:

. . . the new technology is against old art; it demands a new kind of art that comes straight out of the new technology. The old principles of individual creativity and expression are replaced by new impersonal and functional products. The result is a state of crisis in all the arts, a kind of hysteria that seems ready to abandon all known distinctions between art and non-art, all aesthetic principles, and yields to the process of mechanical transformation. ("The American Pavilion" 54)

One could not, in other words, "put on" the servo-mechanistic apparatus of mass man, including the "cool" style of theoretic detachment (the theorism that Heidegger denigrates), without soon being reduced by those new clothes. In this regard, Dudek was prescient indeed, as *mcluhanisme,* the word the French have coined for the McLuhan style (dissociation, acceleration, mosaic configuration, simultaneity, and Symbolist do-it-yourself sleuthing), has become all that is left of his work. The misreading of McLuhan's message for his medium has become an epidemic, and long after Dudek cautioned that form and content were not the same—that satirists, in an age of folly, are sometimes taken seriously; and that the con can easily become a contagion. It is an outcome that McLuhan, too, no doubt, would regret. Dudek, we must also remember, lived to see McLuhan bastardized month after month in Wired magazine and other assorted high-tech industry organs. And it was Dudek who lived to see what he once considered the best of the high-modernist McLuhan lost: the notion that "real control comes by study of the grammars of all the media at once" *(Verbi-* 53); the notion that "education will become recognized as civil defense against media fallout" *(UM* 305); the notion that "consciousness will come as a relief [from collective dreaming]" *(MB* 128). For a thinker as practical and "catholic" as Dudek, McLuhan's detachments seeded doctrine while they also somehow avoided what was most urgently needed—"disentaglement, clarification, [and] plain good sense" *(CIV/n* 89)—thus making McLuhan a duplicitous agent provocateur. In exasperation, Dudek would ask: "Is it too much to hope that McLuhan, hardening into radio's Mechanical Groom, . . . will wake up and face the job to be done? *(CIV/n* 91).

Perhaps, in this light, Dudek's quarrels and obsessions make more sense, as does the way he cultivated his difference from McLuhan into a formative drama that impassioned his work for a lifetime. We should remember, as well, that Dudek fashioned similar quarrels with Irving Layton and Northrop Frye, claiming always that his *Gegenteil* narrowed (as in the case of Frye's "anthropocentric vision" ["Questions" 24]) or coarsened (as in the case of Layton's "crudity and vulgarity" ["Irving Layton: A Vicarious Rebel" 184]) the civilizing values that were his sacred trust. In both these instances—mirroring his criticisms of McLuhan, John Sutherland, and H.A. Innis—Dudek reacted to an "exasperating megalomania" *(CIV/n* 86) that put the rhetoric of the personality before art, thus reducing "the thing made" to the peculiarities and fiction of its maker. "The Sermon on the Mount," Dudek reminds us, "is without rhetoric" ("Questions" 11). Literature or criticism produced by any sort of distillation through the ego (Layton) or archetypal concourse (Frye) is naturally reductionist and can rarely bust through the quotidian to the "unchanging essence" that is "an eidolon of the good" *(Europe* 140). And so we are left with the image of Dudek always fighting, quarreling, and feuding to make room for the transcendent, for the possibility of art and reason in an increasingly vulgar age.

I belabour the Dudek-McLuhan association to illustrate how Dudek not only embraced his formative moment and fashioned it into a functional poetics, but stoically stayed the course while his *Gegenteil* were receiving greater scholarly attention, media celebrity, and critical praise. He accepted critical neglect and isolation as a consequence of his principles, becoming, in the process, what Robin Blaser and others have called a "walking loneliness" *(Infinite Worlds* 28). Lonely, yes, but Dudek was never paralyzed nor ambivalent in the face of what he knew he must do. In that regard, and against his own natural inclinations to the warmth of the folk and the popular amusements, he was always the unrepentant idealist.

∾

So what are we to learn from these formative moments? At the risk of cliché, there comes a time when we all stand at a crossroads or, in David's case, at the span of a bridge. Today, in a confused and equivocal age, an age in which many consider virtue to be more about compromise and accommodation than hard choices, we might be tempted to say that Dudek's resolve in accepting the sentence of loneliness and neglect for principle was Romantic, stubborn, or elitist. We might also be tempted to say that the right choices today are clotted with the agendas of market-driven collectivism, that capitulation to social consensus is a survival skill, and therefore, that the choices we make are infinitely more complicated than in Dudek's time. Saying that, however, lets us off the hook and discredits the sacrifices of a figure like Dudek, who chose not to succumb to the glitter that had sparkled for McLuhan. Surrendering to equivocation in complex political times is a particularly maudlin response, a New Age pathology that purports to be different from the kind of paralyzing ambivalence that stifled David, but really is the same in the end.

Rather, the lesson of the two formative moments I illustrated provides a clear view of options: either to be nullified at the crossroads, unable to force the moment to its crisis—"neither leave[ing] nor stay[ing]. . . . neither one thing nor the other"—or to be enabled, and, so charged, to accept a lifetime of quarrel. Neither option is easy, nor do I want to suggest that the Dudek choice is right for everybody. What I do want to say is that, for Dudek, the compromise position somewhere between the two—that is, teaching and writing about popular "clutter" in order to undermine it, which he saw as McLuhan's method, the method of the doctrinaire in a secular age—was dishonest and unacceptable. The compromise was also, and especially, offensive to the artist in Dudek, to that moral part of him that saw attention to "clutter," if only as subterfuge or scholastic prank, as fraught with the neglect of the good and the artistic, the material worthy of ideas and attention.

Dudek would have agreed with Raymond Williams, who cautions that we must never let that clutter become the cacophony that overwhelms our critical, rational, and artistic capacities:

There are times, in the depth of the current crisis, when the image materializes of a cluttered room in which somebody is trying to think, while there is a fan-dance going on in one corner and a military band blasting away in the other. It is not the ordinary enjoyments of life that are diverting serious concern, as at times, in a natural human rhythm, they must and should. It is a systematic cacophony which may indeed not be bright enough to know that it is jamming and drowning the important signals, but which is nevertheless, and so far successfully, doing just that. (18)

Dudek and Williams, contra McLuhan and the Stuart Hall/Birmingham School culturalists, are not calling for what essayist George Steiner terms "more elbow-room for sensibility" (85)—that does sound elitist to all but those with an aptitude for high literacy—but for some, if only small, attention to the idea that works of art and literature, the study of music and history, acts of worship, and all those unquantifiable instances of human imagination really do matter. They matter because they celebrate a non-technical, non-material, non-boisterous humanity: the mind in deep and silent thought, the heart in love and anguish, the soul in contemplation of things other and greater than itself. We should read Dudek's quarreling, then, as an impassioned warning to us to move away from and against what he sees McLuhan endorsing: in Steiner's words, a state of "domestic comfort . . . in which intellectual passions are not only curiously luxurious, but positively the enemy" (87).

And so it is only fitting that I close with one of Dudek's "important signals," a beacon of light that pulses beneath the dunghill. Why end this way? Because Dudek's quarrels with McLuhan reveal a final truth that must be inferred: namely, that passion and critical thinking are, in themselves, not enough. Thus, Dudek's final question of McLuhan must be this: where do ethics, art, and aesthetics reside in the person who can think passionately and critically, but, neutral and detached, hasn't been taught to value anything? Dudek's creative work provides an answer to this question, as the following passage, echoing Eliot's "Little Gidding" and the long passage down the tradition, illustrates:

Time and the wars have destroyed it all, but the Acropolis
standing there, crumbling with infinite slowness,
                              in the sunlight,
is all that it ever was, will be, until the last speck
of the last stone is swept away by the gentle wind.
Strange, that a few fragile, chalky, incomplete blocks of marble,
worn away by time, thievery, and gunpowder,
should be enough, and all that we have come for,
to erect in the mind the buildings
        of the Greeks who lived here, and their city—
akro-polis against the blue sky of heaven.
I have said of the sculptures, such people
will never again be, it is more
                than we can really believe in.
Shall we ever again see such buildings? Heaven
        seemed near then so that the hand could touch it.
But we have the light years,
                the immeasurable solitudes.

I sit here, drinking in sunlight
from the clean candid marble,
        thinking the thoughts of Plato,
of Solon, and the perfect republic.

(Europe 110-11)

Works Cited

Buckler, Ernest. *The Mountain and the Valley.* 1952. NCL Edition. Toronto: McClelland and Stewart, 1970.

Collins, Aileen, ed. *CIV/n: A Literary Magazine of the 50's.* Montréal: Véhicule, 1983.

Dudek, Louis. ""The American Pavilion at Expo 67." *In Defence of Art: Critical Essays & Reviews.* Ed. Aileen Collins. Kingston: Quarry, 1988. 54-55.

, ed. *Dk/ Some Letters of Ezra Pound.* Montréal: DC Books, 1974.

. *Europe.* 1954. Erin, ON: Porcupine's Quill, 1991.

. "Irving Layton: A Vicarious Rebel." *In Defence of Art: Critical Essays & Reviews.* Ed. Aileen Collins. Kingston: Quarry, 1988. 183-85.

. Infinite Worlds: *The Poetry of Louis Dudek.* Ed. Robin Blaser. Montréal: Véhicule, 1988.

. "Marshall McLuhan Defined." *Louis Dudek: Texts & Essays.* Spec. Issue of Open Letter. Ed. Frank Davey & bpNichol. 4th ser. 8-9 (1981): 181-82.

. "McLuhanism in a Nutshell." *Louis Dudek: Texts & Essays.* Spec. Issue of Open Letter. Ed. Frank Davey & bpNichol. 4th ser. 8-9 (1981): 183-85.

. "Questions (Some Answers)." *Louis Dudek: Texts & Essays.* Spec. Issue of Open Letter. Ed. Frank Davey & bpNichol. 4th ser. 8-9 (1981): 9-38.

Frye, Northrop. *The Modern Century.* 1967. Toronto: Oxford, 1969.

McLuhan, Marshall. *The Gutenberg Galaxy: The Making of Typographic Man.* Toronto: U of Toronto Press, 1962.

. *Letters of Marshall McLuhan.* Eds. Matie Molinaro, Corinne McLuhan, William Toye. Toronto: Oxford, 1987.

. *The Mechanical Bride: Folklore of Industrial Man.* New York: Vanguard Press, 1951.

. *Understanding Media: The Extensions of Man. New York:* McGraw-Hill, 1964.

. *Verbi-Voco-Visual Explorations.* New York: Something Else Press, 1967.

Pound, Ezra. *Guide to Kulchur.* 1938. New York: New Directions, 1970.

Sanderson, George. Letter to the Author. 15 February 2002.

Steiner, George. "Culture: The Price You Pay." *States of Mind: Dialogues With Contemporary Thinkers.* Ed. Richard Kearney. New York: NYU Press, 1995. 82-92.

Williams, Raymond. *The Year 2000.* New York: Pantheon, 1983.

The good thing is something that sounds revolutionary
until you get to know it

Sometimes I feel I'm really getting there
the words
little ladders

from *Continuation I*

PIERRE DESRUISSEAUX

À Louis Dudek—
Le voyage est un poème

LE VOYAGE est un poème
composé avec une extrême rigueur
qui pour le dire tout haut
est bien trop près du cœur pour passer
à voix basse il semble que l'été nous
brûlions tout le jour
trop de lumière trop d'étoiles
s'éteignent dans l'échancrure des arbres
moi comme une barque faute de la parole
je ne peux que te faire entendre
ce que je suis ce n'est pas être dans ton rêve
mais partir ce soir pour d'autres champs
et d'autre chose qui m'appelle.

Dans le souvenir
il y a une habitude triste
et bien des semaines de tous les jours
jusque dans les rues la croix
crie au loup le soir
j'entendais hier des réponses faute d'images
dans le souvenir la vie devient habitude
avec tant d'indulgence
tant de pitié s'épaissit à mesure
que le temps de nous entendre
ouvre le chemin de vivre.

J'ai écrit trois vers comiques
Pour Fernande petite et chic,
Pour Fernande que j'adore
Trois vers sonores.

from "Trois Vers" in *The Poetry of Louis Dudek: Definitive Edition*

Louis Dudek, summer 1956.

Louis Dudek, Gregory Dudek, Steve Luxton, Bruce Whiteman,
Nancy Marrelli and Simon Dardick of Véhicule Press,
celebrating Dudek's 75th birthday at the Dardicks' home,
Montreal, February 1993.

Amicitia

THE FRIENDSHIPS OF writers tend to be intense. The hard work that writers do is carried out in something like solitary confinement; and released from that, a poet will seek out like-minded companions who comprehend the nature of that work and are equally needy for talk about it. It—that talk—is almost as important as desire, and contributes equally to making work possible. Such friendships can flare and subside (think of Flaubert and Maxime Du Camp) or they can last most of a lifetime (think of Creeley and Olson); and when they leave a written record, they can be as fascinating as the work itself.

This book provides ample evidence that LD made many friends over the course of his long life in poetry. With his contemporaries these relationships seem often to have been uneasy, most notoriously in the case of Irving Layton, but perhaps no less straightforward with the other poets whom we think of as his coevals: Souster or Waddington, for example. With students it was different. LD had a long career teaching at McGill, and many of his students remained close friends, from Mike Gnarowski in the 1950s on down. LD loved to teach, and the poets who found their way to his classroom often became real allies and maintained contact long after they had ceased to sit at his feet. Ken Norris is perhaps the best example, but many others could be cited.

I was never a Dudek student, and indeed came to know him relatively late, so I had nothing like the claim on his affections or attention that many others did. In the early 1980s, he was giving one of his rare readings in Toronto at a gallery just north of Queen Street near the Don Valley Parkway, in a series curated by the poet Richard Truhlar, and Ray Souster told me I should go along and introduce myself. I had come to LD's poetry largely through Pound and from being asked by *CVII*, Dorothy Livesay's Winnipeg-based literary magazine, to review *Dk/ Some Letters of Ezra Pound* (1974) a long while after the book appeared. Indeed by the time my review was published, *Dk/* had gone out of print, or so I heard. I went up to LD rather shyly after the reading, having formed an impression of him that was confected half of respect and half of intimidation. Of course he was immensely cordial and not intimidating at all, and we had a good talk. LD did not actively seek out acolytes, but clearly he was attracted to younger writers who had something of his own bifurcated love for poetry and learning, governing passions which are notoriously difficult to nurse with equal success.

In 1988 I moved to Montreal to work at McGill as a librarian. I was editing John Sutherland's letters at the time, and that if nothing else would have brought me into LD's orbit. Like many others, I had lunch with him from time to time at Ben's, the delicatessen on McGill-College at de Maisonneuve (no bars for him, I'm not sure I ever saw him take a drink), a short walk from the McLennan Library for me and a longer but not unusually long walk for him from his Westmount home. He would show up with a book, always, and once I remember it was Dostoevsky in Russian. The talk was always about poetry and literature; and although he did like to pontificate, he also knew how to listen and was curious about other views on his "authors". I had books for him occasionally, books of my own, and he always read them carefully and wrote a letter of thanks. He was uncharacteristically offhand when I presented him with a copy of my Sutherland letters in 1992, and Ken Norris, who was there, noticed it too; and although I felt hurt at the time (it had taken ten years to compile and edit), looking back now I can see that the period of his life that included his friendship with John Sutherland might not have been remembered by him with unadulterated affection, and perhaps the book evoked emotional trials and poetic rivalries that made him ill at ease.

Ken Norris was living at that time, as he still is, in Maine, and teaching at the University in Orono. But he was in Montreal as often as he could get away, and we became good friends. Ken was acutely aware of LD's importance over a period of time that by then stretched to almost four decades, as he also knew (all of LD's friends did) that public recognition had by contrast been rather slim. It was Ken who proposed that we get a group of writers from across Canada to contribute to a special award for LD. This we did, and many poets and writers sent us money that went towards a cheque for him, as well as a certificate that Fred Louder printed letterpress. We put on a day-long program of readings at McGill in the old anatomy theatre (somehow it seemed appropriate); and although LD had always maintained that awards were divisive and meaningless, he seemed genuinely pleased.

> If you are still living, and already in anthologies,
> That's bad, very bad
> (Confucius might have said)[1]

Maybe so, but like all artists LD craved at least some validation from his peers. Endre Farkas blessed me that day by saying that, as the co-organizer of the Dudek award, I was now a genuine Montreal poet. Claude Lemoine, the head of the Literary Manuscripts section at the National Library of Canada, unfortunately chose that day to tell me that LD had decided to sell his papers to the National Library of Canada instead of to McGill. So it seemed that I was a newly anointed Montreal poet but an unsuccessful Montreal librarian, proving once again that it is hard to be both a poet and something else too.

I moved to Los Angeles in 1996, so I knew LD best for the eight years between 1988 and the early summer of 1996. It was instructive to watch him in the company of old friends like Ralph Gustafson or Alec Lucas. For all that LD's poems seem to lack artifice and can be blindingly honest about feelings, in conversation he seldom divagated beyond literature and ideas into small talk, and he seemed especially guarded in the company of writers who were of his age. He was not suave like Ralph nor gruff and demotic like Alec, although he clearly valued the friendship of both men. He and Aileen came to dinner once when Leon Edel was in town to give a lecture at McGill, and LD, I suspect, somehow resenting Edel's scholarly achievements, rather badgered him about missing the lie that John Glassco had perpetrated concerning the date of writing of his *Memoirs of Montparnasse.*

> Good to have some old friends
> > To amuse and abuse
> Left over, among life's odds and ends.[2]

On the other hand, and despite his repeatedly returning to the subject of the ignorant young in his poetry, LD could be extremely generous to young writers and had young friends to the end of his life. Crabby at times, apoplectic on certain subjects such as the media, dauntingly well-read and never without several books on the go (among the poets I have known, only Robin Blaser perhaps was more devoted in this sense), LD nevertheless recognized the spark if a young poet had it, and did what he could to help, not least by treating such a younger writer as a colleague. That meant a lot to a lot of writers. It certainly meant a lot to me.

I found him finally an extremely private man, and I retain an image of that privacy—privacy intermixed with solitude and perhaps a deep sense of grief—from one of the few times I visited him at home. In fact, thinking on it, this was the only time I was in his house, and it was because we had got to talking about music that he invited me over to listen to a recording of Bach's *The Art of the Fugue* played on the piano. Uncharacteristically, I have forgotten the name of the pianist—was it Andràs Schiff?—but at the time I knew the piece only in a performance played on the harpsichord by Gustav Leonhardt. LD did not have musical training, but art music had been a comfort to him since his college days. It is not surprising that he would like Bach, and even less surprising that among Bach's works *The Art of the Fugue* would capture his imagination, for it is the very epitome of a hugely formal, even olympian intelligence embodied in sound. ("Order, kosmos, the knowing process./Without it there's only the flux.").[3] LD sat on a bed or a daybed while we listened to the music, and as the sun declined and his body began to be shaded by the disappearing light, I formed an image of him that bespoke such absolute loneliness that I have never forgotten it. Perhaps it was only concentration that gave him that aspect, but I did not think so then and do not think so now. The poetry bespeaks the same quality often. "Only the lonely are free,"[4] or "The trainwreck inside the heart/in the meantime."[5]

Almost forty years ago, LD began an opinion piece in the *Montreal Gazette* by remarking "Sometimes I'm just fit to hate mankind."[6] But he was not a cynic, much less a misanthrope. Neither variety of human could entitle a book of essays *Paradise,* as LD did in 1992. In an essay on Ken Norris included in that book, he talked about Norris's search for the paradisal in the South Seas, and observed in that context that such a search "is a measure of the hunger of the heart, an elevated idealism, which is the most precious gift of the poet, and the greater it is the greater the promise of lasting work."[7] The particular hunger of the heart that poets know is the basis for long-lasting and passionate friendships (whatever else it is the basis for), and LD knew that lesson well. He was a Ciceronian friend: demanding at times, wanting above all to elaborate an intellectual common core, unforgiving only to those he thought had betrayed their own ideals, their own potential. It is hard to imagine LD talking conspiratorially with a friend about girl

problems or money problems, but where friendship really mattered he was staunch. It was a grace to enjoy his companionship even for a few brief years. It made me—as I suspect it made many others—a better writer, and a better human being.

NOTES

1. Louis Dudek, *Continuation II* (Montreal: Vehicle Press, 1990), p. 91.
2. Ibid., p. 44.
3. Louis Dudek, *Atlantis* (Montreal: Delta Canada, 1967), p. 117.
4. *Continuation II,* p. 15.
5. Louis Dudek, *Continuation I* (Montreal: Vehicle Press, 1981), p. 33.
6. Louis Dudek, "Is Pornography Invading All the Media," reprinted in *In Defence of Art: Critical Essays & Reviews* (Kingston: Quarry Press, 1988), p. 47.
7. Louis Dudek, "Ken Norris in the Twentieth Century," in *Paradise: Essays on Myth, Art, & Reality* (Montreal: Vehicle Press, 1992), p. 43.

Photo Courtesy of Stephanie Zuperko Dudek

Louis Dudek, Montreal, 1970.

**Louis Dudek at Restaurant Capoli, Montreal,
October 2000.**

Photo by SAS

Interview with Louis Dudek

[The interview took place at Louis Dudek's home on June 25, 1992.]

IT IS A HOT Montreal morning in late June. A breeze wafts through the trees as I drive from the Outremont plateau, along the tortuous Côtes des Neiges down into the corridors of the city. The streets are quiet. Louis Dudek lives in a street nestled in Westmount, not far from the park and the library. It's from this quiet corner that Dudek has carried on his work as a publisher, editor, professor, and poet. Dudek, Frank Davey observed, is the most influential of "any poet in Canadian literary history."

He has been associated with First Statement, Contact, CIV/n, Delta, *and* DC Books. *He has been committed to the development of literature throughout his life. This can be seen in his dissertation,* Literature and the Press, *his interest in Ezra Pound, and his desire to keep art independent of commercial influence.*

It is a modest two-story red-brick house. Dudek appears relaxed this morning, although he is recovering from Bell's palsy. He speaks about giving his last lecture, his last reading, and an upcoming book. One is immediately aware of an order in the house, a definite clarity of arrangement. Along the wall there is a twelve-foot bookcase. In fact, there are bookcases throughout the house, even in the Dudeks' legendary basement filled with magazines, periodicals and books. There are paintings by Louise Scott, influenced by Betty Sutherland, Irving Layton's second wife. ("Aileen has arranged everything," Louis says.) On a side table are several vases created by Wanda Rozynski, who was associated with CIV/n. *There is Aileen's Henry Moore sketch, "Drawings of People in the Underground," from World War II. Dudek comments, "I'm not much in favour of it. I like people fully awake." There are two art books on Borduas and Miro. In the staircase there are paintings by Stella Sagaitis, mother of Dudek's first wife. He says he has enjoyed living with these because they are filled with flowers and trees. In the dining room there is a reproduction of Da Vinci's "Madonna of the Rocks" and his unfinished picture of Saint Anne. Against the opposite wall there is a Macintosh which Louis uses to write on and play chess against Sargon. A copy of* Open Letter *sits beside it. In the middle of the dining table is a bouquet of chrysanthemums. Louis says, "they cry out to be praised." We start the interview with Louis reading Sidney's translation of a Petrarch poem followed by his own version and inviting me to compare them.*

LH: In the poem "Life and Art," you wrote, "Life first, / and art after, if a choice must be made." Is this an accurate statement of your aesthetics?

LD: Yes. First, you notice that the phrasing contains an aesthetic quality, or what I think of as the "electric charge." But why life first and art after? Because a choice must be made. That's the key. And of course it's simply true. It's made in a sharp epigrammatic way, but in fact I am affirming an order of values. My position has always been that art exists in order to serve life, to represent life, to discover some new possibility, a breakthrough for life itself. That's what it's all about. If we imagine something, we imagine something we might do, or could do, or could become.

LH: Why were the 1950s in Montreal so crucial for the development of literature in Canada?

LD: It's not something that happens to us; it's something that we do that makes a period important. In the Nineteen-fifties we did that. When I came back in 1951, I came to teach at McGill. I came with the perfect confidence that I was coming where I had to be to do my important work. It was not just for myself that I was going to do this work, but for this city and this country. I was ready for it, and I knew it was going to be important. We were going to change our world, so to speak. Somehow that involves the many things I had learned in New York. I had studied modern poetry there. I had studied under Lionel Trilling, Jacques Barzun, and Emery Neff. I was full of the sense of what the modern is, and the transformation that modernism must bring to poetry and life. So I came back and a friendship was soon renewed with Irving Layton, and we began to publish together. The first book was *Cerberus*—three poets together, Layton, Dudek, and Souster, with prefaces by each.

At first it was just ourselves getting off the ground, but we were going to publish others. Daryl Hine was in Montreal at that time and his book soon appeared. Leonard Cohen turned up at McGill and he wanted to bring out a book, so actually I proposed that the McGill Poetry Series start with his book. After that other books followed. At the same time Contact Press was bringing out books through Raymond Souster in Toronto and ourselves jointly in Montreal. And the first bunch of those I was editing from McGill.

Before us, a very important generation, the first modern generation had done work from 1925 to 1940, but they had not started presses. They had published some magazines. These magazines, however, were not really little magazines in the real sense of young poets making very radical statements of their own. In the 1940's in *Preview, First Statement, Contemporary Verse,* you got that for the first time. Since then, this kind of originality has spread all over

Canada, a branch of independent writing and publishing. Because that other phase had preceded in the 1920s, the new one in the 1940's looks so important since now there was a lot of momentum behind it. The two generations joined together.

L.H. In the 1950s a number of poets were associated with Frye: James Reaney, Jay Macpherson, D.G. Jones, and Eli Mandel. Mandel, in fact, called the fifties an "age of mythopoeia."

LD: Sure, Mandel was one of the mythopoeic poets himself, so he would be inclined to call it that. It certainly wasn't mythopoeic in the 1950s. It contained the mythopoeic group appearing for the first time, as well as more general modernists who were still dominant. Now, John Sutherland was one of the first admirers of James Reaney's book *The Red Heart* in 1949. I also thought Reaney was wonderful. I mean one was interested in any poet that really had that kind of jazz, that really had something alive, something exciting and different in him. You didn't want poets to be copies of one another. Of course, Raymond Souster was the ideal poet of our kind who was simple, straightforward and dealt with the contemporary world, people in the street. He had a humanitarian sympathy for everybody. Raymond Souster was representative that way, but at the same time he was of course limited in what he could do or say. One has to grow intellectually as well. Reaney was something different, formalist in his methods, and eccentric in his behaviour. Very bright.

LH: Also, his mythological interests are connected to the earth and local history. The Donnellys *and other works have a strong sense of the local.*

LD: That's true. That's probably often forgotten. In the mythopoeic group, whether in James Reaney or Margaret Avison, there's a strong local realistic particularism that makes a firm bridge between them and the Montreal group. That realistic touch, that's the Canadian character. In films it becomes the documentary of the NFB [National Film Board], you see, utterly factual.

LH: The local.

LD: They were beginning there. In the fifties the mythopoeic group was beginning and important works by Northrop Frye were coming out. Then *Delta* came out in '57. I published a review of Jay Macpherson which was very critical of her traditionalist mythopoeic kind of writing. However, she sent me some poems in response, and these too I published gladly. They were good things. So, they were part of the mix and part of a lively debate. Controversy is good for poetry and for groups. There had been a controversy between *Preview* and *First Statement*. And now this controversy between the mythopoeic poets and the social realists. But then, who were the social realists? Is Irving Layton a social realist—my God, he's really some kind of a surrealist I would say, a rhetorical surrealist. Am I a social realist? Hardly at all. I'm more or less a transcendentalist in poetry. It's hard to say. Raymond Souster is the nearest to being a social realist, but even there, I would say this would be a very soft social realism.

LH: Do you see a connection, then, between this social realist school and yourself, Irving Layton, Raymond Souster and the mythopoeic school? You have myth in your work in the same way the mythopoeic poets have an anchor in experience.

LD: The point is that we were opposed to each other because of the exclusive concern with myth on the part of Frye and the actual rejection of the social realist position by Frye, with damaging remarks about it in the essay "Tarzanism in Canadian Poetry." "Tarzanism" he called it. He was often offensive, in his mild way, to the school of reality. There's a real temperamental opposition between the two, and one has to look at what's at the root of that. So, I don't think that there's any congruence between the two things at all. The mythopoeic school was leading Canadian poetry in directions that were not helpful in the way that I thought we could develop in Canada.

LH: I want to ask you about the change in the fifties from a more formal literature, with its emphasis on the formal properties of literature, moving toward the poetry of voice, the poetry of experience as represented by Tish.

LD: Yes, now that would be in the 1960's that another kind of poetry came in, not mythopoeic and not social realist, but very much concerned with voice and sound. Reading aloud would never appeal to me nor the notion that some kind of new aesthetic would come out of this kind of plain sounding of poetry. I know all about the history of oral literature, of course. Homer and all that. But that was in an age of oral poetry, before the advent of writing. If you know that, then you must also know that literature was soon written on a scroll, and that later still it became very strongly scripted, so that our experience of it was no longer pronounced with the lips, as the Romans still did, reading with their lips and reading aloud. We eventually learned not to have to do that at all because as human beings we had learned how to listen inside our heads. And the experience of reading that way became more analytical and more attentive to what's there on the page. It's not less aural. It's imagined. It's much more imaginative.

LH: There's a strong sense of voice in your poems, a sense of colloquial speech, yet accompanying it is a structure, a philosophical argument. How did you develop the balance between these two aspects of your poetry?

LD: I don't see any opposition. These two things are entirely compatible. You can have something that is extremely philosophical with an extremely formal and pompous tone of voice. You can have the philosophical with the colloquial, which brings it to life, which probably is what philosophical ideas need. They need somebody to make them come alive [laughter]. So, you get this kind of voice. Primarily, the issue can be stated like this. I believe a poem ought to say something, because a poem that just babbles along and says nothing at all is just a pain in the ass. I don't like to hear somebody just sounding off out of vanity. I want meaning to be conveyed, at least some images that I can think about, if not some idea.

LH: The short poem "The Sea", for instance, is a very beautiful poem, rich in its qualities and voice. It foreshadows and contains many of the elements that are later expressed in your longer poems.

LD: Yes. It's strange that you bring that up, because on Friday I'm visiting a class at McGill, and I've just agreed to talk to the students about this poem! And with the poem, I want to tell them just what you said, that this poem of the sea existed before I had ever seen the sea at all. It's full of the sense of a meaning that appears later in *Europe,* this whole idea of the sea is the unifying concept of that book. It's extraordinary that I hit upon an idea, a metaphor, which was going to do so much for my poetry later, not only in *Europe,* but also in *Atlantis* and other poems. So, of course, the Frye group would say that this is a deep image of the archetypal sort. Perhaps so, but it need not be that. There is W. H. Auden's book on the subject of the sea, *The Enchaffèd Flood,* the turbulent sea. All about the sea in literature, how much has been written about it. The whole question, then, is whether there's an archetypal image here or perhaps an experience so moving that it represents whatever ideas you may need—even as Niagara Falls does, or the starry sky—and you would be surprised if somebody thought there was nothing at all there, just a lot of water and empty space. You know, we're moved, we're so moved by the sea—I'm so overwhelmingly moved—and propelled into thought, by the sea, that I have it all in the very first poem I wrote on seeing the sea: "On Coming Suddenly to Sea in My Twenty-eighth Year."

LH: You have been critical of Frye's view of literature yet you use myths in your own writings, for example in Atlantis. *How is your use of myth different from Frye's?*

LD: Now, the definition that I would want if we're talking about myth philosophically, is something like 'a story that has religious symbolism embedded in it, and is collective in its belief content,' as in the Christian myth, or the Greek myths. If we limit it to that we'll be making sense of what we're saying because then other things that are not like that will be free of contamination. Words like "the sea" in my poetry are large metaphors; they are not really mythological. If I say in *Europe,* "And I would not be surprised if the sea made Time / ... or if the whole fiction / of living were only a coil in her curvature..." Now, how could the sea make time? It's an absurd statement. You could say that's absurd in a way that most mythological statements are absurd. The sea, the ocean could not make, create time. How could it create time? And yet when you read it in a poem and when I wrote it, it seemed perfectly valid poetically because metaphorically it is. But when I say "the sea" in the poem *Europe,* I am referring to something behind that word. It is that something that made time. And, "the whole fiction / of living were only a coil in her curvature..." of that creative process. So, there is a creative reality of some sort as the source of all that exists. And you may say, if you are of a religious persuasion, "Oh, he obviously means God." Well, you can rush to your own conclusions if you wish. But I don't have any formulation about that as yet. I am completely open on that question, and the point of this open-mindedness, which is very important to me, is to distinguish between what we know and what we do not know. What we know is what we know with our eyes, our ears, and our human relations, and through history so far as we know that. What we do not know is what we can suggest and intuit in poetry. It's very beautiful to know that we do not know it, that we can speak of it as the sea... or as "Atlantis", say, in another poem.

LH: This is the source of your long poems.

LD: That's right! You create another kind of metaphor. "Atlantis" is another large metaphor. The sea is the ocean which is visible. Atlantis is an imaginary continent that sank in the sea, and now it emerges bit by bit. It is used as a symbol for an ideal world, a utopia perhaps, an affection of some kind that surfaces out of the ocean, that surfaces out of reality. This is a metaphor of rich possibility, but it's not what it seems to be; it's only a metaphor for that something which also surfaced when Aileen brought a heap of chrysanthemums, white and red and pink, the beauty of those things sitting there on the table. They emerge out of somewhere, you see. That's where everything comes from, Atlantis. Here's a bit of Atlantis before us. [laughter]

LH: It's interesting how you use the iceberg. Writers feel differently about icebergs. Roberts' iceberg is very different from Pratt's or from Purdy's iceberg.

LD: You're right, Laurence, because it is the thought that surrounds the idea of an iceberg that will make it feel different for different people. For me it's the idea of Atlantis, and the iceberg is somehow related to that infinite source of visions, perfections, utopias... and death also with its coldness. So that it has a richness of feeling in it, that makes it seem different. And it's at the end of *Atlantis* that the iceberg appears. So I would say that there are in my poems of the sea a whole cluster of metaphors. "Europe," itself, is a symbolic word and place. Interpreted, you could probably say it means something like "the civilized life." It means cities and nations with cathedrals, museums, books, and cultures, with all those possibilities of civilized life. *Europe.* I go to the heart of it, to the Parthenon from which everything in *Europe* derives. *Europe,* the sea, *Atlantis.* Is the sea *Europe?* Yes and no. *En México* is the jungle which is also an aspect of the sea, an aspect of the creative process, but here its negative aspect. The point of the jungle is that there everything is crowding everything out. The birds are shrieking, murdered. Everything is dying, choking inside that jungle. I've written an epigram, "In nature all forms of life are stunted."

LH: Generally critics have not observed the importance of formal patterns in your work. There are exceptions, of course, such as Dorothy Livesay and Frank Davey. These formal patterns are important in the longer poems Europe, En México, *and* Atlantis. *Could you comment on formal elements such as line arrangement, rhythm and sound pattern.*

LD: For a poet writing these are the chief concerns. I don't think about the idea of the poem very much when I'm working on a poem, or I don't think about anything but the words of which it is made, how it flows together and how it is architecturally shaped. That is the poem. Because ultimately . . . suppose I've got a poem and it's a pretty good poem, but mediocre . . . the last line has a very bad word there and it just flops, it's lousy, the poem's no good. It's no good unless I'm terribly lucky and I find a replacement for that word in the last line that'll just lift it suddenly and make it a better poem. So you see, it's just that one word and you could prove it by taking any line of Shakespeare and changing it. You know, "the multitudinous seas incarnadine."

LH: I was just thinking of that word.

LD: Change "multitudinous" into something like "incarnadine multiplicity" and you know there's something wrong with that word "multiplicity." Unless you find the right word, you haven't got a poem. Everyone knows that. Finally the words are what the poem is made of and the words are, in a sense, magical. They are fitted like pieces in a jigsaw just exactly to fit into that position. That's it. Click! It works. But that perfection is actually in the words. Now, let's see if we answered the question about the importance of formal elements, such as line arrangement. Very important. Line arrangement. You see, I think that literature, poetry or the human mind itself, have always had a very dangerous failing, a tendency to slip into the rut of mathematical counting, of lines, syllables, lengths, and thinking it has got a form when it has measured it out with a ruler or counting device, ten syllables to the line. So you have the heroic couplet, you have the French couplet and so on. This is really a perversion of artistic form, since the mathematics should be invisible, like that of flowing water or clouds. The twentieth century discovery is that form in the arts is more like modern dance, that it has an infinite number of forms that are made by free movement actually, with language and words. The only way to do it is the intuitive way, which is through feeling, or aesthetic awareness.

LH: Some of your poems are almost like the forms of paintings or ideograms, the way you see them on the page.

LD: Absolutely. The beauty of an arrangement on the page that hits the eye, I love that. I want to read the poem when I see that it's a lovely scattering of a certain kind. I can see that it is done sensitively like a Japanese awareness of space. One of the articles in *Delta* magazine was about the importance of space by a Japanese student.

LH: The Macintosh allows you a wonderful sense of kinesthesia of the poem.

LD: The Macintosh helps, but of course the typewriter did it too, so this technique has a history. The line arrangement means that you don't indent all lines to the margin on the left hand side. You don't have a straight margin entirely. You indent in different ways and there are various points of indentation. And then not too much of that either, so that it doesn't look like a Ferlinghetti scattering: it's not salt and pepper. Actually there is a pacing. The way lines move in and back to the margin is a kind of lovely movement, more or less graceful, the way tropical fish move in the tank. It should be delightful and it should be well-paced.

LH: It's also art, dance and music...

LD: Yes, beautiful. Art, dance, music, in the way the words are moving around from the margin into the middle and so on. That's it. So therefore, line arrangement.

LH: Critics often ignore these important aspects, even silence or the space between words.

LD: Yes, but you see, for a critic to write about this is very difficult. He may perceive it and feel it, but then what's he going to say about it when he can't reduce it to mathematics? The only thing he can say is "isn't that fine the way this line drops here?" Now, in *Atlantis,* very often I found I'd have a line of about five-six words, then a break, with a highly indented part of a line with about four words, and then back to the margin with two or three or four words. This kind of three-line stanza must have some relation to the *terza rima.*

LH: Exactly, I was just thinking it's Dante...

LD: Inevitably, but it's so irregular that you could say it's got nothing to do with *terza rima.* There's no rima in there and there's no definite metric. But there's a threeness there. A kind of ta ta ta—ta ta—ta ta ta. This three-line shape has form; three is an interesting number, you know. Three-leaf clover. Nature must have discovered it and used it quite a lot. A rhythm. I guess a repetition is necessary. You could scan some of these things, but rhythm and meter are two different things. A rhythm and a meter. Sound pattern is the most beautiful way, yes.

LH: You said in a recent interview that you consider Continuation *your best work.*

LD: I suppose I do because it is the most completely worked out, a case of finding a voice for myself in the poetry. I explained that in the interview with Louise Schreier in *Zymergy 8*. In *Continuation 1* and *Continuation 2* I have at last found a voice where I could say exactly what I want to say, and everything I want to say, in the most amazing fragmentary way.

LH: And you don't find the absence of a larger structure restricting?

LD: Now what you want to say is "don't you mean it has a flaw in it?" Yes, maybe it has. Even I may be aware of that, but you have to take risks in poetry. What is poetry trying to do on the page? It's trying to represent the poet's thought. If that's what it's trying to do, then ultimately you have to create a fictitious form that is doing that. Not one that is spurious, but the actual thought with all its fragmentary wayward digressions. And yet, if you read *Continuation 1* and 2, you find that it's really not digressing so very much. It's actually obsessively concerned with only one kind of subject.

LH: Essentially, the poem is concerned with process, getting closer to process.

LD: The process is the internal monologue, only that part of it in the mind, which deals with this question, which is poetry. But it's as if you were listening to me thinking as if it were recorded.

LH: It's an important "as if."

LD: As if. And I think eventually anybody can read that and say that it's easy as pie. They'd say, "I've learned how to read him because I know what he really is deeply concerned with. That's what he's thinking about all the time and it's very amusing."

LH: But still some of those individual lines are very well crafted. They have a subtle sense of sound, image and metaphor.

LD: Sure, Laurence. Individual lines are well crafted. You may still have the feeling that somehow one line and the next one are not connected enough. That is a criticism that I've heard here and there.

Maybe people have to get rid of the expectation that there's going to be a Wordsworthian boring exposition going on for six hundred lines on the same subject, that this talking old sheep is going to go on and on. This is not what this poem is doing. This poem is going to be exciting, or surprising, from line to line. But then, you no longer expect a connected essayish kind of mind here, or an old bore to be talking like Wordsworth. Then you may say, "This is very much like what happens in my own head."

LH: So you should revise expectations...

LD: Yes, expectations; but you also know that this is true, that this is true to nature, that this is true to your own thoughts. As you are sitting there your thoughts are jumping around. And since that is what is happening, that's what we want from literature. We want to know how human thought jumps about. And I guess it jumps about a little differently in every head and in every age. As time goes on, this poem is going to be dated and then they will say: "So that's how they thought in 1989... '60 or '70."

LH: What are the problems facing the English Quebec poet?

LD: I would say there are none. The poet will be writing poetry whether there's a revolution or a war going on or not—as when Goethe during a war was quietly writing his poetry. During World War II German poets were writing when the bombs were falling and the concentration camps nearby were steaming full blast. The poet goes on writing for some reason. You might curse him for this, but that's the way it is. He does his work. The one thing to understand about the big events, the wars and revolutions, is that while the revolution is in progress, the people are still going to see plays, they're going to buy their lunch, and they're sitting and talking in cafés. Life is still going on even in the worst of times. That's so, always. The English-speaking population of Montreal is declining, and of course that affects the English Quebec poet, but they were never a great reading audience anyway. Our readers are scattered throughout Canada. We could be only ten people writing poetry in Quebec and no other English people here and we could still be known to some readers across Canada. That would still be possible. So as poets, we have no problems, really; you write your poetry. And for your lifetime, it will probably continue to be that way. On the other hand, there are immense problems of a practical sort. I am extremely critical of nationalism, which is a mode of transferred religious fanaticism. You know, that's what it really is, a group identity manifesting itself with a religious enthusiasm. Nationalism compensates for a sense of inadequacy or inferiority, and it ought to be dealt with at that level; we ought to do something about ourselves, do something positive rather than get up collectively and start yelling about how great we are, what giants we are. Today's *Gazette* deals with that, how the French see themselves as giants in Quebec. They aren't, of course, because they don't feel that they're giants. They're compensating. Well, I'm not a prophet and I don't want to be one. I hope these problems that we have in Quebec can be resolved. It's the only way we can prosper together, the French and the English both. I am certain that if we break up we'll be poorer and sadder and less productive in every way.

LH: Do you see much interchange between French and English writers in Quebec and also in other parts of Canada?

LD: Take a group like Guernica. Antonio D'Alfonso does have contacts with French writers. He is doing something. I know Claude Péloquin. He's a very good poet, very well known, and there's a translation of one of his books brought out by Guernica for which I wrote a preface. But that's a very rare exception. We have very little interchange between French and English writers. A few months ago Liberté asked for a response from English writers about the Quebec problems. I contributed to that; others did. The most memorable ones came from Henry Beissel and myself. We said what we really thought of this question. And they published a whole number of English responses to the French problem. Interchange there is little enough, but there would be enough if we read the French writers in their own texts and that's something that every English writer should do. I would say this to every writer in Canada. Read the other poets. Don't read only your own work and write your own poetry. Read and study the other poets so that you understand what each poet is saying in his own particular way. Read the Québec poets too, and consistently study them, to find out what it is that each poet is saying, each as a separate voice. Don't be too quick to generalize about French writers.

LH: À propos of this in Zymergy 6, *David Solway says, "And I think as English poets we have an immense amount to learn from French poets in this country and they are on the whole the better poets."*

LD: It's an impression one will get certainly from time to time, if you read French poetry and you talk to them, but it's much more complex than that. The French tend to be quite uppity, I would say, and that's one of their problems. Their intellectual life is very arrogant, and therefore cut off from their own people. A magazine like *Liberté* has no hopes of being read by very large numbers of French people. It's only for intellectuals and the university crowd that it's written. Its tone is quite wrong, I would say, as a literary magazine. They don't have any magazine of the kinds that we have had in English, like *Matrix, Delta,* or *Northern Review,* that is magazines for the general reader that have relevant things to say about the whole culture and are open in a general way.

LH: There have been exchanges between Québécois *feminist poets Brossard, Cotnoir, Bersianik, Mouré, and Marlatt.*

LD: You see that's true, and there was an exchange between Frank Scott and Anne Hébert, though I don't know all the contexts that exist. There are the human interchanges between individuals and there are the books. I think it is more important that we read the books. There are two literatures here, not one, two language literatures. You cannot merge them into one, but you can build relations, and it's very enriching to do that.

LH: What is the relevance of critical theory to poets?

LD: Well, by critical theory you mean structuralism, post-structuralism, deconstruction, all that. I hope it's a passing fashion; it's junk, it's horrible, and its effect on literature and especially on the study of literature in universities has been totally negative. Critical theory, apart from that, as thinking about the nature of art, is very important. So, that has to be distinguished. Current "critical theory" is a specific kind of fundamental, metaphysical approach, mainly denoted by the word "deconstruction." It is a linguistic metaphysics, which asks, "What is language? What are words and communications? What do we mean when we say, 'This is a fan.'" And finding that we don't know, or we don't mean anything, and that all languages are essentially ambiguous or meaningless, that nothing exists: this is the old philosophical nonsense about whether this table exists. 'We can't prove that anything is so because of the nature of language,'—it's that sort of thing.

LH: Is that what they're saying?

LD: Of course. They're throwing great doubt on the nature of the literary act and communication itself. Certainly they are. The plain synonym for deconstruction is destruction.

LH: But aren't they suggesting the many ways in which one can approach a text?

LD: We always knew we can approach a text in many ways. What you really have is an approach that makes it impossible for most students to take literature now at the university. They don't want to study this subject. It's not literature anymore, it's become something else. It's something called "a philosophical theory about the nature of literature and language." They should set up a department in the philosophy of language and leave literature alone for those who want to study literature. As most poets and novelists will tell you, literature deals with telling a story or writing a poem. The thought about what that means is secondary and also many-sided. You can say many things about the same story or the same poem. Your response of course is very important, the kind of imagination and emotion you bring to it and the thoughts that you produce as to what you think it means. All that matters, of course, and it's a whole variety of things. But critical theory, as the French have developed it, is a kind of *a priori* methodology or metaphysics, and it's also a language. It's an incredible jargon which is only putting off the general reader. That's what its purpose is. And it should be very simple to see that a language is one that either wants to include people or one that wants to exclude people.

LH: At McGill you encouraged young poets. It was a very healthy situation.

LD: I myself am not typical of anything, since I was a maverick, and I did a few things out of my own convictions. But today's universities . . .how far have I looked into this? It's just a few casual contacts and the people I know who tell me what's happening at universities. Yes, the universities have been invaded by this critical methodology. Then they also have been invaded by Marxism in a very widespread way. It's all hush-hush about this, you don't want to stir up a new wave of McCarthyism. But Marxism, it seems, has taken over the universities, it has infiltrated everywhere. And what do we think Marxism is—a fine theoretical way of thinking? It's a program for revolution, don't you know? And here it is, all over the Political Science Department, Sociology, Literature. It's everywhere, and behind critical theory, too, there are Parisian Marxists whose purpose was to overthrow the entire, so to speak, liberal humanistic civilization of the West, the death of the author being one of their latest findings. At first an idea, but then obviously later on it will be a reality when they put us up against the wall and shoot us. The death of the author is a figure of speech, but it can become quite a reality. They don't want the individualist author to be an important personage any longer. Individualism must go. They want just the text, and they want you to treat it in such a way that literature cannot be used as a support for individualism, or free thought.

LH: What are you working on now? In "The Idea of Art" you speak about poets developing new forms of poetry. What are some of these possibilities?

LD: The new forms of poetry are infinite, I believe. They do have affinities with preceding poetry because everything grows out of something else, but they also branch out in an incredible way, almost the way that plant life develops into a multitude of plant forms and leaf forms and so on. It is in this way that poetic forms can develop.

They don't have to be mathematically structured, as we said earlier, but once they are released from that, there's no end of possibilities. You want to guard against two things: against a mathematical and geometrical structure, guard against that because it's too rigid, it freezes the process. The other is to watch that it does not become prose, that it does not go into the prose paragraph. The rhythm or the patterning—whatever it is—that movement or feeling with which you started determines that this is a poem. And once given, that you have that, that you're writing a poem, you can make many poems.

LH: It's very much up to the individual poet. The young poet has a map of what he wants to do like Wordsworth or Rimbaud, "The Poet at Seven." He is constantly looking for new forms as you did in the early work and later in Continuation.

LD: That's my development of the form; it evolves like a plant. But, take certain experimental forms that I developed. If you go back to the seventeenth century, the emblem poems in which a poem imitates the shape of something, well, that was the first of its kind. Then, the next important step, I would say, is Mallarmé and the poem *"Un coup de dés"* ("A throw of the dice"), where the words are scattered, because he's trying to say something about chance. *Un coup de dés n'abolit pas le hasard* (A throw of the dice does not abolish chance.) Of course, rather a self-evident statement. Anyhow, that's a wonderful poem of Mallarmé's that had a powerful effect upon me. The emblem poems, and Mallarmé, show that you can take words out of the rigid form of the coffin-like quatrain, you can really scatter the words and you can do something strikingly new, like the extreme innovations of Walt Whitman, or Apollinaire, or Cummings. Whitman was aware that he had released the poem from the quatrain by making this long line of his of various lengths and letting it speak—a wonderful release. But he also had the emotion that made sure it never lapses into mere prose. He's compelled by an almost transcendental quality of feeling. That's it. Now, starting from that, and looking at what other poets have since done, depending on your individual temperament, there's no end of forms that can emerge and one would want to live forever to see what poets will write. That's where the infinite worlds are, in part.

LH: Each decade you can develop different forms, do variations on them.

LD: Variations, yes. Let's think about that. In music, you make a melody, then you compose variations. That's very important for structure in music, because in music they develop the structure of sound by making variations on a theme. You think of "The Goldberg Variations" or the "Chaconne." So, in poetry perhaps we haven't thought much of variations, but if you look at *Continuation 1* and *2* you may say "What he's got here are variations." As Mike Gnarowski said: "You know, you're saying the same thing over and over." I never repeat myself entirely, but actually if you examine it, and you number these things or see them in different colours, you might get a sense of variation in the way it occurs. It's the way the ideas turn and return. There's the possibility here that variation may have a future in poetry. Remember that Eliot worked *The Four Quartets* on the theory of imitating musical form. Ezra Pound said there was a fugal form in *The Cantos,* an idea which I don't think he carried very far, but he had it in his mind in the early cantos. Ezra Pound is important here because of the form, let's say, in the *Pisan Cantos*—very highly-charged poetically and very free in the way the lines move. That's the nearest to the kind of thing I eventually did. But I have never really followed Ezra Pound. I found my own form in my own way.

Dk/
Some Letters of Ezra Pound

Edited with Notes by Louis Dudek

All that we have left
      of some ancient poets
is what happened to be quoted by this critic or that
      in a rhetoric book.

from "The Ultimate", *The Poetry of Louis Dudek: Definitive Edition*

Photo by Geof Isherwood

Louis Dudek attends a reading by Ken Norris at Montreal's Double Hook Book Store in 1988, with (left to right) Antonio D'Alfonso, Raymond Filip & Aileen Collins.

Antonio D'Alfonso

9 April 2002

for Louis Dudek

My DAUGHTER IS as tall as my mother
I'm teaching her the meaning of the ocean horse
The ice cap over the Antarctic is melting
I could slice a cube of the sky
And blow it into your lungs
What good would that do
People are into schemes of rhyme
Instead of learning the merits of ambiguity
The paradox of story is that the more you become self
The more you belong to collectivity
Poets want to adhere to the Academies of Royalty
They imitate the monarchy
And forget that the shovel is what created the museum,
I'm reading Victor Hugo right now
And realize that to emulate is the enemy of loving
My daughter tells me that gold too bends
Under the weight of suffering
It's spring and the world is fast asleep
Respect has no need for me to vote for your party
Voices at dawn are what cardinals in the morning turn to fire
We can never be taller than the modern world

If you say in a poem "grass is green,"
They all ask, "What did you mean?"

"That Nature is ignorant," you reply;
"On a deeper 'level'—youth must die."

If you say in a poem "grass is red,"
They understand what you have said.

from "Poetry for Intellectuals", *Collected Poetry*

**Louis Dudek with his nephew
Colin Babin, circa 1985.**

MOHAMUD SIAD TOGANE

(From left) Ruth Taylor, Endre Farkas, Louise Schreier, Ken
Norris and Louis Dudek, after Norris presented Dudek with The
Canadian Writers Award. Ben's Delicatessen, March 2, 1990.

A Toast and a Tear For Louis Dudek

Which of us has known his brother?
Which of us has looked down into his father's heart?
Which of us has not remained forever prison-pent?
Which of us is not forever a stranger and alone?

ADD THIS TO Louis Dudek's "and no one on earth knows his true
being." You might well be apt to conclude that Thomas Wolfe's
poignant lamentations are true, too true up to a point for, as Somalis
say, "You never get to know a person if you don't succeed in taking
their proper measure and sizing them up within the first hour of
encounter." Having spent more than an hour with Dudek, therefore,

I would dare say that I knew him. In fact, I got to know him very well for—as, once again, Somalis say, "Since you are not going to endure forever, leave behind some wit, some wisdom, some waggery, some bonbons, some bon mots." And my friend, Louis Dudek, did leave behind a wealth of wit and wisdom and waggery for: consider Dudek, decked out in his own lilies of the fields of imagination on which he toiled and farmed and cultivated throughout his life. Even Solomon in all his glory was not arrayed like one of those lilies of the field which Louis cultivated and cathected.

So we (his readers) would dare claim that we got to know the real man, the imagination. The late and unlamented, terrible tyrant of the Somalis, known as "Afwayne" used to brag, "I know Somalis better than anyone else (a) because I rule over them and they daily kowtow to me instead of Allah; (b) because more times that I cared to count, when I fled to Mogadishu as an Ogaden Marehan refugee from abysmal Abyssinia and even long after that—need necessitated that I beg from better-off Hawiye Abgal and Majerten Somalis. I still owe some money to Dal-fà and Siyaad Togane and Ali Madoabe and Joone and Oonlaaye for the tabs I ran up in their greasy spoons, from the days when the British lion lorded it over us all freshly-caught sullen Somalis, 'half devil and half child ...lesser breeds without the law' in savage Somalia."

Likewise I got to know Louis Dudek pretty well because once a sore need necessitated that I ask him to recommend me to the Canada Council. After reading a book of poems that I had then just published, without hesitation and with an assist or two from his friends, Irving Layton and Henry Beissel, Louis scored a grant for me that lifted me out of the low, degrading doldrums of the dole to the majestic heights of self-respect and *amour-propre* and poesy. Louis met my need just the way he met life—with a *yes* that blessed me for

Yes
Is made to bless
With natural largesse.
Yes
Is no less
Than God's excess.

His *yes* was the moral shot in the socket of my soul that I then sorely needed—for it was shortly before that an *ofay,* that soi-disant sympathizer and groupie of Third World pseudo-revolutionaries, that not-so-lyrical leftist, that silly celebrant of Turd World tyranny, "A", rudely, crudely and cruelly put me down in my proper 'pickaninny' place by pulling rank on me at a certain Montreal university—and given me the bum's rush from the highfalutin' hackdom of "the sweet recess and the studious walks and shades of the groves of academe." Thus proving my friend Ray Filip (who was also a friend of Louis') to be right on. Which is why I hereby soar and roar as I jam with Filip, the lip from Lithuania:

I call me Ishmael
I am the father and the founder of the black pariah people
I am an uppity Somali Arab nigger wog refugee immigrant
I am Mahmud
I am Muhammad
I am Ossama
I am Hassan
I am Hussein
I am Saddam
I am Muslim
I am your infidel enemy
I am the eternal enemy of Christendom
I am the darker brother
I am the duskier brother
I am the visible enemy
I am the risible enemy
I am first fired
I am last hired
I am no Canadian content
I am a Somali bushman with no Canadian experience
I am the mighty buck
I am the immigrant fuck
I am the melting Pot Luck
I admit being tongue-tied for
I am the language that is lost
I am the name that is changed
I am hard up for money
I am a hard-on for money
I am the inalienable right to alienation
I am the Canadian Mosaic
I am the melting pot on ice
I am the victim of this 'sanctimonious icebox'
I am the American buffalo soldier from Africa
I am the citizen of the world in exile

I am the common loss
I am always the next generation
I am that child grown up writing in English now
I am Caliban cursing out Canada our Lady of the Snows
I am the nigger with no place to be somebody
I am nothing left to be but Canadian.

Dudek had nothing to gain from helping me and my kind—such hapless hobbled hoboes! He simply helped me because Louis was a good man. And a good man is hard to find in Canada or anywhere else. The day I met him was a blessed day. Today I am proud to call myself a Canadian, a *Québécois*—a Somebody to Be Reckoned With, Somebody Not to Tangle With. For me, Louis was one of the few Canadians who exemplified, who lived out this touchstone, this Canadian ideal that his friend and fellow poet, F. R. Scott, composed as his credo—which has now become the secular, unofficial credo, the very ideal Canada and Canadians aspire to, and which Dudek characterized as "unflinching in its humanistic commitment":

The world is my country
The human race is my race
The spirit of man is my God
The future of man is my heaven.

Even now I can hear the cynics and the skeptics snickering away: "Togane, get off it! You've got to be kidding! You say Dudek was a good poet? Fine! But also a good man? Why, that is an oxymoron no moron could or would utter or buy! A poet by definition cannot also be a good and decent human being! A poet is nothing but a slobby, solipsistic slop of a son of a bitch simmering if not over-boiling with

A zoo of lusts
A bedlam of ambitions
A nursery of fears
A harem of fondled hatreds
A jungle of green-eyed jealous monsters
His name is legion.

A poet by definition is bad news! A poet cannot also be a good and a gentle man! The usual rule and the common truth and the typical reaction pertaining to poets are: "Read the poems but flee from the bitch! Read the poems but beware of the bastard, whose bite and bark are more fatal than any dog's! A poet is an egotistical egoist who is the only begotten son of his own silly selfish self!"

Louis Dudek was that rare exception who did indeed cancel and confound us all by calling into question that whole canned cliché of the mad *maudit* poet. Was it not Dudek who wrote:

I want no harm to anyone, have no enemies
And for myself ask only one thing
your happiness)

Louis meant every word—preached it not only with his lips but also with his life. That is why I am here to bear witness to the goodness and the integrity and the dignity of the poet as well as the man. I know among poets and writers the rule and the truth are more in keeping with that of the late American writer, William Saroyan, who wrote of the finest feelings and hopes and dreams and of the magical mystery the human heart harbours—and yet who, in his own life, lived out in living color the raging and gaping contradictions and confusion between the noble utterances of his oeuvre and his ignoble dirty daily deeds. This is the man who exclaimed upon the birth of his own son, "His nose is too big! He looks too Jewish!" Meaning that he found his own flesh and blood too ugly to be loved and even looked upon. No wonder the son, Aram Saroyan, grew up to write a "Daddy Dearest" as harrowing as Christina Crawford's own *Mommie Dearest*.

To explain this not-so-funny phenomenon, this crazy contradiction between the word and the actions, between the theory and the practice, between the lousy life and the lyrical lays, in his essay "The Wound and the Bow", Edmund Wilson resorts to the Greek myth of Phyloctetes and his bow: the Greeks need Philoctetes when they are at war, because with his bow he never misses and is ever the scourge of the enemy. But the fly in this sweet ointment, in this balm in Gilead, is that they can't stand his wound that suppurates with such a horrible smell; which is why, whenever peace breaks out, they exile him, marooning him on an island. Likewise society entertains similar ambivalent attitudes towards the poet who harbors not only his own deep anguish but society's as well and "whose lips are so fashioned that the moans and the cries which pass over them are transformed into ravishing music"—which enables us all to cope with hope. Not only does he forget his own woes by singing them, he also gladdens our hearts despite our own woes.

The price the poet pays for his genius is that not only is he often unbearably obnoxious to others, but also is often unbearable to his own society. I suppose this is what Wordsworth had in mind, when he lamented,

> We poets in our youth begin in gladness;
> But thereof come in the end despondency and madness.

My friend Dudek died sane and sober, and now lives with us in his legacy of the word and the wit and the wisdom he left behind—for us and for Canada and for the world. At his funeral, two years ago, we were all sad and solemn and serious. Yet Louis looked death, the nose-less one, in the face—and couldn't help but laugh. He considered death "The Joke"; his attitude was no different from Donne's:

> Nor dread nor hope attend
> A dying animal;
> A man awaits his end
> Dreading and hoping all...
> Man has created death

Louis didn't dread death but laughed at death! "The Joke" celebrates his own rendez-vous with death:

> When they plunged the first knife in
> I laughed my head off.
> And when they tore my bowels out
> roared with laughter.
> But the best was
> when they brought the box
> with the bows and the flowers,
> and forced me in, I died laughing.

Parenthetically, when I was a child, before "snivelization" set in and wrought its dirty hypocritical job of rendering me into a professional weeper and griever and copious shedder of crocodile tears at funerals. This was exactly my reaction to the death of one dear to me—Togane Dhuhulow Carboni—not only had I burst out laughing at the news of my grandfather's death, I clapped and danced as if I were at a wedding! Louis lived laughing too and today he is in Paradise because not only did Louis love laughing, he lived laughing and he did die laughing and his laughter was so contagious and infectious, he is still making me and countless others in Canada and in the world laugh—nurturing us all with the legacy of light and lightness born of his wit, of his wisdom, of his waggery.

So my dear friend, Dudek, thanks again for all you did for this Somali bushman who once was a Taliban and a Caliban—exiled now in this alien land of snow. Rest now in peace for you fought the good fight; you finished out the course of this life laughing; you kept the faith in God, in your friends, in Canada and in your race, the human race.

Bon voyage et à la prochaine!

TEXTS CONSULTED:

John Carey. *John Donne: life, Mind And Art,* 198. London: Faber and Faber Limited, 1981.

Christina Crawford. *Mommie Dearest.* New York: Berkley Publishing Corporation, 1979.

Louis Dudek. *The Surface of Time.* Montreal: Empyreal Press, 2000. p.51

Sandra Djwa and R. St J. Macdonald, editors. *On F. R. Scott.* Kingston and Montreal: Mcgill-Queen's University Press, 1983. p. 36

Endre Farkas. *The Other Language: English Poetry of Montreal,* p.27. Dorion, Québec: The Muses' Co/La Compagnie Des Muses, 1989.

Raymond Filip. *Somebody Told Me I Look Like Everyman,* p.13. Vancouver: Pulp Press, 1978.

Alfred Kazan. *The Portable Blake.* New York: The Viking Press, 1968. p.1

Rudyard Kipling. *Collected Verse,* pp. 215 and 219. New York: The Sun Dial Press, 1940.

C. S. Lewis. *Surprised by Joy.* New York: Harcourt Brace and Company, 1955. (p.34)

The New York Review of Books, March 29, 2001. p.52

"Sanctimonious icebox": A term for Canada coined by Wyndham Lewis: See Irving Lewis. *The Selected Poems of Irving Layton.* New York: New Directions Publishing Corporation, 1977. p. 7

Aram Saroyan. Last Rites: *The Death of William Saroyan.* New York: William and Morrow Company, 1982.

Roger Sharrock, editor. *Selected Poems of William Wordsworth.* London: Heinemann, 1958.

Louis Untermeyer (editor). *Treasury of Great Poems.* New York: Simon and Schuster, 1948. p. 24

Edmund Wilson. *The Wound and the Bow: Seven Studies in Literature.* New York: Oxford University Press, 1947.

Thomas Wolfe. *Look Homeward Angel.* New York: Charles Scribner's Sons, 1929. p.1

STEPHEN MORRISSEY

The First Person In Literature

AFTER I COMPLETED my B.A. in literature at Sir George Williams University, I went to McGill to do my M.A. I chose McGill because I wanted to study with Louis Dudek. I remember that first day, finding Dudek's office. It was a large spacious room with a window facing Sherbrooke Street, just above the main entrance to the Arts Building. Three years before, I had published my first chapbook, *Poems of a Period.* Sir George Williams (now Concordia University) had an active English Department that brought in poets from across North America and England to give readings. Visiting poets included Patrick Anderson, Alden Nowlan, Diane Wakowski, Robert Creeley, and Allen Ginsberg. I studied creative writing with the poet Richard Sommer. I took a course on British and American Literature with the writer Clarke Blaise. Walking up to Dudek's office that early fall day in 1974 was another part of a natural progression in finding my own voice as a poet.

The graduate seminar taught by Louis Dudek was entitled "The First Person in Literature." That same year Dudek had published *Dk/ Some Letters of Ezra Pound.* This was a collection of letters Ezra Pound wrote to Louis Dudek over a twenty year period, with commentary Dudek wrote on each letter. In our graduate class, Louis was discussing the English novelist Ford Madox Ford; the topic was literary hoaxes in relation to Ford's autobiographical writing. Dudek felt that Ford Madox Ford was more concerned with self-mythologizing than with the truth.

Louis drew me into a practical joke he wanted to play on the class. In *Dk/ Some Letters of Ezra Pound* there are reproductions of typewritten letters by Ezra Pound. When you entered Louis' office, there was a bookshelf behind the office door and on the top shelf was a portable typewriter. The joke Louis wanted me to help him play on the class was as follows: I was to claim that the typewritten letters from Ezra Pound were forgeries. I was to expose that they had been typed on the portable typewriter in Dudek's office.

Louis thought this joke would bring to life the concept of writers' falsifying the truth in their writing. Dudek was concerned with the whole notion of truth versus fiction in autobiographical writing. Of course, the letters in Dudek's book are authentic letters from Ezra Pound, but Louis loved a joke almost as much as he loved honesty. Being shy by nature I didn't carry off this practical joke very well, but I do remember with fondness the minor conspiracy Louis brought me into that day. It helped me to know Louis Dudek the man, not only Dudek the professor or poet.

During that year-long seminar Louis also discussed in class Douglas O. Spettigue's *FPG, The European Years* (1973). This is a fascinating book that reveals the early life of the Canadian author Frederick Philip Grove. Spettigue discovered that Grove's real identity was completely at odds with the persona he created for himself in his autobiographical writing. Dudek was intensely interested in the connection between autobiography and fiction. Dudek believed autobiographical writing is best served by honesty and truth.

Dudek was a great supporter of John Glassco's *Memoirs of Montparnasse* (1970). But Louis became critical of Glassco when it was later revealed that Glassco had fabricated parts of this famous book. Frederick Philip Grove's deception was part of a complex psychology. Grove had needed to divest himself of his old life in Germany in order to create a new life in Canada. Glassco's deception seemed much more self-serving and full of literary ambition. In his *Notebooks, 1960-1994* (1994), Dudek discusses both Ford Madox Ford and John Glassco. He writes that "For some years now I have noticed that I cannot read any of the autobiographical writings of Ford Madox Ford; that is, ever since I realized that he was a habitual fabricator, utterly unreliable in his account of things." Dudek then goes on to write, "For the same reason I have been unable to reread any part of John Glassco's *Memoirs of Montparnasse,* although I once praised it as 'The best book of prose written by a Canadian.'" I feel that this very strong statement by Dudek is significant, for it shows how deeply committed Louis was, as a man and a poet, to truth and honesty in writing.

Louis Dudek's many students as well as his fellow poets loved Louis. He could bring the world of the intellect and poetry to life. As a student in Dudek's graduate seminar he made me feel that the life of the poet was the only one worth living. Louis was dedicated to literature and he was a champion of poetry and poets.

Dudek served poetry and the literary community not only through his teaching at McGill and his influence on many younger poets, but he also served as a literary small press publisher. He initiated the McGill Poetry Series in the early 1950s, and published Leonard Cohen's first book of poems. From 1957 to 1966 he published *Delta*, a literary magazine. In 1967 he began a new press, Delta Canada. A few years later, Dudek and his wife Aileen Collins began DC Books, a literary small press that is still active, now owned by the Montreal poet Steve Luxton and novelist Keith Henderson. In the late 1940s and early 1950s he was associated with several poetry magazines of importance in Montreal, including *First Statement* and *Northern Review*.

It might seem improbable that a moral conservative like Louis Dudek would praise Henry Miller whose books were banned as pornographic for many years. But I remember discussing Miller, whose work I had always admired, with Dudek once when we were together on a Montreal city bus. In an interview in *Quill and Quire* (August 1982) Louis talks about the odd combination of influences on his writing, ranging from Ezra Pound to Matthew Arnold and Henry Miller. Dudek comments in this interview that the voice in his work is a combination of Henry Miller's conversational style with Matthew Arnold's critical faculty. Robin Blaser, who edited *Infinite Worlds: The Poetry of Louis Dudek* (1988), a selection of Dudek's poems, writes in his preface: "The practise of his poetry, which fascinates from the first poems to the latest, has led him into a flowing, radiant form."

Stephen Morrissey with Louis Dudek, circa 1988.

I am writing this memoir "The First Person in Literature" practically a year to the day after Louis died. I have beside me a collection of Dudek's prose books. Dudek's critical writing shows a lively and engaging intellect. Indeed, his critical and artistic contribution to Canadian literature is significant. His reviews and articles on Canadian poetry are written with an enthusiasm and perceptiveness that is immediately communicated to the reader. One time he wrote, "I am not an expert, just a compiler." Most of Louis' scholarly writing is in the form of collections of his critical essays and book reviews, commentaries or statements on poetry, a series of lectures delivered on CBC radio. These books include his *Epigrams* (1975), his *1941 Diary* (1996), his *Notebooks 1960-1994* (1994), and academic papers delivered to various conferences. His doctoral thesis was published in 1960 as *Literature and the Press.*

Louis Dudek was a poet, a teacher, a man of letters, and a supporter of literary small press publishing in Canada. But in the long run, Dudek the intellectual, teacher, and poetry publisher is secondary to Dudek the poet, Dudek the creative man. While Dudek was conservative in his lifestyle, he was always adventurous in his poetry. He was aligned with the Modernist tradition. In fact, Louis Dudek played a very important role in bringing Modernist poetry to Canada.

When the Vehicule Poets, a group of young poets with whom I was associated in the 1970s, were active, Dudek published a book with us, *A Real Good Goosin', Talking Poetics, Louis Dudek and the Vehicule Poets* (1981). Frank Davey dedicated an issue of his magazine *Open Letter* (Spring and Summer 1981 issue) to Dudek, as well as writing a book-length study, *Louis Dudek & Raymond Souster* (1980). For Robin Blaser, "Dudek is Canada's most important—that is to say, consequential—modern voice."

My own favourite book by Louis is *Atlantis* (1967). The experience of reading Dudek's poems today is that they aren't in any way dated, they're as timely as when they were written. What Louis wanted was that his poems be read in the future. For Dudek and other poets, that is the only true test for poetry.

Although Dudek had a long and distinguished teaching career at McGill University he was never really a part of any establishment. When he was young he was isolated, partly by his intellectual interests but also because he was from a Roman Catholic, immigrant, working-class family. In the turbulent years of the late 1960's he was also an outsider, critical of the hippie movement and the radical social changes they represented. He seemed on the surface quite a reactionary, usually wearing a jacket and tie and highly critical of the changes society was undergoing.

I loved the weekly seminars at Louis' office above the main entrance of the Arts Building. You could see Sherbrooke Street from his office window. In the late afternoons of November and December there were office buildings with their lights on, visible across the McGill campus. If it was snowing the city seemed magical and distant. Usually, half way through the seminar, Louis would serve tea and biscuits to his students. Often visitors would drop by and sit slightly away from the table around which we sat; sometimes they participated, but often as not they just listened. They were there to listen to what Dudek had to say. There was Louis' wonderful teaching, his inquiring mind, his unique ability to listen with interest to the ideas of young people, his encouragement, his advice, and his obvious love for teaching and literature. I enjoyed sitting with him and listening to him talk; I enjoyed his physical presence and his kindness which was so reassuring.

Louis was part of an older generation whose poems we read in high school. He was the same generation as Irving Layton but there was also the generation before Dudek and Layton, such as Frank Scott, with whom Dudek was a great friend. We younger poets respected the older poets, not only for their work but because they were poets. The poets in Montreal created an environment in which to be a poet was a possibility, not something alien and foreign. We didn't have to look to England or the United States for our example of what it meant to be a poet. Established poets lived among us, we saw them on the streets where we lived, we read their poems at school, and we read reviews of their books published in local newspapers.

I know that Louis did a lot for other people. As a poet, publisher, and university professor he was in the position where he could help people. He was always writing letters of recommendation for jobs and grants; publishing new poets; meeting people who wanted to talk with him. I remember showing Louis my poems in his office in early 1975. I remember how much it meant to me that he liked them. After that meeting he always treated me as a poet and not as a student. I left his office that day feeling on top of the world, knowing that the rest of my life as a poet was ahead of me. He wrote a short introduction to my first book, *The Trees of Unknowing* (1978) and offered to publish my second book. I participated in a group reading at McGill in 1990 that honoured Louis. In 1993, I nominated Louis for a life membership in the League of Canadian Poets, an organization he helped to found in the 1960's. Later, I introduced Dudek at the League's Annual General Meeting, held that year in Montreal, where he was presented with this honour.

During the early 1990s, Bruce Whiteman, who was head of Rare Books and Special Collections at the McLennan Library, McGill, organized a series of poetry readings. After the reading a group of us would walk down to Ben's, one of Dudek's favourite restaurants. I remember sitting in Ben's Restaurant in the Poet's Corner with Louis on those occasions, under photographs of Montreal poets he helped to have displayed. He devoted his long life to writing poems, to the literary community, to teaching, and to his family and friends. I have happy memories of him, he changed my life for the better, and it is an honour to have known Louis Dudek.

Susan Stromberg-Stein, a fellow student in my 1974 graduate seminar with Dudek, later wrote *Louis Dudek, A Biographical Introduction to His Poetry* (1983). Stromberg-Stein introduces her book with a quotation from Louis: "At the core of every work of literature stands the self, or the psyche of the author; it is the first and most readily available ground for interpretation, the meaning from which all universal meanings spring..."

I studied at McGill University only because I wanted Louis Dudek as one of my professors. He was the best teacher anyone could have. He acted out of love—he encouraged my writing, he wrote the preface to my first book of poems; he offered to publish my second book *(Divisions,* Coach House Press, 1983); he wrote letters of reference for me for grant applications; he wrote a letter of reference which helped secure the teaching position at Champlain College that I have held for twenty-six years now. It is with great fondness that I remember Louis Dudek and his long influence on my life.

Homage to Louis Dudek

A COLD WIND sweeps down
from Mount Royal
to the city below;
this bitter winter
ending with a death.
When a poet dies
a light goes out,
a bit of brilliance
is extinguished,
although poets know
no death is greater than another,
the homeless man surrounded
by plastic garbage bags,
or the former prime minister,
his body carried by a train
slowing at each station.

At the funeral, I listen to Louis' poems
being read, each reader celebrating Louis' life
with anecdotes and poems, a life
dedicated to poetry and teaching.
Louis has moved from temporal
to eternal, from flesh to word;
no more poems will be written by him,
no more meetings in restaurants
to discuss books and art and ideas.

A final grief, a final salute:
the old poet is dead,
the books are written,
the poems recited,
discussions into the evening
come to an end
and we prepare to go home.
We linger at the door

and say "Louis' life
was lived for love of others,
his poems were written out of love."
Outside the March day has turned to night,
we return to our usual lives
feeling diminished by his death
and the world seems
a lesser place.

જી

Louis Dudek, Way's Mills, 1990.

Photo Courtesy of Aileen Collins

from "XIV"

THE CITY'S long
tradition of poets
am klein
john glassco
fr scott
irving layton
louis dudek
leonard cohen

violence or the lack
of violence is something
also to remember

(bombs in mail-boxes
kidnapping
political murder)

call this winter city
Leningrad, Petrograd,
St. Petersburg
city of literature
deconstructed

midnight on March 31st
and April begins with 7 inches
of new snow

none of the above
an April Fool's joke

from "Winter"
© Carolyn Zonailo 1998

Photo Courtesy of Stephanie Zuperko Dudek

Louis Dudek circa 1946.

Louis Dudek: Canadian Poet

THIS FRAGMENT OF a poem is an excerpt from my long mytho-political poem "Winter". It was published as a chapbook by Morgaine House, Pointe Claire, Quebec, in 1998. "Winter" is a poem in celebration of the diversity of cultures in the long literary tradition of the city of Montreal. My poem links the winter city of Montreal with the historical and literary city of St. Petersburg. The poem proceeds via metaphorical associations—as diverse as Hades, Anna Akhmatova, and Jim Morrison—rather than by literal event. When the chapbook was published, Louis Dudek wrote me a letter. This is what Louis wrote:

I first visited Montreal in 1978, for the League of Canadian Poets' Annual General Meeting. F.R. Scott was at that meeting. So was Ken Norris—he and Cathy Ford and myself were the youngest and newest members at that time. I came home with a copy of Michael Harris' recent book, *Grace*. I was introduced to Artie Gold in his book-filled apartment in the McGill ghetto, and to poets Endre Farkas and Tom Konyves.

I returned to Montreal a couple of years later to perform with jazz musicians Al Neil and Howard Broomfield. It was during a bus and metro strike, so I arrived from the airport just in time to step on stage. I didn't come back to Montreal again until I attended a Writers' Union conference at John Abbott College, in the spring of 1991. Strangely enough, six months later, I moved to Quebec. I came only for a weekend and I am still living here a decade later. When I moved to Montreal I had not yet experienced the great difference in climate between the West Coast and Quebec. Living through several winters here led me to connect with my Doukhobor Russian ancestry and to write the long poem "Winter".

Within a month of moving here, I met Louis Dudek, in the winter of 1992. It was at the McLennan Library, McGill University, where several poets and poetry enthusiasts had gathered to hear a reading organized by librarian and poet Bruce Whiteman. The poetry readings were held in the basement of the library. I happened to take the elevator with Louis to the main floor. As we stood beside the elevator, waiting for the others to join us, Louis Dudek introduced himself to me. He welcomed me, as a fellow poet, to his much loved city of Montreal. Louis said to me, "Growing old is a terrible thing." He was in his early seventies at the time. He also told me that he had finished writing poetry, saying he had just published a book of epigrams, satires, and very short poems *(Small Perfect Things,* DC Books, 1991).

But it turned out that Louis Dudek was a creative man, and a poet, right up to the end of his life. From the day I met him, Louis had another ten years of life ahead of him, during which time he would enter another whole decade of poetic flowering. *The Surface of Time,* Louis' final collection of new poetry, was published by Empyreal Press, Montreal, in 2000. Louis Dudek died in March, 2001. I attended a moving, sad, and celebratory funeral. Poets who had been students of Dudek's at McGill University gave testimonies and read aloud Dudek's poems. Louis Dudek was truly a great poet in a city of poetry.

Louis Dudek with Ralph Gustafson, Way's Mills, 1993.

Photo Courtesy of Aileen Collins

Cottages like Chinese lanterns
shine in the soft dark
I breathe the moist night, by the lakeside

from "At Lac En Coeur", *Collected Poetry*

Louis Dudek,
Way's Mills, 1997.

BETTY GUSTAFSON

Louis and Ralph

"And to the east closer to the Vermont border is Way's Mills. Here Louis Dudek owns a farmhouse and gives hospitality to all the literati near and far: poet Ron Everson from Montreal comes every weekend in summer and contributes the benefit of his art and learning. Here Louis Dudek and his wife Aileen, once-editor of that seminal periodical *Civ/N,* grow their gardens and settle the problems of literary Canada. Louis, publisher, critic and poet—mostly all poet—has been settling with balance and common-sense poetic matters for years. When the problems interfere too much with graceful living, Louis takes up his guitar and plays music."

Ralph Gustafson, from "Some Literary Reminiscences of the Eastern Townships"
(Plummets and Other Partialities, Sono Nis, 1987)

RALPH GUSTAFSON AND I first met Louis Dudek in New York City, circa the late forties, where we all happened to be living at the time. He was going to Columbia University. On one occasion, we joined him and Stephanie for dinner at Sherry's Restaurant, along with Lorna and Ron Everson. Sherry's was the dining room of the Old Metropolitan Opera House at 39th and Broadway. We all attended the opera, "Il Trovatore" and it was a wonderful evening: three Canadian poets talking about poetry and then the opera. I don't recall whether the Dudeks were opera fans; however, I do know that Louis did like music very much: I even have a photo of him playing a musical instrument.

When we moved to North Hatley in 1963, our friendship with the Dudeks and Eversons grew even more profound. We would have great meetings at the Ripplecove Inn in Ayer's Cliff. The men talked of current poets being published, among them Ron Everson, Louis Dudek, Raymond Souster and Mike Gnarowski. Frank Scott would join his fellow-poets later in the day. Thus the League of Canadian Poets was started, although the official first meeting actually took place in Toronto. Over the years, we continued to meet the Eversons, along with Louis and Aileen Collins, either at The Ripplecove Inn or at the Dudeks' home in Way's Mills. Those were wonderful gatherings of poetry, art and music. Many years later, after the Eversons had moved away to Ontario, we were joined by Sonja Skarstedt and Geof Isherwood. I recall how strongly Louis felt about awards: he thought that the Governor-General's and other prizes for poetry were far too political. Ralph, Ron and Louis never received the recognition for their poetry that they certainly deserved. Louis had been writing so much for so long. Bruce Whiteman, Director of McGill University's Rare Book Department, invited Ralph and Louis to read their poems one afternoon in 1992. That was one outstanding event!

I will never forget Ralph's last birthday celebration in 1994: on August 14th of that year, Aileen asked us to come for supper. Ralph's birthday occurred two days later, so I made a birthday cake and placed it in the trunk of our car. When we got to Way's Mills I hid it in the refrigerator. We had a wonderful meal and when I brought out the birthday cake, was he ever surprised! Ralph read some of his poems, Louis read some of his and they, as usual, entered into lively discussions of poetry and the poetry scene in Canada. They both kept in touch with what was going on: who was writing poetry, the future of Canadian poetry.

After Ralph's death in 1995, I would see Louis and Aileen in Montreal and in Way's Mills: they were so very kind to me. One day, Louis remarked on a statement I made back in the early 1960's, when Ralph accepted a teaching position at his old Alma Mater, Bishops University. Ralph was unhappy for me because I had had such a wonderful position at Harkness Pavilion, the private pavilion of Columbia Prebysterian Medical Center, in New York. I was an Evening Head Nurse, and happened to meet all the celebrities who

Photo Courtesy: Betty Gustafson

Louis Dudek, Betty & Ralph Gustafson, Way's Mills, 1991.

went there for treatment, from Fritz Kreisler and Elizabeth Taylor to Edna Ferber, and many others. I told Louis what I had told Ralph: "You know what the bible says. 'Whither thou goest I will go!'" Louis was very impressed by that. Many of our meetings in Way's Mills were just so filled with meaning, and flashes of those lovely times come back to me with warmest emotions.

TODD SWIFT

Louis Dudek playing the flute
in North Hatley, early 1960's.

The Idea of Louis Dudek

I HAD WANTED this to be a longer essay—perhaps a study of Louis Dudek's wonderful long form poem *Europe*—but several projects intervened: a new collection of poems from small press DC Books, and a global anthology of new English-language poetry, as well as a CD of recorded verse for a Montreal label. I mention these things not to draw attention to myself, but to make a very important point about Louis Dudek: none of these works of mine would have been thinkable, and barely possible, if not for Dudek—and the idea of Dudek, as literary predecessor.

Unlike many other Canadian writers in this book, I cannot pretend to a personal relationship with the great man (and great he was, in the European sense of cultural significance he himself argued so openly for). I never ate with him at Ben's, or studied with him. Indeed, I only met him, physically, on two occasions: first, at a national poetry gathering, where we stood on the steps of a Toronto library and chatted for a few minutes; and then, again, at the memorial service for long-time CBC radio man, and fine unsung poet John Bishopric, who was part of the Knowlton circle. Though I will say that I was struck by his friendliness, and interest in a then (very) young poet's enthusiasm, these chance meetings are not the legacy he passed on to me, and my generation of "fusion poets" now just entering their mid-thirties.

Instead, it is the Idea of Dudek which has so captured me, and, less intangibly, the praxis that came with this idea, or set of ideas, which has proved so inspirational, and useful, as a guide to being an anglophone poet from Quebec. Louis Dudek is an exemplary figure. Like few other major poets—Yeats, or Pound, or William Carlos Williams—he was able to fuse a love of poetry with a didactic activism on its behalf, and carry these twin necessary dedications through a long life and work span. He is an exemplary figure simply because he is the single best example we have, in Canada (and there are precious few of his kind elsewhere, either, on the cosmopolitan stage) of the rigorous, serious, committed poetic life, full of achievements at every stage.

A life, let us admit, lived not in the self-interested hullabaloo of the spotlights, as some of his peers' were, but in the shadows cast by other more ancient (and modern) role models; nonetheless, for a poet who eschewed prizes and ceremonies and the attendant laurel leaves of "big press" publication, and "big name" recognition, he was, for his time, remarkable for his involvement with—his direct action upon—the means of production, and the agents of discourse (including the media). For instance, his Phonodisc recording, *The Green beyond: Poems* which I have had since I was fourteen (having rescued it from an uninterested church sale), or his appearances on the CBC's "Ideas" programme, are key and early interventions in new broadcasting and recording media; using his *vox* to reach the people.

His exemplary status means that, by the very choices he made in his literary life, and by his very interests, he established the field on which I am now able to play. I alluded to this before, but let me return, now, to elaborate. Louis Dudek has made a difference in my life of poetry, and for that I will always be grateful.

Firstly, Dudek's very question *"Où sont les jeunes"* and his editorial call, in January 1952, for young poets to emerge, is continually relevant, and was, as I started to think of a career in poetry, very meaningful. Secondly, his almost single-handed (there were other hands, but none as steady) invention of the small press movement in Canada, centred in Montreal, meant that Dudek's own Delta Canada (now DC) was—by a none-too-difficult leap of the imagination—to publish my collection, *Budavox*, in 1999. In Hungary, at Budapest University, this press was known, once its lineage was traced back to Dudek. With some pride I tell people that my press is one of the key modernist presses in our history.

Thirdly, there was Dudek's McGill Poetry Series, which introduced the world to Leonard Cohen, and Co. As Cohen has always been a more popular touchstone for my generation, this was a way back to Dudek for those whose sense of iconography might not be so austere. So it was that William Furey and I ran, from 1987-1989 "The New McGill Reading Series" in direct (if cheeky) reference to Dudek's pioneering efforts.

Fourthly, Dudek's poetry activism and involvement with Pound, and his ongoing cultural defence of poetry, basically sanctioned all the renewed-*zeitgeist* action (and manifestos) centring around the little magazine *Agent,* and the shows *Vox Hunt, Yawp!* and the label *Wired On Words.* Naturally, this association with Dudek has not always been recognized, but such is the nature of influence, pervasive as air, and often as unseen.

Fifthly, it was small press publisher Simon Dardick, who agreed to publish a key landmark of our young generation, *Poetry Nation.* Dardick's decision to support our work, with an anthology, can be directly traced to the generosity of spirit, and the critical curiosity, of Dudek, whose own anthologizing/editing instincts and involvements are, once again, seminal for Canadian poets. Dudek's was the keen eye, in the 1950's, scouting for the next poets coming over the horizon.

In the 1990s, his belief that editors should always keep a look-out for the next wave, bore fruit anew. After all, this is the man who left New York (and a circle of exceptional US poets) to return to Montreal, to establish how it could be done here. When Anne Carson, or Julie Bruck, or myself, are published in New York, we are in no small way expatriating the poetic confidence that Louis Dudek originally repatriated by putting Montreal on the modernist map: and keeping it there.

Knowing that Dudek had paved the way, after having fought the battles on the same turf, it was easier for myself and my peers to pronounce an "English Quebec Literary renaissance" in 1988, and become our very own D-I-Y Poundian impresarios. This would have been culturally bankrupt, and intellectually silly, if not foregrounded upon the stage set by Louis Dudek.

And here, to be honest, I must speculate on the question: would Dudek recognize this spoken-word based scene in Montreal as his "bastard child"? I fear that, in some ways, he would not have been amused by the arrogant assumption of patrilineage (but then again, perhaps secretly touched, nonetheless?). Dudek took McLuhan to task over too heady a celebration of hot and cold running media; he did not like competition in poetry, so no doubt found the advent of the slam and multimedia poetry in Montreal somewhat repugnant; and much of the new poetry being written for the page and stage in Canada today would seem slack and lacking in a credible respect for tradition.

However, strong literary figures, like Pound, or like Dudek, are often mentors despite their own intentions, and their generous resources, renewed for each generation, spill over from their own fields of force. Furthermore, the energy, commitment, and urge of the latest generations, struggling themselves with Philistine society to "make poetry new" and get poetry heard—by more than "200 out of 200 million" people—that cultural expenditure he would always approve of.

Louis Dudek is proof that a poetic center can be imagined out of any cultural wasteland, let alone Montreal, and his many fertile enterprises have yielded almost every route possible for emerging poets and poetry advocates to take.

It is time Dudek not be taken for granted, and be embraced by my generation, and the one (or three) coming up behind us. This will be said again and again in this book, I suspect, but it bears repeating: Dudek deserves more. More praise, more recognition, more gratitude, and finally, more readers. The Idea of Dudek is the idea that poetry can happen here, and when it does, it matters. Now let us turn from the idea of the man, to the man's own words. These matter too: very much.

Photo Courtesy of Stephanie Zuperko Dudek

Louis Dudek, circa 1970.

Making All the Difference

FIFTY YEARS have passed since I made my way three times a week at five o'clock to a class in Comparative European Literature. The professor, whose name meant nothing to me then was tall, angular, with human parts branching out in all directions so that at first glance he seemed disconnected. I felt the same way about his syllabus both that year and the next, an assemblage of books that ranged from Voltaire's *Candide* and Young's *Conjectures on Original Composition* to Goethe's *Faust* and Proust's *Remembrance of Things Past*.

I can't remember whether the texts ever got connected. I suspect most of them didn't. But it didn't matter. His courses were the beginning of my education. I was there—the son of working class parents—to discover, among other things, the mysteries of the ologies (psychology, sociology, anthropology etc.), and Louis Dudek's course was to be nothing more than a wayside stop. I never realized that the stop would become a full time enterprise, nor did I have an inkling of the role that he might play in my choice of vocations—teacher and poet.

Try as I may, I can't recollect specific things he said about specific books, but I do remember that he rarely spoke at length. He let us, his students, do that. What he did do was listen carefully, poking occasionally at what we said with an offhanded remark that seemed to come through the slice of an open window, as though Louis Dudek were merely the innocent carrier of some fresh, but crucial news. In any event he kept the conversation—and our reverence for those books—growing, not merely throughout the class meeting, but afterwards from one week to another, until those books became as indispensable as breathing.

The magic of those classes stays with me, more so than any of the other items that might fall into a summary of Louis Dudek's life and career. I find myself less interested in whether Louis expressed the ultimate wisdom on any of the books we read; less interested in the debate on the merits of his poems though some of his lines will not leave me (and I was delighted to hear his *Europe* quoted at a recent poetry reading in Germany). In recent years, when we occasionally got together for a cup of tea, usually close to his home on Ingleside, he'd start the conversation with a jab at something that had appeared in the newspapers or on an aesthetic position that I'd taken. But inevitably we'd come back to reminisce about the excitement of that class. I believe it meant as much to him as it did to me.

At his funeral in March 2001, I recall seeing three classmates from that class of '52. I suspect that our accounts of what we shared, those stews of literary, political, and social debate, would vary somewhat. (In a well-made stew it is not unusual for each of the ingredients to emerge with its own added flavours.) What we would all share is an acknowledgement that those classes played a shaping role in our lives.

I've always felt suspicious about conversion experiences, people who liken themselves or others to Saul of Tarsus, smitten and fully reshaped after dropping from his camel on the dusty road to Damascus. As for a single person, experience, or event making "all the difference," as it does in "The Road Not Taken," I'm sure that Frost himself would not stand behind that judgment. Louis Dudek did not make all the difference in my life, but he made an enormous difference, and for that I will always think of him with fondness and gratitude.

TOBIE STEINHOUSE

Louis Dudek, circa 1980.

Louis

L OUIS WAS, for many years, a friend of my late husband, Herbert
Steinhouse, and of mine. I am including some letters from him:
especially important to me was his letter of February 4, 1972, and
the many pages, selections of his poetry, that he sent to me when I
asked him to do the introductory page of my portfolio of eight etch-
ings called "Sanges et Lumières" which was published by La Guilde
Graphique in 1972.

There is also the letter from Louis of February 20, 1960 regarding his publishing in *Delta 11* (Spring 1960 issue), of a poem by
Pamela Fry about "Tobie Steinhouse—Impressions of Her Painting".

As well, Louis and Herb were old friends dating back to McGill
in the forties—and their friendship and mutual esteem continued—
with Louis writing a critique of Herb's last book (manuscript) not
long before his death in 1996. I also include, on a more humorous
note, the poem Herb wrote about the article in the *Westmount
Examiner* about Ingleside Avenue—February 25, 1993, and Louis'
letter in response.

The world misses Louis—and I do too, very much.

BOOKS

February 4, 1972

Dear Tobie,

        I've typed a few pieces, enclosed.
Each is a separate selection, except the
KEW GARDENS, which goes into page two. In other words
you can consider any separate page of these as a possible
choice, or the Kew Gardens, both pages.

        The one thing the pictures and the poem should
have in common, I think, is the aesthetic. As a tribute
to you, I find that the only poems of mine that in any way
fit your pictures are the high points of my poetry, i.e. where
I get at the ultimate and, one might say, incommunicable
essence-- which, frankly, I don't do very often. It's the
Mallarmé element. I'm astonished that you can stay at
that kind of intensity all the time. I've got to descend
into the grbage of reality and see what I can pick up from
there--

        In a way, it's one vast slum,
                       the world.
        Or a rich garbage dump
        on which gaudy flowers and delicate pinks
              sprout, clamber, float..."

Otherwise I'd probably start faking. Anyway, I've got to
find God, or the Platonic, in the garbage. It must be there,
or I don't want it. I'm always working on this problem.

        Don't worry if none of these fit your sense
of what the portfolio needs. There is no reason why my poetry
and your pictures should find a match.

Dudek/Collins (editors), 5 Ingleside Avenue, Montréal 215, Québec, Canada

① ~ ~ ~ ~ ~ ~ ~ ~ ~ ~

This is our gift, to extricate joy
             from earthly things,
what is distilled of transcendence
                 out of the visible. . .

· · ·

p. 272.

The greenery of many mounting trees,
with nary a cloud, a spot of light
                 held in the memory.

· · ·

Like dreams before they begin, a tunnel
             at the end of which a blue grotto,
silently set with shrubs, shines.

Silence, in the glass light of so much meaning
it looks like indifference, and purpose so large
             the details are left to chance.

p. 279   ~ ~ ~ ~ ~ ~ ~ ~ ~ ~ ~ ~ ~ — from "ATLANTIS"

Who thinks the living universe?
I think it but in part.
Fragments exist
         like those infinitesimal separate stars . . . .
~~I saw, lying on my back on the cushions~~
~~last night before the storm:~~

omit →

their union, as powers
             but as wheels on the one axle,
and as form--
         a drawing by a master hand.

We have united some few pigments
         (all that is in museums)
but the greater part, all life, was there
                 united when we came--
and grows, a copious language of forms.

Who thinks them?...
         Their being is a thought....

My thought, a part of being-- is a tree
of many thoughts, in which a yellow bird sits.

p. 217.

~ ~ ~ ~ ~ . ~ ~ ~ ~ from "LAC EN COEUR"

(2.)

In the daylight of departure from the shores of light,
the sea was a white burning cloud all afternoon.

Locks hanging over the counterpane
                    or grapes spilling
out of the bright horn.

"Light."

Only in the reflection of portholes
                              gulls
flash across mirror, a dumb sequence.

            The sea as an escritoire.
                        That pale blue
                  and violet
                        heaven.

AT LAC EN COEUR *— title could be omitted*

The sea retains such images
    in her ever-unchanging waves;
for all her infinite variety, and the forms,
inexhaustible, of her loves,
she is constant always in beauty,
    which to us need be nothing more
        than a harmony with the wave on which we move.
All ugliness is a distortion
of the lovely lines and curves
    which sincerity makes out of hands
        and bodies moving in air.
Beauty is ordered in nature
    as the wind and sea
shape each other for pleasure; as the just
know, who learn of happiness
    from the report of their own actions.

The shapes, I think them
    as of waves coming in
    lapping the curve of the shore,
        and wind carving clouds,
may be or not be as I perceive
but the fruit of the maple, pine cone,
seed of the cedar (proving Goethe's principle,
    every compartment
a form like the flattened branch and whole tree)
formed out of the flux, are there
atomic, mobile--
    unities that persist,
real as in a mind.
With Riemann, & Einstein,
with Hoogstraaten's peep-show,
and Vermeer, the fascination of symbolism.

A heap of straw, in which a needle of truth lies hidden,
    Turner's "Evening Star"
        over the sea...

Violet last shadows of evening
                on the high cliffs.
Darkness is in the current, reflective colours.
In the mountains, even the dusk is brief,
        for sunset, over the peaks, comes early.
And the strenuous life takes its toil.

Then the cooler trees, cedar and fir, in the hollows,
damp, dark,
            thoughtful.

Turn away from it all.
What is it?

A circular movement of matter,
                        swirling, atomic salt.
Distant, the dark trees, the snow patches,
            turbulence of waters
indistinct in the night--

a glimmer, a dot, lost
        somewhere in the void

where everything good is possible.

KEW GARDENS

Have you seen the weeping beech
          hanging like a green pavilion?
Or the tulip tree
          reaching up to heaven?

Have you seen the cedar?
The kakee tree, the gingko, the lobed sassafras
    --have you inhaled their fragrance?

The glistening leaf of the strong oak, suber,
    the slender white birch,
                    the dappled maple,
the tough sticky pine, swelling with rosin?
Have you sat on the moss among the brown cones?
Have you seen the contours of the leaves?
Or listened to the silence in their shadows,
          or the rush in high winds?

I have gone to the green pavilion of morning
    and watched the dahlia open her eye.
I have seen the violets breathe in the blue light
          under pendent leaves.

Ilex Aquifolium, the pale-fringed holly.
The Strelitzia like a tropical bird,
    _   the hanging lamp of the purple fuchsia.
The rose Spiraea and the royal lily.
(And birds come to eat from your hand--
                would you want to harm them?)

Gleditschia   Dietes   Regal Lily

I have seen the parts of a flower
          floating, detached from the stem,
yet knowing somehow what to do.
Growing, drinking in rain.

Callamandra   Zantedeschia   Gloriosa

And an orange tree, with dozens of fruits.

The fruit of the Magnolia of Yunnan
                opening their great pods
and the Cashmere Cyprus of Tibet
          that hangs like drapery, green and brown.

Nymphaea and tropical fish

But the rhododendrons were not in flower.
"The rhododendrons were not in flower!"
     "Ah, you must come back another time."

(next page)

To see the famous roses
    Mme Butterfly, Sutter's Gold, Masquerade,
    Christopher Stone, Misty Morn.

(Was it Mandeville wrote--
    "How Roses First Came Into the World"?)

Primula Japonica...

Ah, Waste Land!

(end)

" .... I find that the only poems of mine that in any way fit your pictures are the high points of my poetry ...: "

— Louis DUDEK
'72

DUDEK, Louis, OC, MA, PhD

Poet, critic, professor, editor, man of letters

On Thursday, March 22, 2001 at the Royal Victoria Hospital, Montreal, after a short illness, Louis Dudek, aged eighty-three. Dudek was a professor in the English Department of McGill University from 1951 to his retirement in 1983. He was Greenshields Professor of English from 1969 to 1983. Among his many honours were Doctor of Letters, York University, 1983; Professor Emeritus, McGill University, 1984; Order of Canada, 1984; and honorary doctorates from Lakehead University and St. Thomas University. His literary papers are in the National Library of Canada, Ottawa. He is survived by his wife Aileen Collins and his loving son Gregory from an earlier marriage to Stephanie Zuperko, daughter-in-law Krys and grandchildren Natasha and Nicholas. Survived also by his sisters Lillian and Irene (George Lewinski) and nephews Konrad (Jane Agnew), George (Alison Gopnik) and John-Anthony (Cheryl) and great-nephews Nicholas, Alexei and Andres. Also survived by niece Mary Stewart (Michael Babin) and great nephews Colin and Adam and great niece Caitlin. Louis Dudek's intellectual vitality and honesty, breadth and profundity served as an inspiration to all who knew him. Visitation at the Centre Funeraire Cote-des-Neiges, 4525 Cote-des-Neiges, Montreal (514) 342-8000 on Sunday, March 25 from 2 to 9 p.m. and Monday, March 26 from 9:30 a.m. to 1:30 p.m. Funeral service will be held in the chapel of the Centre Funeraire at 1:30 p.m. In lieu of flowers, donations may be made in his name to the Canadian Diabetes Foundation.

Eternity is the surface of time.
As Parmenides says, a reality
unchanging, one, undivided,
from which creation uttered.

Louis Dudek, from "Continuation III"

"DELTA"

781 Beatty Avenue
Montreal 19, P.Q.

Feb. 20, 1960

Dear Tobie,

The poem is fine, and I'll be running
it in Delta 11.
I hope it will be all right to change
the title slightly to read

TOBIE STEINHOUSE
Impressions of Her Painting

since the title as it now stands: "To Tobie
Impressions of her painting" will not be clear to most
readers. Might as well let them know you.

Unless I hear from you within two
weeks, say, I'll use the title suggested.

It's a pity I do not have a halftone,
or line cut, or woodcut, of your work that I could
run in the same number. It's a platen press, with mag
x page size about 6 x 9, so the cut should be 5 1/2 by
8 1/2. Got anything?

Sincerely,

Louis Dudek

Dear Herb,

March 28/93

Yes, the poem looked very well in the Examiner. I was worried that all the attention to that question, beginning with the editorial "Why Ingleside" would lead to the end of our good luck in getting the street cleaned; but it made no difference, we were spick & span a few days ago, when you couldn't walk on Ste Catherine or Metcalfe.

The fact is, the workmen like to begin here. And the street is not for residents at all, its a parking lot for anyone in the surrounding neighborhood. Cars are always cruising around looking for a place to stop.

Anyhow, thanks for the tribute and all. Love to Tobie.

Louis,

RONALD SUTHERLAND

Photo Courtesy of Stephanie Zuperko Dudek

Louis Dudek, circa 1953.

A Thoughtful and Generous Friend

L OUIS DUDEK CAME into my life about a half century ago when as
a 16-year old freshman at McGill University I wandered into one
of his courses. During a meeting with him after the class, upon
learning my name he wanted to know if I were related to John
Sutherland, his fellow editor at *First Statement*. I told him that I
wasn't really related to any Sutherlands because I had been adopted, and we thus discovered that we had something in common. He
too, in a sense, had been "adopted," since Dudek was not his blood
family name. "But what does it matter?" he said.

Then we discovered that we had another thing in common: unlike ninety-nine percent of students and faculty at McGill at the time, we were both born and raised in the largely French-speaking east end of Montreal. In fact I sometimes went to Saturday night dances at the Dom Polski Hall near Frontenac and Ontario Streets, a place he knew well.

I soon got into the habit of dropping into Louis' office. I felt him to be a kindred spirit, and he seemed to feel the same way about me. He always had time to talk to an insecure, struggling kid who traveled an hour on the streetcar from the east end every schoolday to attend classes. For me, as for many other aspiring writers and poets I'm sure, he was the "Miss Appledaisy" of McGill University.

A few years ago, an extensive study was conducted by pedagogy researchers at McGill on the career of an elementary-school teacher, in a school in Point St. Charles, I believe, who had a Greek name but was fondly known as "Miss Appledaisy." The study sought to evaluate the lasting effect she had had on her pupils, who were randomly selected for one of the school's three Grade One classes. Tracing former pupils over several years, the study established that Miss Appledaisy's group consistently achieved higher levels of accomplishment in life than the pupils who had been in the other two Grade One classes. What was the explanation? Apparently Miss Appledaisy had the gift of instilling self-confidence in her charges, and it served them a lifetime.

Louis Dudek had the same gift. I recall showing him some primitive literary efforts. He was critical. In fact, Louis was the most honest and fair critic I have known. He would neither flatter nor trash. But he would find something positive, a reason to continue and a direction to follow. Self-confidence.

After I left McGill and went to the University of Glasgow, then to Wayne State University in Detroit, I did not see Louis Dudek for several years. Back in Canada with a post at l'Université de Sherbrooke, I settled in the town of North Hatley. Not long afterwards, at one of Frank Scott's legendary birthday parties, I met Louis again and found out that he had a summer place at Way's Mills, not far from North Hatley.

Our friendship took up again where it had left off. Louis was in the hall when I delivered the first paper on Comparative Canadian Literature (Learned Societies, 1966). He approved the initiative, much to my relief and satisfaction, and thereafter he supported me wholeheartedly in attempting to foster the comparative study of English-Canadian and French-Canadian literature. I guess it was an appropriate field for two former east-end Montrealers.

For me, then, Louis Dudek was always a thoughtful and generous friend, an inspiration and a positive force. But I know that's exactly what he was for so many others, including my friends Leonard Cohen and Doug Jones, and for the whole enterprise of creative writing and publishing in Canada.

Alan Pearson,
Irving Layton
& Louis Dudek,
circa 1956.

Photo Courtesy of Betty Gustafson

To that tree, seen by my lover
at the other end of the line:
       Shine, green bonfire
into her eyes, make them green
            with desire.

from *Small Perfect Things*

Louis Dudek, summer of 1954.

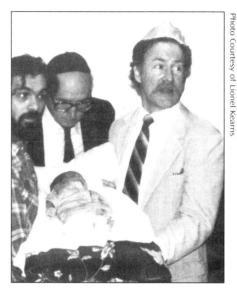

Photo Courtesy of Lionel Kearns

(Left to right) Endre Farkas,
Louis Dudek & Lionel Kearns
with son Louis, 1983.

Cultural Commitment

I OWE A LOT to Louis Dudek. For more than thirty years he helped
and encouraged me in my writing career. Without his presence
and support, I doubt if I would have published a poem. I am sad
that he is no longer with us.

I first connected with Louis in the late 50's. I was a naïve kid
who had come to Vancouver from the B.C. hinterland. I had the idea
that somehow I would end up as a writer, but I did not know exactly what that meant, or how to go about it. I was writing the odd
poem and short story, but I did not know what to do with them after

I had written them, and I hesitated to show them to anyone. I did not know any other writers, but I kept my eyes open for literary events, read *Canadian Forum,* and I listened to Robert Weaver's *Anthology* program on CBC radio. Somewhere along the line I heard about Louis Dudek and his Montreal based literary magazine, *Delta,* copies of which I eventually tracked down.

On the pages of *Delta,* which Louis was putting out on a hand press, I read short insightful comments and articles on writers as diverse as Ezra Pound and Wilhelm Reich. I also read the poems of Al Purdy, Doug Jones, Daryl Hine, Leonard Cohen, Alden Nowlan and George Ellenbogen, none of whom I had ever read before. Delta gave me my first sense of a community of poets in Canada. It also gave me a context in which to place my own literary interests and writing activities. At one point I got up enough courage to send a small bundle of my poems as a submission to *Delta.* Louis replied with a letter discussing my work, pointing out what impressed him, and what did not, and he accepted three of my pieces. I was ecstatic. It was my first publication.

Louis came out to the West Coast in 1962 to teach a summer course at UBC. By then I was connected with a group of young writers who had come together to put out the *Tish* poetry newsletter. Some of the Tishers enrolled in Louis' course, and some of us just sat in on the seminars. It was an enjoyable and enlightening experience. Louis conducted it as a kind of forum, guiding the discussion and offering his considered and informed observations, which frequently conflicted with our narrow and sometimes biased opinions. Louis wanted to open us up, to make us look beyond our immediate restricted area of focus, to put our writing into the wider arena of history and learning. It was a good tonic for us at that point of our development.

I kept in touch with Louis after that. He invited me to read my poems several times at McGill, and during the year I spent in Montreal as writer-in-residence at Concordia (1982-83) he invited me to his classes. That was a treat, because Louis' students were bright-eyed and interested. They listened and asked good questions. It seemed that he had instilled in them a deep interest in world literature and a healthy respect for contemporary writing, and writers.

Our last child was born that year, and we named him Louis.

Could there be a more auspicious name for a Montreal son? At the *bris* the older Louis put on a yarmulke to complete the minion of male poets participating in the ceremony. There was toasting and joking and reading of poems, much to the consternation of the *mohel*. The older Louis was very interested in the traditional part of the proceedings, and leaned over to see what the mohel was about to do to the baby, who was lying on a cushion, naked and hollering. Just as the sacred act was about to take place, the baby Louis shot up a stream of pee that hit his namesake in the eye and soaked the three of them. It was a kind of baptism that seemed entirely appropriate for that raucous and memorable occasion.

That same year my wife and I attended a dinner party at the home of Frank Scott. We sat down to servings of exquisite food and good wine, and listened to Frank and Louis recount stories of their literary adventures, and misadventures. The repartee was a relaxed and spontaneous, but the anecdotes were measured and shapely and performed with a style and elegance that was quite marvelous. I remember thinking that if this was an example of civilized behaviour, then I was all for it.

When I associate that term, civilized, with Louis, it does not have its usual ironic clank. Louis believed passionately that culture was a process to which we must commit ourselves, individually and collectively. He had little time for the over emotional or the selfish or the silly. However unfashionable poetry might be in the modern world, he reminded us in his writing, in his teaching, and in his life, that it was a serious, worthy, and important undertaking. That is a message which I take to heart.

SONJA A. SKARSTEDT

Geof Isherwood, Sonja Skarstedt, Betty & Ralph
Gustafson, Louis Dudek, Way's Mills, 1994.

"Pourquoi Jean Narrache?"

"In the 1970s, I translated a batch of poems of Jean Narrache with great enthusiasm, out of affection and gratitude."

Louis Dudek[1]

WHEN ONE CONSIDERS the pantheon of poets whose work is cry-
ing out for translation, it is fascinating to consider why Louis
Dudek devoted over four decades, on and off, to rendering the verse
of Jean Narrache—*"ami des petites gens"*—into English. Two years
before his death, Louis asked me whether I would consider publishing the result of his meticulous labour. *"Pourquoi Jean
Narrache?"* I quipped, as he handed me a care-worn manila envelope neatly packed with a cross-section of Narrache's poems and a
delectably-researched introductory essay.

He traced his fascination with the poet in an essay published in
Open Letter: "I think it was (Maurice) Watier who brought me to the

Photo by Aileen Collins

poetry of Jean Narrache, a popular poet then still at the height of his fame."[2] A number of the translations in that envelope had appeared in *The Tamarack Review* (Number 69, 1976). In the years to come, Dudek would add thirteen more. What, I wondered, was the story behind these poems, aside from Dudek's determination to broaden public awareness of an exceptional poet? Did his persistence have anything to do with the fact that Narrache, so wildly-popular in his heyday of the Depression years, had passed away in near obscurity, during the turbulent years of Quebec's not-so "Quiet" Revolution? I also hoped to glean some further insights into the rhyme and reason of Dudek's own literary motivations. Dudek himself noted that Narrache "wrote his best poetry in Montreal between the late 1920s and 1939, when his books were published."[3]

In her thought-provoking discourse on the exacting, often breathtaking feat that is translation, Cynthia Ozick zeroes in on the paradoxical nature and demands of the work at hand, thus the plight of the individual who dares to undertake this potentially monumental challenge. Is it humanly possible to bring a poem to reasonable comprehensibility, after wending one's way through the confines and demands of another language; to transmit an accurate facsimile encompassing a poem's original emotional and intellectual impact? "The poem and its translation are two separate artifacts," cites Ozick, "each equal to the other; and not only 'equal' in the sense of being 'alike,' but each having become the other."[4] According to Ezra Pound, "the rhythm set in a line of poetry connotes its symphony" as "the rhythm of any poetic line corresponds to emotion" and thus, that "it is the poet's business that this correspondence be exact, i.e., that it be the emotion which surrounds the thought expressed."[5]

Dudek faced a daunting task, bringing to life Narrache's highly original colloquial slapstick while preserving the poet's meter and rhyming sequences. An accomplished poet in his own right, Dudek was willing to subject himself to serious constraints for the sake of accuracy. Determined to present readers with as authentic as possible a rendering of the original poem, he fastidiously adhered to Narrache's voice, questing after the most precise English equivalents to the *Québécois* colloquialisms that shaped Narrache's street-hobo persona, right down to filaments of Victorian phrasing. If there was no available English equivalent, Dudek would leave an original word or phrase intact. Not only does this enhance the "Narrache" voice, but also serves as a useful rhyming device:

> The good old movies, what a world!
> Full of high life and grand amours,
> They make you forget for just a while
> That poor, flat, common life of yours.

("Winter Night on Rue Ste-Catherine")

Dudek's English versions of the poems come across with the same crackling, vivacious energy as Narrache's originals: from the clipped pronunciations of "p'raps" and "b'fore" to the merry-sour slurring of "Canayen". Under Dudek's auspices, the dank and sputtering lives of these victims take the helm, yet he also ensures that each woebegone tirade is shored by Coderre's wistful infusions:

> *Ici, on peut rêver tranquille*
> *d'avant l'étang, les fleurs pis l'gazon.*
> *C'est si beau qu'on s'croit loin d'la ville*
> *ousqu'on étouff' dans nos maisons.*
> *(<<En rôdant dans l'parc Lafontaine>>)*

> Here you can dream real pretty
> By the lake, the flowers on the lawn,
> You'd think you were far away from the city
> Where people choke from dawn to dawn.
> ("Wandering in Parc Lafontaine")

A year and a half before his death, Dudek spearheaded the translation of Quebec poet Pierre DesRuisseaux's *Graffites* (to which I happened to contribute). During this time, he revealed a mainstay of his own translation methodology, i.e., that it was better to err on the side of exactitude than to take any liberties that might send the poem flying off into any unfamiliar galaxy. He handed me back my preliminary versions of DesRuisseaux's poems with a series of admonitions, disagreeing with several of my word choices. I argued my "case," stating that my own versions were less constricting, where it came to making the poet's "sound" as smooth and natural as possible. "Better not take any serious risks," he insisted. "One can destroy a poem that way."

Dudek's scrupulous approach produced gratifying results: the Narrache *oeuvre* provides a touching, down-to-earth picture of everyday Montreal life circa the 1930s and 40s. The poems' titles in themselves comprise a looking-glass through which the reader can enter the perspective of an average, beleaguered citizen during those years: "Election Time," "The Charity Balls," "Winter Night on Sainte-Catherine," "No Learnin'," "Reflections On a Five-Cent Piece," "Wandering in Parc Lafontaine." Likewise, Dudek's poems, minus the rough-and-tumble Narrache persona, provide a vibrant time capsule of that same era, even if Dudek's titles reflect a more sophisticated, meditative (and obviously less rampaging) outlook: "East of the City," "Looking at Stenographers," "The Jungle," "Puerto Rican Side Street."

The poetry of both Dudek and Narrache resonates with a profound determination to expose those very hypocrisies that help keep the poor beneath the heel of the rich. For Dudek the individualist, not ending this cycle would lead to a disaster: by choking off personal freedom and respect, those domineering factions would snuff out the intellectual oxygen supply that necessitates human cultural evolution. As one who was brought up as a Roman Catholic, Dudek would have immediately empathized with Coderre's highly-strung anti-hypocritical stance.

But who was Jean Narrache? As Dudek writes in his unpublished introduction, Emile Coderre became a public figure when, in the 1930s, "he changed his name to Jean Narrache *('J'en arrache,'* colloquial for 'I scrape for life') and turned overnight into a very popular poet."[6] The young Coderre's was no easy existence: he was born June 10th, 1893, to a tubercular mother who died when he was three years old. His father, a pharmacist, died when Emile was seven. The boy was adopted by his father's sister and husband, who brought him up in the stimulating atmosphere of their Viger Square pension in Montreal.

As fate would have it, the house happened to be a gathering place for the cultural élite of the day. Prominent poets and musicians, from Germain Beaulieu to Theodore Botrel, would provide an undeniably edifying impact on young Coderre, who eventually "published a first small book under his own name in 1922, *Les Signes sur le Sable...* The poetry was conventional, in classical hexameters."[7]

In direct contrast to the hoboesque pseudonym he would adopt, Coderre was well-educated. "His uncle financed his education at Séminaire de Nocolet,"[8] where he "edited the student newspaper" and "published some of his early poems."[9] He continued his studies at Université de Montréal, earning a B.A. In 1919, "he earned his professional License in Pharmacy."[10] However, ill health forced him to give up his pharmacological career and become a travelling salesman. He eventually settled in to teaching at Université de Montréal, "writing in weekend newspapers, appearing as a guest speaker and radio commentator."[11]

The timing of his first book, *Quand j'parl tout seul*, in 1932, was significant. The Great Depression was beginning to sink its teeth in: "the Quebec people were easily exploited by English industrial interests in league with the government," writes Dudek. "It is here that the seeds of present-day troubles were planted."[12] Given the pattern that the darkest circumstances often spur the most high-voltage humour, it is hardly surprising that a sensitive and responsive individual such as Coderre chose the guise of the down-and-outer—complete with soup kitchen sensibility and colloquial patter—as a viable platform from which to spread the truth about the hypocrisy that was roiling around him. This he would accomplish with a nearly head-spinning ferocity. No figure, no institution, was exempt from Narrache's truth-seeking missile of a pen. Even the Saviour ("At Christ's Manger") betrays evidence of a pampered existence, reflecting the intentions of those who held the soul's pursestrings: "Little Jesus, smiling in a manger,/Holding out your chubby hands:/Have pity for those in trouble and danger—/Even if they do not understand!"

The soon-to-be famous ramble of the Narrache persona, at once worldwise and battered by the grind of survival, has much to impart about the tumult of life Coderre observed. Jean Narrache's ironic manoeuvering often places Christ at the crux, which serves to amplify the question: who truly needs praying for: those at the end of their ropes (who reflect the genuine, selfless and bedraggled Christ forsaking all pleasure and comfort as he died on the cross) or the callous, heartless rich (who would sacrifice their souls for the brief, damning riches of this world)? The educated, well-read Coderre knew only too clearly what lies at the root of poverty and despair:

> When I was a kid I hated books.
> School, barely six months I took;
> And so, I scrounge for what I lack
> Like a flea on a stray dog's back.
>
> ("No Learnin'")

The endless cycle—collusion of Church and government, their hold over the public and the resulting reams of anxiety, hunger, drinking, relentless procreation—would inevitably come to an end, but not soon enough for Narrache and his fellow sufferers.

Yet Narrache's verse wasn't all bombast: he tempered his street-jargon hellfire with evocative descriptive passages. His subjects are all too precariously human, laced with flaws and ecstasies, visited by heart-rending complications. As I absorbed each addictively rambunctious stanza, I realized that Coderre and Dudek had more than a little in common, poetically and biographically-speaking. Apart from Coderre's having hailed from an older generation, the similarities in their lives are in fact well worth noting. Each came of age in working-class Montreal at a time when the French-speaking Quebec people were forced to swallow a less-than-equal relationship with the English-speaking corporate faction. Both Dudek and Coderre received (one might say, endured) a Roman Catholic upbringing—it is thus not surprising that the literary accomplishments of both, from early points within their lives, set out to expose and decry the appalling disparity between rich and poor. Such unchecked hypocrisy can tarnish, even destroy, much of the good inherent in any belief system. In one of Dudek's briefer essays, "Religion," he ponders the emotionality inherent in various faiths, surmising that maybe he is a Catholic after all, "in a rather obscure and roundabout way."[13]

Dudek and Narrache are equally keen on exposing the deadly mechanisms of romantic delusion. For example, the dreamy-eyed ideals of young lovers soured by the domestic-economic realities that set in, too often, within the paltry space of six months. Narrache revels in this opportunity to spotlight nature's biggest lie, its aiding and abetting by greed-stoked human treachery. "Wandering in Parc Lafontaine" depicts a girl who "nests her head" on the shoulder of a boy whose mind, in response, "is going tweet-tweet":

> But if they knew they'd be amazed,
> That eternal love, like it or don't
> Is often just like a permanent wave—
> You're lucky if it lasts a month.

No aspect of societal struggle is left untouched by Narrache's jocular and merciless pen, from the "needy" (who "sell their votes, what horror!") of "Election Time" to "Our Little Mothers" ("Who is it that manages to still get by/When the husband's paycheck suddenly stops?") to saying "Farewell to My Old Shoes" and a "Sunday Afternoon At the Cemetery" during which "The woman sometimes, or maybe the gent, /Becomes an "angel" to th' one who survives —/... Seems like one improves, after one dies!" Whereas Dudek's intonation is more somber, slightly formal, infused with a perceptible longing, a hinting at glory that might yet be. Yet Dudek is also capable of unleashing poetic wrath when there is human suffering at stake: for example, in his sinuous and grimy "Old City Sector," his rage and disgust are as deeply etched, if not as deliberately torrid, as Narrache's: "they work and wait for their simple Sundays,/for the evening show, or sex,/always in the grip and tension of this intestine,/the small capitalist's greedy space/of warehouse and foetid factory/where tight-fisted profit is squeezed out"[14]

Where Narrache's money-eyed archetype is guilty of being blind to the plight of the poor, Dudek's tyrant is also guilty of "ignoring the soft sun, and the imaginary note of the chanticleer somewhere singing."[15] The corporate kingpin's heart is necessarily cold and sterile: to permit fine poetic oxygen to permeate the armour might signal the death-knell for his success. In the following stanza from "To a Literary Patron," Dudek's Christ doll offers its own sarcasm from a luxurious vantagepoint: "And said I would, and we drank tea or coffee;/The carvings on the table scattered ice,/And a little Jesus in a bed of amber/Grimaced at the spearpoints of electric lights."[16]

In Narrache's realm, there is no energy left for anything more than scraping by. Steeped in that deliciously accessible drunkard's persona, the poet's outrage bubbles forth like an awry burst of lava. Still, that unyielding, accusatory finger looms beneath the hobo's boisterous brooding:

> The government spends like all the rest;
> It doesn't save a bleeding sou.
> The money they take will dance around,
> But they waste it just like any fool.
>
> ("Prosperity")

In Narrache's signature poem, "I Talk Away," ("J'parl'pour parler") wisdom and sarcasm appear like beacons amid the apparently rag-happy swerving:

> I talk away, not just for my own plight,
> But for all the ones who are in pain:
> And that's the majority of common men.
> I take their side, and that is my right.

This street philosopher, or *"philosophe dans la rue"* uses his battered position to slip what might well be the seeds of revolution into the ears of a hopefully not-so-drunken audience, an audience so beaten down by adversity, that the voice of this hobo provides solace, a form of emotional sustenance—perhaps even a means for escape. Dudek's tip of the hat to Narrache's moments of outright yowling, mingled with his own fervent desire to expose the monsters of hypocrisy, finds its balance in Narrache's surprisingly meditative, softer lyrical segues. For instance, the sorrowful, acutely-aware musings of the first person narrator in "Sunday Afternoon At the Cemetery"

> Before those rich stone monuments
> With weeping angels at the posts,
> I don't see people praying, bent....
> They don't need it, those that have the most.

can be perceived as a parallel to the following excerpt from one of Dudek's earliest poems. In "Sound for Orchestra" a series of images captures that sensuality inherent in the commonplace, which lures its victims into a dizzy escapade that leads, inevitably, back to square one: "The stops break and the wind breaks—/you bring the boy and the girl together, and the kazoo./But the ecstasy will finish fast as sex;/they will sit building/hills and mountains like a diastrophism."[17] The spectres of the cheap kazoo and crude breeze cast a heavy prescience over the briefly-enraptured lovers.

Dudek succeeds in getting at the core of Narrache's intent, transcribing the sarcastic and indignant thrusts of the *Québécois* bard into an English further authenticated by the inclusion of French words such as *"patates frites"* and *"tourtière"* as well as the names of Quebec landmarks and historical figures from Cartier to Dollard Des Ormeaux. Where the latter are concerned, Narrache emphasizes the lack of awe, the disenchanted sneers, apparent in the heirs to this colonial legacy: "They say we're descendants of old France, /From Poitiers, Bretagne, or Normandy—/ But I don't look for the difference/ When once I'm a Canayen, me." ("The Discoverers")

For all of Dudek's determination to preserve his subject's original voice, there can be found throughout his translations of Narrache inevitable traces of Dudek: that meditative and visionary, yet cautious, voice of reason and subtle rendering of order out of chaos that pervades his poems. Note, for example, the following passage from "East of the City", in which Dudek questions the 1930s present-day behemoths whose calculated cruelty can be traced back to those barbarisms of prehistory:

> Out of the ruptured cauldron, the green factory
> Whose ogre eyes gleam in the sooty night,
> Railed wrists stretch over hard, broad hills,
> The cold coal and straight strata, iron and steel;
> The belly boils, and peal its shattering bells
> Of hammers and cranes, flying their halleluyas.

The factory is an "ogre" bent on tormenting, squeezing the life out of its "shattered" victims who exist in a soot tarnished world, and whose hungry prayers fall on indifferent ears: the colloquially-spelled "halleluyas" swing cold and sarcastic.

There is even an epigrammatical side to Narrache, to be found in a series of poems with one-word titles, whose force is comparable to mincing bolts out of the blue. Like Dudek's trademark epigrams, these four-line encapsulations of Coderre's opinions on everything from bilingualism to rock and roll refuse to pull any punches—there is no holding back on the sarcasm here:

> Bilingualism! What a boon!
> Now on the radio you can tune
> Soap operas by double lots
> And twice as many idiots!
>
>   ("Bilingualism")

In all, Dudek culled a selection of thirty-two poems from the two most popular Jean Narrache volumes: *J'Parl' pour parler* ("I Talk Away", 1939), and *J'parl tout seul quand Jean Narrache* ("I Talk to Myself as I Scrape for Life" or the 1963 edition of the selected poems published by Les Editions du Jour), as well as some of the later poems. These rabble-rousing verses enable the reader to stand in the epicentre of the Depression era, magnifying the sting of inequality and the reek of the gutter:

The half-starved head for some eatery,
Get stuffed with pasta and hot-dogs;
Swill coffee hopped up with black chicory,
Fooling awhile their hunger throbs.

("Winter Night on Rue Ste Catherine")

"I read him with great zest and gusto, because the kind of *joual* in which he wrote was the speech I knew from childhood."[18] Dudek was of divided opinion on *joual*, that distinctly-*Québécois* patois whose elements comprised Narrache's poetic intonation. Although he felt that it was "disparaging to call it Joual" Dudek postulated that this language of the streets might "eventually become a language in its own right, a variant of French, as writers give it more dignity."[19] He understood why Coderre, from choosing the "Jean Narrache" moniker to his mastery of the street dweller's apostrophe-peppered syntax, felt the need to "assume the speech and manner of the poor and inarticulate in literature"[20] in order, not only to understand where they are coming from, but ostensibly, to provide them with a voice. Dudek clarifies the role of high art, specifically how "high civilization depends upon the furious churning of muck that occurs at the bottom of society."[21] How the pain of raw survival contains a fiery germ whose energy, through the disciplined and capable mind of the artist, can be forged into finest creative platinum. "There is an energy and fuller breath of life that constantly rises from the bottom," notes Dudek, "to transform and renew every living literature."[22] Without this primeval energy, art, like driftwood, is in danger of turning dry and brittle.

Louis Dudek was determined that his translations of Narrache's poems find a wider audience—that is, outside the microcosm of French Quebec. His reasoning had nothing to do with the nationalist-versus-federalist politics of Quebec. Nowadays, it is perhaps inevitable that wider, especially English, availability of these poems might upset those who prefer to leave behind the grim, poverty-ridden, pre-Quiet Revolution social status of *les Québécois*. It is logical that Dudek, renowned individualist, admired Coderre for his one-of-a-kind perspective: the deliberately-slurred accessibility belying the intellect that carried their message—a mind brimming with music, wisdom and common sense. But perhaps most of all Coderre's inciting people to think for themselves.

All of which reflects an even greater scale: the place of the written word within the world's socio-political agenda. As Dudek realized: "Literature, it seems, is involved with radical social change. But here we are primarily interested in the literary form of that change (...) the grand revolution and transformation of the arts in the twentieth century."[23] Tony Tremblay notes in his recent essay, "Louis Dudek and the Question of Quebec," that Dudek's 1946 poetry collection, *East of the City*, "enumerates the struggles of working-class francophones and, as importantly, brings into focus Dudek's belief in a democracy that liberates rather than diminishes common people."[24] Tremblay also reminds us that "(f)ew other Canadians lived the drama of Quebec as fully as Louis Dudek."[25]

Narrache's rage was firmly directed at those slavedrivers whose chains were fortified by a hypocritical Roman Catholic Church—an institution whose existence dictated the continuation and worsening of an already tormented existence. Cow down, do your duty, suffer in silence and await the afterlife for your true reward:

> And that's where the reward will be
> For chaps like me who have nothing now.
> For if we didn't have at least our beliefs
> What would be left in our dog's life to show?
>
> ("Having Hope")

What impact did Jean Narrache's poetry have on the people of Quebec? The fact that somebody—a poet at that!—was willing to expose the rotten truth, and in such a public, comedic yet infuriated manner, must have been cause for great release, rare relief, for those imprisoned by poverty. Yet once the laughter subsided, there must certainly have been tidal waves of realization: the idea that this was no longer a tolerable situation, and never should have been. Given the afflictions of the mass majority of the Quebec people, Dudek most certainly would have sensed that the province was ripe for revolt. During those years when the Quiet Revolution was underway, Dudek wrote that "all the present trouble in Quebec is really a case of moving things out of the doldrums where they had been fixed for three quarters of a century beyond their due date."[26] Dudek also affirms that, had the English establishment only let loose the reins when it had the chance, before the situation had gone too far, then all hell might then have not broken loose. He also acknowledges the astonishing deep-rooted influence of this 'people's poet': "If there had been no Jean Narrache there would have been no *Couteau sur la table,* no *Prochain episode.*"[27] Like Dudek, and for all his disgust with the English oppressers, Narrache never espoused outright nationalism—only a breaking away from the slavery of poverty, *les Québécois* at last having the courage to stand on their own feet. Like Narrache, Dudek writes, "I am for justice and for understanding."[28] And, in his *Notebooks:* "Tolerance for other people's speech is tolerance for other people."[29]

Do present-day *Québécois* assume that the English will regard them in a negative manner, because the poetry provides such an authentic portrait of *les Québécois* in those days when corporate-religious-anglo-political corruption ruled the province? Or do (as I suspect) the present and succeeding generations have the maturity (and plain common sense) to appreciate not only why these poems were written, but to allow themselves to be dazzled by each irrepressible stanza? There is no embarrassment to be found here—*au contraire!*—only the miracle of pure intelligence rising above the mire and inciting readers not to settle for anything less. There is too much sparkling eloquence, too much mirthful wisdom evident here, to dismiss these poems as mere populist dross.

Yet despite Jean Narrache's personal and profound influence, Emile Coderre died neglected and ignored decades after his triumphant reign. "In the milieu of the so-called 'quiet revolution' that existed then in Quebec," writes Richard Foisy in his introduction to *Quand J'Parl'Pour Parler,* an Emile Coderre anthology, "Jean Narrache entered into a silent seclusion. On April 16, 1967 Radio Canada Television presented *Le Poète Gueux* (Poet of the "Downtrodden"), a documentary on Jean Narrache, filmed at his home, which the director Alain Stanké fortunately had the idea to film. Three years later, almost to the day, Jean Narrache died in semi-neglect, and not even the literary 'cream' reported the event."[30] Continues Foisé, the "name of Jean Narrache, relegated to the shadows of radio, is gradually fading in

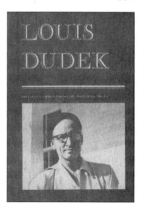

recollection. If it is sometimes mentioned in anthologies, the literary history of Quebec too easily neglects to remember and the global dimension of the *oeuvre* continues to be ignored."[31]

Sadly, when I attempted (on several occasions) to request copyright permission in order to proceed with publishing these excellent translations, and despite my numerous detailed attempts, there was no response to any of my messages. Dudek urged me not to give up: he considered Coderre's *oeuvre* too valuable a cultural touchstone and record of the Quebec experience. Narrache also happened to be one of the few Quebec *literati* cited by Dudek as having made a personal connection with their audiences: "Among the best French Canadian poets there is a great distance between the poet and the audience."[32] Narrache not only "touched" his audience, but elicited a powerful emotional—and even thoughtful—response.

Although Louis Dudek has passed away, his faith in Emile Coderre will continue to resound from his translations of Jean Narrache. After all, the poems are in many ways "as relevant now as they were in their time."[33] The present generation of *Québécois*— English, French et al.—will hopefully discover the radiant legacy of Emile Coderre. His message is perhaps more indispensable during these helter-skelter early years of the twenty-first century—when the boundaries of individual freedom continue to be shamefully, even torturously challenged.

NOTES:

1. Dudek, Louis: from the "Introduction". *Some Poems of Jean Narrache Translated and With An Introduction by Louis Dudek*. Unpublished manuscript, Montreal, 1999.
2. "Getting to Know Nelligan," from *Open Letter,* Spring & Summer 1981. Fourth Series, Nos. 8-9. p. 306.
3. *Ibid.*
4. Ozick, Cynthia. "A Translator's Monologue," from *Metaphor & Memory,* Alfred A. Knopf, New York, 1989. p. 201.
5. *The Translations of Ezra Pound* (with an Introduction by Hugh Kenner), New Directions, 1950.
6-12. Dudek, Louis: from the "Introduction". *Some Poems of Jean Narrache Translated and With An Introduction by Louis Dudek*. Unpublished manuscript, Montreal, 1999.

13. Dudek, Louis. Dudek, Louis. *Reality Games.* Empyreal Press, Montreal, 1998. p. 62.
14. Dudek, Louis. *Collected Poetry.* Delta Canada, Montreal, 1971, p. 37.
15. *Ibid,* p. 33.
16. *Ibid,* p. 50.
17. *Ibid,* p. 2.
18-23. Dudek, Louis: from the "Introduction". *Some Poems of Jean Narrache.*
24. Tremblay, Tony. "Louis Dudek and the Question of Quebec" (essay). 2002.
25. *Ibid.*
26. *Open Letter,* Spring & Summer 1981. Fourth Series, Nos. 8-9. p. 306.
27. *Ibid,* p. 292.
28. Dudek, Louis: from the "Introduction". *Some Poems of Jean Narrache.*
29. Dudek, Louis. *Notebooks* 1960-1994, The Golden Dog Press, Ottawa, 1994. p. 36.
30. Narrache, Jean. *Quand j'parl' pour parler: poèmes et proses (Anthologie présentée par Richard Foisy).* Éditions de l'Hexagone, Montréal, 1993.
31. *Ibid.*
32. Dudek, Louis. *In Defense of Art: Critical Essays and Reviews.* Quarry Press (Ontario), 1988. p. 209.
33. Dudek, Louis: from the "Introduction". *Some Poems of Jean Narrache.*

Louis Dudek, 1954.

Photo Courtesy of Stephanie Zuperko Dudek

Coming Suddenly to the Sea

Coming suddenly to the sea in my twenty-eighth year,
to the mother of all things that breathe, of mussels and whales,
I could not see anything but sand at first
and burning bits of mother-of-pearl.
But this was the sea, terrible as a torch
which the winter sun had lit,
flaming in the blue and salt sea-air
under my twenty-eight-year infant eyes.
And then I saw the spray smashing the rocks
and the angry gulls cutting the air,
the heads of fish and the hands of crabs on stones:
the carnivorous sea, sower of life,
battering a granite rock to make it a pebble—
love and pity needless as the ferny froth on its long smooth waves.
The sea, with its border of crinkly weed,
the inverted Atlantic of our unstable planet,
froze me into a circle of marble, sending the icy air out in
        lukewarm waves.
And so I brought home, as an emblem of that day
ending my long blind years, a fistful of blood-red weed in my hand.

from "New Music" (Section 4), Dudek's *Collected Poetry*

GEORGE HILDEBRAND

Louis Dudek circa 1970.

The vertical text on the right of the image reads "Photo Courtesy of Stephanie Zuperko Dudek"

A Modernist Raid on the Romantic Sublime

> But I had not known the sea would be this splendid magnificent lady:
> —*Europe,* Section 10.

L OUIS DUDEK'S MOST popular poem among editors of anthologies is "Coming Suddenly to the Sea," the only poem common to four of five such textbooks I have lying around my office. Internally dated as 1946 ("in my twenty-eighth year"), the poem first appeared in 1956 in *The Transparent Sea.* In 1998 the poet included it in his definitive *The Poetry of Louis Dudek* (62). "Coming Suddenly To the Sea" is also a poem that students like and certainly one that I have always loved. In the classroom, it is read as a fine example of a modernist poem, an objectivist epiphany exemplary of mainline modernism, which itself can be summed up in such slogans as "the objective correlative" (Eliot), "contact" and "no ideas but in things"

(Williams), "the proper and perfect symbol is the natural object" (Pound), or "the baptism of the gutter" (Yeats). I value the poem not only because it reiterates and renews a major tradition but also because it is such a tightly written and witty ocean poem, and ocean poems like Masefield's "Seafever" and Carman's "The Ships of Yule" were some of the first poems that ran around with me as a child.

In the context of the complexity of Dudek's thought, the poem is seminally grounding. In it one finds concrete poetic evidence of his philosophical concerns, a conceptual imagery that does justice to the secular transcendentalism of early modernists, and a dramatic affirmation of confidence in himself and in his vocation as poet. As such, the poem calls for a closer reading. The natural symbol of the ocean is central to Dudek's imagination, and in "Coming Suddenly to the Sea" he provides the script for a remarkably consistent poetics grounded in the natural world. I mean the whole complex of intellectual and emotional meaning caught up in "sea" and "seeing," seeing "weed" in the sea, and hence poems in the sea and cities in the sea. The poem is consciously located in the long tradition of what I like to call ocean-motion and ocean "e-motion" poetry, poetry that explicitly takes as its subject the natural sublime in the form of ocean. And Dudek's "Coming Suddenly To the Sea" is an incisive and witty summing up of the tradition. It is also an ironic renewal of and response to the 18th century sublime, which was a new aesthetic category and a new descriptive poetry taking the sublime as its subject.

The title and the first line introduce an intense personal initiation, the poet's first and apparently unexpected experience of ocean, his arrival at the shores of "the inverted Atlantic" ("inverted" as he told me once, because he first encountered the ocean in France from the side "other" to North America). A modernist drama of perception, the poem is organized by five scenes or movements, each an extended sentence.

The introductory action phrase of the title, repeated in the first sentence, establishes the dramatic situation. The poet discovers the seashore for the first time, implies that it is rather late in life for this experience, specifies his astonishment at seeing "the mother of all things that breathe," and presents his reaction: He is "at first" blinded but then he acknowledges seeing sand and "burning bits of mother-of-pearl." The second sentence extends and re-emphasizes the first reaction. The speaker reminds himself "But this was the sea" reiterating his inexperienced "infant eyes" that now see the "terrible" light "flaming in the blue and salt sea-air." The third movement or scene is the central revelation of the poem: the poet notes the details of the amoral death-dealing if life-giving ocean, summing it up as "the carnivorous sea, sower of life." The fourth movement is a stepping back, way back, with a panoramic overview beginning with (perhaps) a weedy shore of direct vision—"The sea" has a "border of crinkly weed"—but it then becomes "the inverted Atlantic of our unstable planet," a pre-satellite vision of the ocean perceived inter-continentally. The emphasis is on the poet's state of mind. He has been frozen "into a circle of marble," but then this state of astonishment is broken by a dramatically understated action, the fifth sentence that closes the poem: the speaker carries home "a fistful of blood-red weed," noting that his "long blind years" have been ended.

The poem works of course in many complex linguistic ways to reinforce and extend the central drama caught up in the meeting of the seeing man and the blinding sea, an episode of sight and insight, and finally a case of the manifestation of the mystery of forms and poetic meaning out of chaos, a cheeky affirmation of human action, of the poetic action of seizing meaning, rapaciously and violently, and bringing home the concrete emblem of the "blood-red weed."

The sentence structure reflects the oppositions of the poem-making I and the subliming sea, and the human resolution. First there is the action and the qualified contradiction: "Coming suddenly to the sea" is coming to see but leads to "I could not see anything" [but sand and shells]. "I could not see anything" is followed by the sentence "But this was the sea" with the major coordinating conjunction "but" (stating opposition) and the state-of-being verb introducing the sea as an objective reality confronting the poet-speaker as something absolute. The next sentence is transitive, an action sentence introduced as a dramatic addition with the coordinator "and" (stating addition) and the adverb "then" (suspense) leading to a powerful predicating catalogue of noun objects and active participles, a complex series completing the verb "I saw," the climax of the coming. The poet comes to the sea and the sea enters his eye.

It not only enters his eye but also freezes him. The sea is the actor and the speaker its pacified object: "And then I saw the sea" is followed by "The sea [...] froze me." However this stasis leads to action. The frozen "I" breaks out of the spell with a sort of understated closure: "And so I brought home [...] a fistful" not of the sea but of a sea border, a form from the sea, the emblematic "blood-red weed."

Patterns of diction, subtle and not so subtle, increase the resonance of the central drama of seeing, cognizing and re-cognizing, and then acting. I have already noted the central expansion of the homonyms "sea" and "see." "Coming suddenly to the sea" is also coming suddenly "to see." The chiming of "sea" (six repetitions, including "blue and salt sea-air") is linked by echo to "I could not see anything" and then to "And then I saw." The waves-to-weed motif is emphasized by the doubling of these words (more of that later). A major pattern of diction is the movement from the concrete to the abstract, in terms of both nouns and participles. Thus, the concrete action participles in sequence are "coming" (suddenly), "coming" (suddenly), "burning" (bits of mother), "flaming" (sea), "smashing" (spray), "cutting" (gulls), "battering" (sea), and "sending" (the icy air).

These actions have a consequence in the powerful stasis of "The sea [...] froze me," but then they also extend to the more abstract participle phrase, "ending my long blind years." A similar pattern, the imagistic induction of a mental movement involving not sentiment but objective concept and thought, is available in the nouns. Consider the concrete plural nouns, the powerful catalogue of sea-things seen with the poet's "twenty-eight year infant eyes"—eyes surrounded by and overwhelmed by images: "things" (that breathe), "mussels and whales," "bits" (of mother-of-pearl), "rocks" (spray-smashed), "gulls" (angry), "heads" (of fish), "hands" (of crabs), "stones," finally modulating into "long smooth/ waves" and "luke-warm waves." The epic catalogue of plural nouns leads to mentation, the poet's reflection: the list comes down to the abstraction of "years" (the ending of his "long blind years"). The plurals, though, also lead to the concrete singulars, to the "crinkly weed" and "blood-red weed" and then emphatically (terminally) to "in my hand."

The sound symbolism of the poem is provocative and supportive. The sibilant "s" sounds (23 initial, 2 medial, and 18 terminal) dominate the poem, creating the swish and spatter and smash of the sea and signing the apparently absolute otherness of sea with a variety of human meanings. The patterned consonance, especially of the third sentence, tells of a pattern similar to the movement of concrete-to-concept specified above. The consonance, terminal and initial, links the concept "carnivorous sea" with the more human idea "sower of life" [emphasis added].

The opposing pair, conceptually paradoxical, are associated (and submerged) by ocean motion music. The harsh plurals, "rocks" and "gulls" and "stones," are associated by sound to "hands" and "heads"; finally they are also linked by sound-symbolism to "needless." The sound effects force "needless," at least glancingly, to modify the amoral brutalities of the sea, these perhaps almost as needless as "love and pity." In the patterns of the "s" sounds and in the strange alliterative dance of the "f" sounds, the suggestion is that all are but "ferny froth." The long "ee" sounds move in a similar apparently paradoxical way: from "sea" to "see" to "weed" and, slantingly dissonant, to "years."

There is more in the music of the words. Hear the soft "w" pattern, from "whales" to "waves" "waves" to "weed" "weed." Significantly enough, not only do the "w" words (the first three) end the longest lines (and so were often set by editors onto a separate line), but also the poet himself in the definitive edition moved "whales" and "waves" and "lukewarm waves" to separate lines, apparently for purposes of association and emphasis. The gentle and positive sound group (whales and waves) moves dissonantly towards "weed," that which the poet takes from the ocean and carries home.

Poetry is, as I have been implying, first and always an investigation of language and a celebration of the concrete and physical way in which we "have" it. I mean kinaesthetics. The primary poetic action of "Coming Suddenly to the Sea" is found in the transformation of the "way" sounds into the "wee" sounds. Place two fingers lightly on your lips and say "mussels and/ whales," say "long smooth/ waves," say "crinkly weed," say "luke-warm waves," and finally say "a fistful of blood-red weed." This is where poems work— and do not even start to think or to ask whether it is intentional. Here is Louis Dudek in the poem "Taking Shape" (62) speaking directly about such subtle effects of sound: "So consonants close/ (wings!) in a whorl/ of vowels—"

In this way the poem "Coming Suddenly to the Sea" comes

down hard on "blood-red weed," the only sequence of spondees in the poem. Three stressed syllables go wham wham wham-blood-red weed [emphasis added]. Include "fistful of" and you have wham wham da wham wham wham. Way Way Wee! says the poet to ocean, rather joyously or exuberantly or wittily violating the Mother by taking her blooded crinkly weed.

Perception is more than seeing. Poeming is more than providing camera images of realistic perspectives. This transcendental realism of the modernists and of Louis Dudek is cunningly embedded in the imagery and paradoxes and ambiguities of "Coming Suddenly to the Sea." Consider first the way in which the poet gender-busts the ancient allegory of the sea. The classical allegorical representation of "mare oceanum" was masculine:

Poseidon was god of the sea. Louis Dudek does not use the latinate word "ocean." It is always the "sea" of Old English, and when he touches the ocean into life with a traditional personification he makes the ocean a woman. The sea is "she." The personification appears not as a sense impression but as a traditional pre-concept or cultural memory. The sea as a special case of Mother Nature is "the mother of all things that breathe." Blinded as he is by light, he remembers the scientific fact that life arose in the oceans (or as contemporary biology has it, where ocean meets land, as Rachel Carson details it in that fine book The Edge of the Sea) and that indeed the sea is a "mother." The figurative domestic reduction and pathetic fallacy are immediately subverted by the literalness of the phrase "burning bits of mother-of-pearl." The hints of the personification return in "the sea, terrible as a torch/ which the winter sun had lit." A humanizing and anthropomorphic image, the sun as torch lighter is emptied of its pathos somewhat by the adjective "terrible." Further the literal and concrete image "heads of fish" carries over into the frisson of "hands of crabs," with the personification now reversing itself into a foregrounding of the slaughtering amoral sea.

It could be argued that the phrase "sower of life" is more pathetic fallacy, but I think the juxtaposition with "carnivorous sea" creates a tension that further subverts any traces of humanization or sentimental anthropomorphizing. It morphs all right, but it moves toward the needlessness of "love and pity." The central transformations are whales/ waves into weed, and salt water into imagistic blood. And the objective "iciness" of the poet can be found in the identification of the crab's amputated claw-hand with the poet's hand, fisted and blood-filled. All this comes to a witty raid on the romantic sublime, that traditional aesthetic response of the 18th century, which as Ferguson reminds us is "synonymous with irresistible forces that produced overwhelming sensations" (1231). For Burke this meant that we got scared and turned back to society to work harder. Kant repeats some of the English tradition, but he does not (as does Burke) hold a social and functional view of the universal response to sublime scene. For instance:

"Bold, overhanging, and, as it were, threatening rocks, thunderclouds piled up the vault of heaven, borne along with flashes and peals, volcanoes in all their violence and destruction, hurricanes leaving desolation in their track, the boundless ocean rising with rebellious force, the high waterfall of some mighty river, and the like, make our power of resistance of trifling moment in comparison with their might. But provided our own position is secure, their aspect is all the more attractive for its fearfulness; and we readily call these objects sublime, because they raise the forces of the soul above the height of the vulgar commonplace, and discover within us a power of resistance of quite another kind, which gives us courage to be able to measure ourselves against the seeming omnipotence of nature." (Book II. Analytic of the Sublime, 110-111).

Where Kant takes this, for many pages, is to the aesthetic. Kant reduced the mathematical and dynamically sublime to aesthetics because he thought the vagueness and indefinable (the subliminal) of terrifying and awe-ful scenes merely lead to idiosyncratic poetic fancy. Hence the "aesthetics of the infinite" (Nicolson's phrase) that characterized the 18th century response to ocean and mountain and the stars. And Keats of course, in the famous phrase, spoke of Wordsworth's "egoistical sublime."

Dudek however knows precisely what he is seeing. There is a comic and anti-cosmic descent of the tradition here, although the plot of the poem follows the tradition in the first four movements: The speaker sees and is overwhelmed by the sea, by its blazing light and power; he recognizes its powers over life and death, powers greater than his own; he is frozen by the experience, and discovers in himself his own human power. But there is no vague sense of the infinite or the aesthetic in the poet's reply. And he is not interested in emotions. He notes the ocean's icy indifference to the human moral sense, and he identifies with that iciness and appropriates it. He knows what he is seeing and responds with a sign violation and an iteration. He will violate the mother and bring home the weed, form out of chaos, poem out of experience.

REFERENCES

Carson, Rachel. *The Edge of the Sea.* New York: Signet, 1955.

Dudek, Louis. "Coming Suddenly to the Sea." *The Poetry of Louis Dudek: Definitive Edition.* Ottawa: Golden Dog, 1998. 62.

Also in (for example) *Canadian Anthology.* Ed. Carl Klinck and Reginald Watters. Toronto: Gage, 1974. 456; *Canadian Poetry. Volume II.* Ed. by Jack David and Robert Lecker. Toronto: General Publishing, 1982. 34; *The New Oxford Book of Canadian Verse in English.* Ed. Margaret Atwood. Toronto: Oxford University Press, 1982. 206; *The New Canadian Anthology.* Ed. Robert Lecker and Jack David. Toronto: Nelson, 1988. 130.

Dudek, Louis. "Sea and Land." *Europe,* Sections 1-26. From Collected Poems. Montreal: Delta Canada, 1971. 77-86.

Ferguson, Francis. "Sublime: Enlightenment to Modern." *Encyclopedia of Poetry and Poetics.* Ed. Preminger. Princeton: Princeton University Press, 1993. 1231-1232.

Kant, Immanuel. *The Critique of Judgement* (1790). Tr. James Meredith. Oxford: Clarendon Press, 1952. Book II. Analytic of the Sublime. With special attention to Sections 23-29. pp. 90-117.

Nicolson, Marjorie. "Sublime in External Nature." *Dictionary of the History of Ideas.* New York: Scribner's, 1973. IV, 333-337.

Photo by Geof Isherwood

**Louis Dudek with poet
John Asfour, Montreal, 1989.**

We Only Meet In a Poem Now

HOW DO the features of the city change
and when is the present tense no longer applicable?
How do you pass on to the damp ground
and leave poetry unattended to?

You and I
Drilled death, waged war on the poem
And never knew that it would create such a distance between us.
Everywhere you leave something, you leave no one,
leave the books and the music notes,
leave us unable to write. All the lampposts
are plastered with faded paper signs and the trees
on Saint Catherine Street are leafless.

There's no war here but a fabricated threat
of terrorism
the criminal law is rewritten
and racial profiling is permissible.

Children are dying elsewhere,
all the headlines in all the papers
have declared the loss of that familiar innocence
and we all have embraced a nightmare
unlike any our ancestors have lived through. The features of the city
have changed and we have sold civil liberty
after you left. Yet,
why am I full of fear and readily postpone
unearthing you in the poem for a day
and fill you in on how we get on in your absence?
Another Christmas has passed and you have missed
our rendezvous.
A lunch and a coffee and an exchange of gifts
that we both promised we wouldn't buy the year before.
Then, you bring out your notebook
and read to me:
"Our age is not the age of the poem,
and this country will never rise to our ideals,
nor will death change what we are."

Let me ask again:
Where does our soul go
after we close our eyes and is the still
body the only fragment that remains?
Does the poem suffice when all else fails
and where do the memories of languages go?
Your place in history has not been made
and one day, this country will have to transfer
your words and passion into action.
One day, we will all have to die
or be hypnotized by the smile
inside the words you left
by the power of death and the power of your lines.

Let's assume, then, that the mind has it all
yet, it refuses to relate it in a language
or sleep on it
to protect what should have never been said or written.
How is it that you were able to pour all of it out
and be elated by the experience?
How is it that you alone knew the course of events
and the direction this country has chosen to take? When I stand,
here, close to the walls of the library,
it is not the books or the notes that come to me,
not the awards and recognition.
It is not death or music that haunts me, not the fate of our planet.
It is your voice reading and assessing,
explaining and debating concepts and theories
and giving literature its power to renew itself.
It is your passion to live and educate, your love of the poem
to instill human values in all of us.
It is your warm smile and let the critics
accuse me of sentimentality, but, let me ask again:
What is the value of poetry and how can we sustain a country
Or live in a poem void of human compassion?

Aileen Collins with Louis
Dudek, circa 1970.

Louis Dudek — A Radical Reformer

"Education is the greatest obstacle to education."[1]

Epigrams

L OUIS DUDEK WAS A brilliant and provocative teacher. Not for
him the academic deadness which he described so poignant-
ly in the poem "The Classroom":

> When I saw the students coming in
> with their warm, intelligent faces,
>   ready for another bout
> with great ideas, analogies, interpretations, facts
>   and the theories that always defeat us,

each of them independently fighting
                    for his own bit of ground
against embattled knowledge, against the karate of reason:
when I saw their patience, silence, meekness
before the imminent stream
                    of accumulated lore, pouring down from glaciers
of unassuaged desire, the mountainous stupefactions of tradition —
I sat down in pity, and held my head in my hands,
until love opened my eyes, and I bent listening to the chatter
                    of those enquiring minds.

Zembla's Rocks[2]

Hundreds of students took Louis Dudek's courses at McGill University over his long teaching career and many of them have talked and written about the powerful and stimulating experiences that they have had in his classroom. Unfortunately, he was not representative of university teaching in general. In an unpublished notebook entry dated November 9, 1988, he wrote: "I am a poet who at one time infiltrated the university—to see if I could somehow transform the teaching profession. To make it relevant to the concerns of life and of living poetry. And then, perhaps, I infiltrated the newspapers[3], for the same reasons. I have been a radical reformer in this way—but the radicalism is not destructive, it is to bring back the values of our civilization."

Dudek believed in the transformative power of education and applied this belief throughout his life both in and out of the classroom. In the autobiographical memoir which he wrote as part of the Contemporary Authors series, Dudek recalls that by sheer luck he was able to leave the menial job in a warehouse where he had worked since completing Grade 13 at the High School of Montreal, and to register at McGill University. "For me, a new life began in the university, a life without parental supervision, a life of freedom and exploration."[4] In later years, he often contemplated this twist of fate that had made possible his subsequent career in teaching and his accomplishments as poet, professor, publisher, critic and man of letters.

The constructive radicalism that Dudek believed was so necessary for a revitalization of the social institutions and for making literature relevant to students led him to be active in the more public domain of education. In the early sixties, he accepted the challenge offered by the Macmillan Company to edit an anthology of modern poetry for students in Grades 11, 12 and 13 (or first year university), a task that proved much more daunting than he had realized. The anthology *Poetry of Our Time: An Introduction to Twentieth-Century Poetry Including Modern Canadian Poetry* appeared in 1965 to great acclaim. It was used widely across Canada for many years and was much praised by educators and students. It signalled a radical change from the more traditional textbooks then in use.

To appreciate its significance, it is necessary to briefly recreate the educational milieu of the early nineteen sixties. There was a growing feeling that radical change was needed in the educational institutions: demands for new texts and other materials, for new ways of teaching besides the lecture method, and for new power sharing between teacher and student were being voiced. Perhaps the student revolution of the later sixties was too rapid and destructive a remedy to the problem. (Dudek believed that it had destroyed the university.) But most of us agreed that something had to change. In the secondary schools of Québec and probably elsewhere in Canada, literature seemed to be viewed as an extension of the student's moral and religious education. In the available anthologies for senior high school students, many with titles which included phrases like "magic realms" and "worlds of wonder", the poetry was usually uplifting, wholesome, and laden with "message." There may have been some perfunctory attention paid to "figures of speech" but a typical question in class and on exams concerned the message the poet was conveying to the reader. (My late sister, Verna Collins, and I were then teaching English in Grades 11 and 12, and tested some of the material for Dudek before publication—with great success. Imagine the impact of Ginsberg and Ferlinghetti on students after a diet of Kilmer and his ilk.)

Dudek was aware that there would be some resistance to his anthology and acknowledged this situation in his introductory essay "Twentieth-Century Poetry," noting that "many people find it hard to adapt themselves to the new kind of poetry. . . . In this book we take the risk of looking at twentieth century poetry as it really is. *Poetry of Our Time* is an introduction to modern poetry designed to present, vividly, its most characteristic features."[5] A review of *Poetry of Our Time* which appeared in *The McGill Daily*, signed "PDM", on March 11, 1966, started with this declaration: "Well, it's been done. Here's an anthology of poetry—203 poets in all—covering the best of modern 'Western' writing, including a

thick section of Canadian writing, that does NOT have Pauline
Johnson, Bliss Carman or Wilson Pugsley MacDonald. Louis
Dudek has scored over the rednecks and the wool hats and the
PTA and the CGIT. Praise be to him." The reviewer commented
most favourably on the two introductory essays and recommend-
ed that the anthology "should be put in all schools immediately."[6]

The two introductory essays were also highly praised by teachers. "Twentieth-Century Poetry," the introduction to the major part
of the anthology, was considered by many to be equivalent to a university course in modern poetry. Dudek's profound knowledge of
modern poetry served him well here, and his lucid exposition of the
complexities of modern poetry provided a much-needed literary
and historical context for the work of poets such as Whitman,
Hopkins, Dickinson, Pound, Eliot, Marianne Moore, Ginsberg and
Ferlinghetti. "Modern Canadian Poetry," the other introductory
essay, was much shorter and offered an overview of the development of English-Canadian poetry and the poetry of the French poets
of Québec, examining the similarities and differences between the
two. Both, Dudek stated, inherited "the problem of reconciling
romantic idealism with the requirements of truth and actuality."[7] The
differences, he pointed out, were that English-Canadian poetry was
following the path into reality, while French poetry tended to the
inward path of spirituality, subjectivity and idealism. The "Modern
Canadian Poetry" section of the anthology included the poets of the
early phase of modern Canadian poetry such as Pratt, Smith, Klein,
Scott, and Nelligan, as well as Page, Avison, Wilkinson, Birney,
Mandel, Layton, Gustafson, Cohen and so on. A representative
group of French poets of Québec included Saint-Denys Garneau,
Jean-Guy Pilon, Alan Grandbois, Anne Hébert, and Gilles Vigneault.
These poems were presented in French and each poem was fol-
lowed by an English translation by, for example, F.R. Scott or
Dudek himself. Having the French and English poets rub shoulders
in this fashion was a radical move on Dudek's part.

Dudek's next venture in textbook publishing was with Clarke,
Irwin & Company Limited in the early seventies, and the new chal-
lenge was to edit a three-book poetry series for junior high school.
The proposed series was to be called *The Worlds of Poetry* series:
Book I—*All Kinds of Everything;* Book II—*The World We Live In;*
and Book III—*Dream Castles/Cracked Concrete.* Dudek intended

the series to move in Book I from the basic elements of poetry, first stressing the universality of poetry, with poems by children and native people, then demonstrating that poetry is essentially song and music, and last, showing that poetry involves meaning. Book II was to involve students in writing poetry, and having them examine the nature of poetry and some of its subject matter, such as the natural world. In Book III, the changing world was to be the focus, contrasting the past with the present and examining poems from different periods and cultures.

For reasons not fully known, only *All Kinds of Everything,* Book I of the series, was published. Dudek had thoroughly mapped out the developmental direction the series would follow, had completed his selection of materials for Book II, and had the contents of Book III sketched in rough. *All Kinds of Everything,* published in 1973, did not have the immediate spectacular success that *Poetry of Our Time* had had. But it stood up very well in its own right. It was attractively produced and carried Dudek's characteristically generous mix of wide knowledge and unpretentious voice—a teacher talking to kids and other teachers. "Poetry is a form of play."[8] Dudek said this in the opening section "Getting Started" and it epitomized the quality of the anthology. The selection of material was lively and eclectic, including songs such as the French Canadian folk song "I Went to the Market," and lyrics such as Ben Jonson's "Song to Celia"; poems such as the Zuni Indian Poem "Prayer for Rain," a Canadian Eskimo poem "A Wonderful Occupation" and from the Gabon Pygmy People "The Rainbow." Dudek's poem "Electric" and e.e. cummings' "the sky was candy luminous" were part of the section "Word Games".

In the *Teacher's Guide,* always a necessary component of school textbooks, Dudek refrained from dictating any one approach to teaching poetry; instead he wrote: "It is obvious, therefore, that one direction indicated in this book is toward activity—to learn by doing." And he advised teachers to make the anthology their own: "there is no reason why one may not improvise, so long as one uses the material in the book and builds extensions out of it into some form of classroom and home activity."[9]

All Kinds of Everything is still one of the most appealing anthologies around for junior high school students. It fits in perfectly with current pedagogical theory which supports the construction of knowledge by "doing" and the use of a wide variety of multimedia and multicultural materials. Perhaps it presented too radical a choice of material and too open a teaching approach for its time. In any case, let's hope that it will be rediscovered and another generation of students will have the pleasure of reading such an anthology.

Dudek's reputation as poet, professor, little magazine and small press editor was well established by this time and *Poetry of Our Time* made him very well-known in educational circles across Canada. The mid-sixties and early seventies marked the establishment of international and national groups of English teachers concerned with the teaching of language and literature. The now famous Dartmouth conference in the US in 1967 explored the question "What is English?"; the International Conference on the Teaching of English in Vancouver in 1967 and the York '71[10] conference in York, England continued the work started at Dartmouth. The Canadian Council of Teachers of English (CCTE) was formed during the International Conference held in Vancouver, August 21-23, 1967. Louis Dudek and his longtime friend and colleague, Michael Gnarowski, attended the conference, along with Desmond Pacey and other Canadian poets and scholars.

At the Vancouver conference, Dudek delivered a paper entitled "What Are We Teaching?" in which he examined the problem facing English teachers.

Twenty years of argument on paper, of argument over coffee, of listening to students confused by conflicting pedagogies, worried to death by anti-literary disciplines, have led me to the realization that there is something wrong with English studies and with English teaching. The nub of the problem seems to lie in our conception of the subject itself, our lack of consensus on the nature of literature and the study of literature. We do not know what we are teaching. And we are often teaching very different things.[11]

Dudek examined the different schools of criticism from New Criticism to mythopoeic criticism to the psychological critics, and made this pointed connection:

All these are schools of criticism; but they are also schools of teaching. Individual teachers are notorious for following one or another dominant school of criticism, usually the kind of criticism which they themselves were exposed to at the university and which impressed them by its effectiveness as a teaching tool. It is actually in teaching that the schools of criticism reveal their real character; and this is a useful pragmatic test that can be applied to any criticism of literature.[12]

Dudek concluded that "the greatest works of literature have an astonishing complexity which makes them ambiguous, ironic, multiplex
and mysterious, almost like the order of nature of which they are the
reflection and image. . . .these things cannot easily be encompassed
in the classroom or in any one systematic school of criticism."[13]

Dudek became active in CCTE and was a sought-after speaker
at their conferences, and those of their affiliates such as the
Association of Teachers of English in Québec (ATEQ) and the
Ontario Council of Teachers of English (OCTE). The problems that
these associations were examining concerned the need for more
Canadian textbooks in our universities and schools and the lack of
support for Canadian publishers of textbooks, subjects of great
interest to Dudek. As well, he continued his "crusade" for the survival of poetry in the schools and for recognition of its critical
importance in society. Many of the addresses that Dudek gave at
these conferences were published and stand as a testamant to his
lifelong belief that education matters and that poetry matters—and
that this has to be said again and again.

The Ontario Council of Teachers of English invited Dudek to
address their annual conference, held in Toronto, March 18, 1968.
And "Poetry as a Way of Life" was what he delivered—this now
well-known text was first printed in *The English Quarterly*,"[13] the
magazine of the CCTE, in the summer of 1968, and later reprinted
in 1981 in the special Louis Dudek number of *Open Letter—Louis
Dudek: Texts & Essays*.[14] The student rebellion—or what Dudek
calls "the radical revolt of youth"[15]—was identified by him as the
main problem in teaching. He traced the origins of the revolt: "it
comes out of poetry and out of the central movement of literature
in this age."[16] An historical overview from the Renaissance to
Romanticism ("the parent movement"[17] of the student revolt) to
modern poetry examines the changing nature of art and poetry.

The modern conception of poetry, derived from Romanticism, involves the
poet's real existence directly in the creation of the poem. He is no longer
detached as a maker, constructing a work of wisdom and knowledge, but a living man who undergoes the passions recreated in his poetry.[18]

It is the nature of the imagination, Dudek said, to carry "all possibilities, all appetencies and conceptions, to their most extravagant

extremes."[19] This heightening of the passions has been absorbed by students from the great Romantic writers, from books and art, and from the media, with the result that these ideas and attitudes, long underground or outside the mainstream, have surfaced and influenced the entire generation of modern youth. Dudek stated that teachers must "examine the radical implications of primary Romanticism. . . and must turn to poetry as a powerful and radical principle of life, an idea that demands study, understanding, and sympathetic criticism."[20] He concludes with the following:

> We must learn to think of poetry and of life with the same critical understanding; in fact, see them as related to the same moral dilemma—the conflict between reality and human desires and aspirations. Poetry deals mainly with the infinite potentiality of existence; it does not limit itself to things as they are. As such, it pushed us beyond actuality, into the unattainable; and therefore, as life, it pushes us toward impossible actions and often even to self-destruction.[21]

At the First Annual Convention of the CCTE, held August 21-24, 1968, at the Hotel Palliser, in Calgary, the theme was "Canada '68—Directions for English Education." In part of the conference called the Canadian Literature sequence, Dudek presented a paper entitled "The Poetry of the City." (This paper was published first in *The English Quarterly*, Vol. 2, No. 2, July 1969 and later reprinted in Dudek's *Selected Essays and Criticism.*) "Urban realism, as we know, is one of the main characteristics of modern poetry in Canada."[22] This opening statement set the stage for Dudek's exploration of the poetry of several modern Canadian poets. "What I want to do here is examine the nature of Canadian urban poetry for its general metaphorical meaning, for the kind of recurring interpretation which may emerge out of a careful reading of these poems."[23] Using Lampman as an early example, Dudek then looked at poems by Klein, Layton, and himself. What he emphasized in particular was the polarities which realism sets up, and how they were expressed in these poems. "It is a poetry torn in the dichotomy between ultimate good or impending evil, between a possible utopia and a palpable inhuman inferno, between a man-made heaven and a man-made hell."[24] This affective polarity, Dudek said, was the crux of urban poetry and it was the highly charged positive or negative images that gave such poetry its force. He suggested that examining poetry in this manner might be of interest to teachers.

The 1970 CCTE conference in Winnipeg, held August 19-22, had as its theme "English in Canada" and its keynote speaker was Professor Robin Mathews. His address entitled "Literature and National Survival" received a standing ovation. (I remember this occasion vividly—it is difficult now to imagine the excitement generated by that address.) There exists an excellent account of this occasion since Dudek was incensed by the manner in which he was singled out by the media and how some of his casual remarks about popular culture made as part of a panel on Canadian publishing, were made sensational, while the real issues of the conference were totally ignored. The article he wrote reporting this incident, called "Media Should See 'Whole Event,' Not Just Highlights" was first published in *The Gazette* on September 15, 1970, and later reprinted in *In Defence of Art*. The real subject of the conference, as Dudek pointed out, was "the teaching of Canadian literature, its relevance to Canadian life, its emergence from a colonial status of inferiority in the curriculum." [25]

Dudek's address at the 1974 CCTE conference in Saskatoon was called "Poetry On the Page," and was later printed in *The English Quarterly* in the autumn of 1974. Here he challenged what he called "the greatest error current in critical and educational thinking about literature today." [26] This is the idea of the so-called "experience school" who claim that poetry is an experience that needs no analysis; that poetry is best simply recited or read aloud, without comment—all you need to do is close your eyes and "experience" it. He took on John Robert Colombo, who, in a preface to his textbook *New Directions in Canadian Poetry,* recommended to students that they read into a poem all that they want, and that they experience the poems, rather than interpret them. Dudek objected strenuously to this view and countered that poetry as a "sensuous 'experience' does not exist... A poem is a sequence of words entering the mind in a certain order." [27] He added that "the poem is a complex mental experience; it is not merely physical, or sensuous. It requires a good deal of analysis; you have to go at it like a cat threading a hedge; and there are many ways of interpreting the same poem, especially if it is a big complex poem." [28] Dudek conceded, later on in his address, that he had overstated Colombo's position, which he had qualified later in the text, in order to make his own point about poetry.

His last address to the CCTE took place at its conference in Montréal on May 11, 1983. His luncheon address was called "The Seven Ages of Poetry," based on a theory he was developing; he explained to his audience that he was gathering material to support his theory and the result might be a book on the topic.

My project is to divide the lives of poets into seven stages, roughly analogous to Shakespeare's seven ages, and to find characteristic poems for each stage, from many different poets, so that a typical kind of poetry for each stage emerges. I have seven key poets, one representative for each stage, poets ranging from Alexander Pope to Ezra Pound, so that the book would be a study of poetry in its normal human development, and in studying any poet you would know what features in his development are perfectly typical before you began to consider particular deviations.[29]

The speech was later printed in *The English Quarterly* in the fall of 1983. Dudek had planned to write a book on this subject, and after his retirement from McGill University in 1983, he began to accumulate a vast file of material on the seven poets he had chosen for his study. However, the pace of his literary life did not abate: he continued to deliver major addresses, to publish books of poetry and essays, to visit the classes of friends and fellow poets, and to be a sustaining influence in the literary life of Canada. Given these circumstances, the projected book *The Seven Ages of Poetry* was not finished. Alas.

As part of his legacy Louis Dudek should be remembered as the radical poet/teacher who stimulated and provoked all who engaged in dialogue with him; who considered all teachers—elementary, secondary, and university—as part of the same great enterprise; who made accessible to students the best of modern poetry; and who, in the *Guide to All Kinds of Everything,* advised teachers "simply to give it [the anthology] to the class to read, for enjoyment, and not to teach at all." But, being Louis Dudek, he added that "a program of some sort is what we need" and asserted that the teaching suggestions in the *Guide* were made in the spirit of poetry itself—"to make it more enjoyable, not turn it into a painful subject of study."[30] A perfect example of his constructive radicalism.

**Aileen Collins,
Way's Mills, 1975.**

REFERENCES:

1. Dudek, Louis. *Epigrams*. Montreal: DC Books, 1975, p. 32.
2. Dudek, Louis. *Zembla's Rocks*. Montreal: Véhicule Press, 1986, p. 18.
3. "I infiltrated the newspapers..." Dudek wrote articles and reviews for *The Montreal Star* from 1959 to 1964; for *The Gazette* from 1965 to 1980; and for *The Globe and Mail* from 1980 to 1988. A selection of these were published as *In Defence of Art: Critical Essays and Reviews*. Edited with an introduction by Aileen Collins. Kingston, ON: Quarry Press, 1988.
4. *Contemporary Authors* series, p. 123.
5. *Poetry of Our Time. An Introduction to Twentieth-Century Poetry including Modern Canadian Poetry*. Edited by Louis Dudek. Toronto: The Macmillan Company of Canada, 1965. p. 1.
6. PDM. *The McGill Daily*. Friday, March 11, 1966, p. 15.
7. *Poetry of Our Time*, p. 196.
8. Dudek, Louis. *All Kinds of Everything*. Teacher's Guide, p. 3.
9. *Ibid*, p. 3.
10. York '71. The CCTE sponsored representatives from across Canada to attend this conference. Louis Dudek and I were part of the Québec contingent. Dudek did not present a paper at this conference which was structured into working groups called "commissions," with each group studying a problem or issue for the duration of the conference and giving their findings in a general assembly.
11. Dudek, Louis. "What Are We Teaching?" 1967. Reprint of address given, p. 2.
12. *Ibid.*, pp. 5-6.
13. *Ibid.*, p. 11.
14. *Louis Dudek: Texts & Essays*. Edited by Frank Davey & bp Nichol. Open Letter, Spring & Summer 1981, Fourth Series, Nos. 8-9.
15. Dudek Louis. "Poetry as a Way of Life." *The English Quarterly*. A Publication of the Canadian Council of Teachers of English. Summer 1968. Number One, Volume One, p 7.
16. *Ibid.*, p. 8.
17. *Ibid.*, p. 8.
18. *Ibid.*, p. 12.
19. *Ibid.*, p. 13.
20. *Ibid.*, p. 14.
21. *Ibid.*, p. 16.
22. *In Defence of Art*, p. 97.
23. Dudek, Louis. "Poetry on the Page." *The English Quarterly*, Vol.. 7, No. 3. Autumn 1974, p. 12.
24. *Ibid.*, p. 13.
25. *Ibid.*, p. 14.
26. Dudek, Louis. "The Seven Ages of Poetry." *The English Quarterly*, Volume XVI, Number 3, Fall 1983. p. 11.
27. Dudek, Louis. *All Kinds of Everything*. Teacher's Guide. Toronto: Clarke, Irwin & Company Limited. 1973. p. 3.

The final result will be work with a good end, and also the best sort of art. The joy of pure art must be in it, but also a relevance to practical life, and even a solution to pressing problems. This can only come from a good man, whose mind is so directed that he delivers a message, even when he only intends to paint a picture of beauty, or to express himself.

from "2 p.m., Saturday, July 26, 1941", *1941 Diary*

Photo Courtesy of Aileen Collins

The cottage, Way's Mills.

Last Poem

The cloud-filled heavens
    crashed down on us
But we cultivate
    our greens and asparagus
        as we did before

(As dictated to Aileen Collins by Louis Dudek, Friday afternoon, March 9th, 2001, at the Royal Victoria Hospital, Montreal.)

LOUIS DUDEK

Photo Courtesy of Stephanie Zuperko Dudek

Louis Dudek, circa 1946.

Beginnings

[Abridged from the
Contemporary Authors Autobiography Series.]

I WAS LEAN and sickly as a child, a tall skinny boy, and a great deal probably follows from this. It made me introverted and hypersensitive from the start, too much concerned with my health—though perhaps with good cause—and too self-conscious for my own good. ("When a hypochondriac is sick," I later wrote, "he is twice as sick.")

"Show me another kid who is any way like you," said one of my cousins to me, sensing my difference from the rest.

"Your family was always superior," said another, many years later. "Always above everybody else." We were all part of an extended family living in a connected group of houses in east-end Montreal, houses owned by my grandparents and uncles. (My superior family owned nothing, we rented a cold-water flat from Grandma at fifteen dollars a month.) The aunts and uncles very Polish, but mostly Liverpool-born and speaking fluent English from the first generation on. I was second-generation Canadian-born: Montreal, February 6, 1918.

There was Grandma, a large patriarchal mother-figure, and Grandpa, with handle-bar whiskers. A backyard which had a long-stemmed poplar tree going up three stories and then branching out, scattering catkins and caterpillars in spring and summer. There were seven sons and daughters, the uncles and aunts, all but one married and reproducing dozens of grandchildren, who were my sibling cousins. So I lived in a big crowd, though feeling somewhat isolated and different.

Grandmother said within my hearing, when I was five or six, that I might as well be taken out of school since I would not live long. Adults should be very careful of what they say within the hearing of children: it can be remembered fifty or sixty years later and can still be resented. I have long outlived my grandmother, and I was quite fascinated by her powerful personality, but I never forgot that careless remark. After all, it flawed my unthinking confidence in life from the very beginning. I was adult from my fifth year, so far as understanding the fact of human mortality is concerned.

The thought that I was somehow insufficiently quick, both physically and mentally, must have stayed with me, because I have never had much solid confidence in myself. Whatever I have done in later years was partly to prove to my father that I was not altogether a loss, not entirely a disappointment, though my father by then was a long time dead and would not have remembered what that was all about.

(Of course, Father would have been immensely surprised, and shocked, at any time, if he had known that an occasional word dropped, really a reprimand, had sunk so deep. So would Grandmother, who came from a Polish-Lithuanian culture where children frequently died young, and frail ones became predictable white coffins. It was hard common sense to say, "He won't survive." They meant no harm by it at all.)

In my twenties or thirties I invented a "personality test" that depends on childhood memories. Write down the three or four things you vividly remember from your tenth year or earlier (most people will remember no more than that), then interpret these incidents as symbolic memories.

I remember coming home from school in some fear, in my sixth year, having missed a word in an ongoing spelling-bee. (I had lost my first place and dropped somewhere to the bottom of the class.) One of my cousins, or one of my sisters, had run ahead to tell my mother the bad news. I could not face the coming reproaches, and hid under a bed to avoid facing my mother.

Some years later, graduating from Lansdowne School, I missed winning a four-year scholarship to attend high school by a matter of three marks or so. The failure stayed with me throughout my high school and college career, both of which were costly and which we could hardly afford, and it was only much later that it occurred to me, when I sized up the past, that after all I had led the entire school neck and neck with another boy, and came very close to winning! No, actually I had failed.

My mother died, at the mere age of thirty-one, when I was eight years old. My third vivid memory has to do with the time of her death. I am standing in the corridor of my grandmother's house, before the closed door at the end of it, when an overwhelming realization comes over me that I will never again see my mother. Upon this thought I dissolve in tears. And then, on a sudden I realize, with a kind of thrill, that I am now completely and inescapably free. I block out this thought, but I cannot deny it had passed my mind. In fact I remember it now. To this day I believe I am different from others because of that dearly bought freedom at an early age. Much later, reading *Sons and Lovers,* I realized how strong my mother's love

(from left) 7 year old Louis, parents Stasia & Vincent Dudek, with sisters Irene and Lillian, circa 1925.

must have been and how great a hold she had over me. I would have been another Paul Morel. The loss, as well as the sudden liberation, are contained in the symbolic memory. It tells me again and again that I am motherless and free, though I am forever deprived by her death.

In my twenties I looked back over those years and thought I had had the most unhappy childhood imaginable. The loss of my mother was not the only cause. I was always being taken to hospital, or "to see Dr. Ship," to find out whether I was about to die from tuberculosis, whether I would at last undergo that dreaded operation for tonsillitis or for nasal polyps, or some other defect that would either finish me or set me right. At the ripe age of eighteen, when my father managed to get some money together to send me into first-year Arts at McGill, he insisted that I first undergo surgery for adenoids, although by the a time I actually had nothing bothering me, and I did have the operation done—like a necessary castration or initiation rite—after which my real life could begin.

After my mother's death, my father brought a maiden sister from Poland to take care of his three children. She was a frail, sensitive, literate person, who told hair-raising stories—some from Pushkin, I later discovered—and could recite many Polish poems from memory that were deeply moving. Her only punishment for me was to make me memorize poems, which was actually a kind of reward I thought, and through her I came to like Slowacki and Mickiewicz, Polish Romantics, before I ever knew Byron, Keats, or Shelley.

In school, in those days (in the late twenties), we sang songs from the English, Scottish, and Irish tradition: "Annie Laurie," "John Peel," "The Minstrel Boy," "Comin' throu' the Rye." The words were beautiful and the melodies delightful: a singing teacher visited the schools of the Protestant School Board and intoned the songs in his rich baritone voice, without accompaniment. That's how we learned all the songs of the traditional repertoire, songs of which most students today are utterly ignorant.

I say the Protestant School Board, though I and my two sisters were Roman Catholics. We were actually "illegals" in the Protestant system at that time, just as recently there have been many "illegals" in the English-language school system in Montreal, students whom the law wants to propel into the French school system.

In my mind I carry lifetime scars of these early terrors and insecurities. Like Joseph Conrad, I am a lifelong admirer of English civilization, and later, in my poetry, I call England "the best corner of Europe," despite my wasteland vision of modernity. Even in the long poem *Europe,* written in my early thirties, I say that "Courtesy is pleasing. . . And what more pleasant than well-bred English people?" And yet this affection for things English, and for the literature of England, is tempered with a kind of alienation, a feeling that what I most love and admire I really have no proper right to. I am an interloper even where I am most at home. I should add that, despite my troubles in childhood, I was also something of a pampered darling, as a reputedly ailing orphan, favoured by my aunts occasionally with a slice of rich lemon pie or home made raisin tarts, and the effect of this preferment has also left its mark. I may take pleasure in "being made much of," even as I suffer from outward signs of neglect.

Stephanie and Louis Dudek on the beach circa 1947.
Drawing by Stephanie Zuperko Dudek.

In the High School of Montreal, for the study of poetry, I had a battered purple-covered book entitled *Poems of the Romantic Revival.* Here I first discovered the great poems of Keats, Byron, Wordsworth, Tennyson, and Browning. Unlike the present time, when students are offered mediocre poems by doubtful poets "whom they can understand," we were given the great poets without any question of watering them down for young minds. Read "The Eve of St. Agnes," we were told, and be ready for the examination. Look up the words. Study the notes.

I also studied Latin and loved it, translating Horace for my beloved teacher and reading her my translations. (Not Greek, I picked that up later on my own.) But the meaning of great poetry, its timeless beauty, is the same in all ages and in all languages, with the proviso that you have to find your own touchstones, the passages that draw you out, evoke your own nature, and send you—"out of this world," as they say nowadays. For me it was the ending of Shelley's "To a Skylark," as simple as the Sermon on the Mount, and as pure and perfect as undoctored natural speech can be. To this day, nearly sixty years later, I can remember the exact position on the page—top left side—where these lines occur. They are there for me still, and they have shaped my life and my emotions forever after.

So, too, are the triumphant closing lines of Horace's Fifth Ode in Book Three about the Roman general Regulus, who being defeated and captured by the Carthagenians was returned to Rome on condition that he plead for peace. But he urged war instead, for the future safety of Rome, and then he returned as hostage of the Carthagenians to be tortured to death, knowing what his fate would be. He returned, says Horace, "as unconcernedly / As if they were his clients and he'd settled / Some lengthy lawsuit for them and was going / On to Venafrium's fields / Or to Tarentum, Sparta's colony"—

tendens Venafranos in agros
aut Lacedaemonium Tarentum.

I came to this a little later. In high school we studied the usual Horatian odes: "Integer Vitae," "Exegi Monumentum," "Eheu Fugaces," "O Fons Bandusiae," "Diffugere Nives." (I think those were some of the poems.) Also some Virgil. But speak-

ing of touchstones, let me give you Homer, from the *Odyssey,*
Book II, just two lines that for me came to define poetry:

To them grey-eyed Athene sent a favourable breeze,
the fresh West Wind, singing over the wine-dark sea. . .

Tóisin d'íkmenon oúron híei glaukópis Athéne
akraé Zéphuron, keládont epi oínopa pónton.

The first requirement for a student of poetry is to learn the Greek
alphabet and to begin decoding phrases like these. *"Glaukópis
Athéne"* and *"oínopa pónton"* are standard phrases; but why does
the whole thing sound so incredibly beautiful to me?

Not to appear arrogant, I will mention an anecdote. A good
deal later, while giving a public lecture in Montreal, I hazarded
an off-the-cuff translation of a Latin phrase from Ovid for the
benefit of the audience—*si pulvis nullus erit / nullum tamen
excute* ("even if there should be not a speck of dust, brush it
off," I think that's about the equivalent)—but I mistranslated it
somehow, I forgot how, and my old Latin teacher, who was in
the audience, came up afterward and corrected me, gently, as
usual. Well, we never cease to learn from our teachers.

On the subject of *élitism,* since we are touching on it, I say—
let's not insult democracy. Democracy was not achieved to make
us all mediocre, but to make us free and superior, each in his
own way. Élitism is a good thing, and highly democratic, if right-
ly used, on behalf of the majority. My father was a hardworking
man, at one time a fireman, later driving a truck for a brewery
in Montreal, for a time running a hotel and tavern in Hamilton,
in his final years managing a court of roadside cottages in
Orillia, Ontario. He was a literate and refined person by nature,
but perforce struggling as an immigrant in a new country.

Money pressures at home nearly made me drop out of high
school before finishing, but advice from a YMCA counsellor sent me
back to school and I completed the course—Grade Thirteen, at that
time equivalent to first-year college. I then went to work in a warehouse, on St. Helen Street, in the old part of Montreal, an area of
brick, dust, and grime, devoted to tightfisted business operations. I
rubbed shoulders with working people, who were the sort of

people I liked best—deliverymen, truckers, salesmen, and typ-
ists crowded in busy offices. Some years later I wrote the poem
"Old City Sector," whose opening lines well describe my impression of this part of old Montreal:

> This gut-end of a hungry city
> costive with rock and curling ornament,
> once glorious, the pride of bankers,
> reaches each projecting cornice
> over the stomach of empty air, the street
> now deserted.

My view of work and workingmen is contained in the poem
"Building a Skyscraper" written some ten years later, in which I say
that someday "They will be celebrated / more than millionaires,
since without rich men/ nations can run as well, or better, but not
without these men." It is not a passing opinion but a permanent
belief, of the right order of values.

At the time, however, work in a warehouse was a dead end, and
yet I did not see any hope of ever getting out of it. Then suddenly
my father was able to send me to college, I think by persuading his
wife, since he had re-married, to help finance my education; and I
registered as a sophomore at McGill University. This was in 1936,
three years before World War II, but Hitler was already threatening
in Europe and there was civil war in Spain. For me a new life began
in the university, a life without parental supervision, a life of freedom
and exploration. I wrote for the campus newspaper, the *McGill Daily*.
Saw my editorial articles reprinted in other college papers across
Canada. Played chess in the
Student Union to my heart's
content. Fell in love. Discussed philosophy and social
problems with new-found
friends, Reg Harris my philosophical cohort, Guy Royer
my best friend, a French
Canadian from high school,
Norman Hillyer a United
Church theology student,

Photo Courtesy of Stephanie Zuperko Dudek

**Louis Dudek, Stella Sagaitis
& Stephanie Zuperko, late 1940s.**

then a keen socialist who later became a Reverend. (We had great lunches at the Presbyterian College on University Street, bringing our own sandwiches to lunch and sharing tea in common, arguing at the top of our bent.) My friend Margaret, who thought me "a genius," brought a book of poems by C. Day Lewis to my attention, a book out of the library, but I was slow in picking up the scent. I had been scribbling poems from high-school days. I wrote my first around the age of twelve or thirteen, but these were miserable childish verses. Our parish priest, Father Bernard, encouraged my sister Lillian in poetry, and brought her secondhand books as gifts, *The Complete Poems of Sir Walter Scott, The Poems of Thomas Campbell, Thomas Moore,* and other nineteenth-century Romantics. I neglected and disparaged these musty tomes.

In the Carnegie Reading Room, subsidized by the Carnegie Foundation, which was a modest room in the Arts building (exactly where the English department offices are now located), I discovered a small anthology of contemporary Italian poetry and in it a poem of about eighty lines, in three sections, which I copies out and soon knew almost by heart. It was by a turn-of-the-century poet named Ceccardo Roccatagliata Ceccardi.

> *Quando ci revedremo*
> *il tempo avrà nevicato*
> *sul nostro capo, o amore . . .*
>
> (When we meet again
> time will have snowed
> upon our heads, my love . . .)

Ceccardo Ceccardi is missing from most later Italian anthologies. But I carried him around in my head; and some forty years later wrote a poem, "First Love," which echoed his exact phrases:

> You wore a blue coat and white scarf, remember?
> And we walked in the dim night-time, talking.
>
> What does love matter, or all that since has happened?
> What happened is an eternal possession. . . .
>
> (from *Zembla's Rocks)*

A poet may seem to have vanished into oblivion; and yet somewhere, perhaps in a far foreign country, someone may have read his poem, and have lived with it through the years. This is what is called futurity, even if it be in only one reader's memory—immortality, to be reborn in another poet's lines.

Leaving McGill University with a B.A. degree in '39 I had already read Neitzsche, and Ibsen. ("The password is Anarchy" says a poem in the *McGill Daily* in 1951, and I am delighted today, in looking up Ceccardo Ceccardi, that he called himself "an aristocratic anarchist"—thought I was neither an anarchist, nor a Marxist, nor even a socialist in any true sense. I argued against the "Reverend" Norman Hillyer, my dear friend, and he called me a "Tolstoyan liberal," whatever that may have meant at the time.) I also carried Walt Whitman into the fields at Charlemagne (some fifteen miles outside of Montreal) and read him aloud to myself, and probably conversed with him in my hallucinations.

At this time (1942) I met with a group of literati and joined in a literary movement of sorts. Canada just then was still doing its spring cleaning of Victorian dust and cobwebs in the renovation that is called modernism, although our modernism had started a dozen years after the European and American schools of London and Paris, and this was the second wave of "modern poetry in Canada." The Canadian poets A.J.M. Smith, F.R. Scott, A.M. Klein, W.W.E. Ross, Raymond Knister, Dorothy Livesay, and R.G. Everson had started the cleanup in a gentle, quiet way around 1925, writing free verse, appearing in *Poetry* (Chicago) and in other small magazines, writing some vigorous articles, and forecasting the changes to come. Their poetry, however, was less vigorous than their prose. The second wave of poets which I now joined were just beginning, combining their forces with the older boys, to make a more raucous, exciting noise.

The simple idea that modernism was primarily a housecleaning, a sweep-out of sentimental propriety and moral hypocrisy, is now hard to recapture; we have so many complex theories about modernism and postmodernism. But the root problem and the liberation, which the modern revolt brought with it, were then so obvious that the idea could be taken up by flappers and gigolos. "Homme, sois moderne!" was inscribed over a café entrance in Montmartre; and Richard Aldington in his poem "The Eaten Heart" said what everyone in that generation knew:

> We were right, yes, we were right
> To smash the false idealities of the last age,
> The humbug, the soft cruelty, the mawkishness,
> The heavy tyrannical sentimentality,
> The inability to face facts, especially new facts. . . .

In Canada there were already free-verse proponents in 1914. But the main lines of developing modernism can be seen as branchings from the chief modern British and American poets, in a clear order of succession. F.R. Scott and A.J.M. Smith, from 1925 on, are most easily associated with Yeats and Eliot, actually the most traditional and conservative of the moderns. The group with which I became connected, consisting of Irving Layton, John Sutherland (editor of *First Statement* magazine, then of *Northern Review),* Miriam Waddington, Raymond Souster, have a kinship to poets like Whitman, Masters, Sandburg, Kenneth Fearing, or Robinson Jeffers. A much later generation, represented by Ken Norris in the 1980s, shows a passionate devotion, in practice and principle, to William Carlos Williams. (Earlier on, Raymond Souster was also a Williams admirer.) The sequence is fairly simple, with other affinities intervening—to Edith Sitwell in James Reaney; or to Dylan Thomas, in Al Purdy and Alden Nowlan; or to popular ballad and lyric in Leonard Cohen—but it shows a progression, if a bit halting, from tepid modernism to extreme avant-gardism, such as we find in the late poetry of bp Nichol and others, analogous to the experimentalism of Gertrude Stein or André Breton.

For myself, I did not want to take a regressive stance, in which loud vulgarity and forced rhetoric replace the old sentimentality, although there are poems from the 1940s or early 1950s that might illustrate the road not taken. My particular affinity did not appear until the mid-1940s, and then the magnetic pull was to Ezra Pound, the most complex and difficult of modern poets. What drew me to Pound was his aestheticism and his revolutionary modernism in principle.

There is no creativity possible to man that is not the result of an impress from some preceding work or creation. The infinite potentiality of nature cannot appear in its purity, as something made out of nothing. It can only work upon what is there, since everything in this creation emerges from something that is already there, as a variation or progression in things. An artist, therefore, cannot produce an original work of art in the sense that it resembles nothing known before, that it derives from a different world, from a distant planet, or even from a remote culture which he has not experienced.

My contacts with other poetry, with other literature, with music, with paintings, with powerful ideas, are the only source from which I can develop original poetry, forms of art, or ideas of my own. The vest-pocket copy of Hamlet which I carried about everywhere in my college years is one such source; so is the poetry of Whitman, which I recited in my country walks.

Music had a powerful appeal for me. While still at college I borrowed from the library complete scores of the famous operas and played on the piano the parts which most moved me. The prologue to I *Pagliacci* was one such piece, especially the melody part beginning *"Un nido di memorie . . ."* (I swooned in ecstasy over such music; come to think of it, my knowledge of Italian, which made me capable of reading Italian poetry, came from these operas.) *Madame Butterfly,* with its wondrous first act, and the great moments in *La Bohème* were made entirely my own, on the piano, in this way. I thought of Puccini's music as "smoke rolling along the ground," with wonderfully imaginative music, and I resented later, and laughed off, Pound's line about "Puccini the all-too-human."

There was Dean Clarke of the Faculty of Music, in those days, conductor of the Montreal Symphony Orchestra, who gave open lectures to interested students in a small, overcrowded room every Friday before the Sunday afternoon symphony concert at Her Majesty's Theatre on Guy Street just above St. Catherine. I could not afford the concerts, but I got a job as unpaid usher and so was able to hear each concert after Dean Clarke's lecture. This was a musical analysis of the themes and development of the main item on the program. I remember especially the lecture on and performance of Brahms's Second Piano Concerto, of which the opening notes still echo in my ears as I pause for a moment in this writing. "Brahms," said Dean Clarke, "was a passionate Romantic at heart, but he held back his emotions—until they broke through in certain passages of his music." There are some things said that one remembers fifty or more years later, whether good or bad, because they are the shaping influences of our lives. At home we played all kinds of current popular music on the piano, as well as traditional songs. I loved Irving Berlin, and later came to love Cole Porter more than any other current composer. A bit later, in my New York years, I discovered the music of Bach, "The Well-tempered Clavier," in the music room at Columbia, where records could be played and music taken out. I played on an upright piano in our rented one-room apartment on 123rd Street, corner of Amsterdam, fingering the music as well as I could, though I'd never had music lessons. Later, I became an enthusiast and collector of the popular songs of the nineties, the songs of Harry Von Tilzer, Paul Dresser, George M. Cohan, and James Thornton. And there was British Music Hall, a great source of social history and fun. And above all, ancient songs from France, beginning with the troubadours, whom I made out on the piano, and going on to the sixteenth and seventeenth centuries, also the melodious songs of French Canada. And finally, English folk songs, in the collections of Ralph Vaughn Williams, songs like "The Banks of Sweet Primroses," "As Sylvie Was Walking," "The Blacksmith," and many others. I have, in other words, a strain of the popular and of the traditional life of the people in my poetry, a very powerful strain of great beauty and universal feeling, but it may be that the people themselves are today cut off from this experience, so that this is not recognized in my poetry.

A visiting lecturer at McGill, many years later, speaking on Theodore Dreiser, remarked about Dreiser's brother Paul, who wrote songs under the name of Paul Dresser, that he was the composer of trivial and unimportant songs at the turn-of-the-century. Sitting in the audience as a faculty member, I could not interrupt the speaker, though I was deeply incensed, for I admired the songs of Paul Dresser with a special kind of joy and nostalgia. Are they collected anywhere? Probably not. And yet, among the stories of Theodore Dreiser, you will find a long

Louis Dudek,
late 1940s.

short-story—actually a memoir—entitled "My Brother Paul." It gives an excellent account of the music business and of the stirring life of the entertainment world of New York at that time. Paul Dresser's songs were a good part of it, immensely popular, and they are still moving and beautiful, with their gentle and sentimental touch of pathos and melodrama.

At home in our Polish family, or later with my in-laws and relatives after my marriage, there was a custom at Christmastime and on other holidays, to do some old-fashioned group singing at table. The great songs of the Ukraine, of Lithuania, of Russia, and of Poland would be sounded in chorus, and repeated to one's heart's content, while glasses klinked and drinks were poured out. Some singers of talent, my mother-in-law in particular, sang in harmony with the leading melody, a technique of part-singing which they had learned in the folk villages of Lithuania. This music, too, is part of my inheritance, though there is no way perhaps to recognize its plangent melodies and vigorous rhythms in my poetry. Somewhere it must be there, since nothing is lost that moves us deeply and is part of our continuing memory.

Beauty is international. And the enduring works of art, whether we find them in ancient Egypt, China or Japan, India or Africa, are all recognizable to us because they have a common element, which must be a quality of humanity, called grace or beauty. All these songs of many nations, and the many kinds of music, are part of one essence which is intrinsic to human nature, and which goes by the name of beauty. That is the best word we have for it, though all it means is that we respond deeply with all our being to its surface resonance.

I had shown some poems to Dr. Harold Files, a very fine teacher at McGill, and he had advised me to look up John Sutherland, who was then editing the first numbers of a mimeo magazine, *First Statement*. At the same time, Irving Layton, whom I knew from his poems in the *McGill Daily* and whom I had met the previous winter, came by chance to know John Sutherland's sister, Betty Sutherland, a young painter who was working briefly as a cashier in the restaurant where he ate his meals. The result was a union of forces in the magazine *First Statement* between a very strong and authoritative critic, John Sutherland, and a very bold and energetic politically-conscious poet—Irving Layton at that time—and a very unassertive lyrical poet, that is to say myself.

I was six years younger than Layton, and in one's early twenties six years counts for a good deal. He was the dominant figure, but I was not inclined to be dominated, so that our conversations for many years took the form of extremely heated arguments. Betty Sutherland used to say: "You two are such different poets, why don't you just let each other be? Why do you have to fight it out over every single point?" (How right she was, yet how impossible to escape this strife of temperament built into our nature.)

The result is that relations between us eventually ceased, in the mid-fifties, which was about a dozen years after we first met. But much water had poured under the bridge (the Jacques Cartier Bridge, where we first parleyed and resolved together to change the shape of Canadian poetry), before that final separation took place.

There is often a short pause between the first phase and the second phase of a significant artistic change, as if "that first fine careless rapture" required the mind or spirit to catch its breath before a second, and stronger, heave could begin. This was true of the modernism of Eliot and Pound, after the *Waste Land,* and it was certainly true of the modern development in Canada. Not only was there a pause after Scott and Smith's first start in the 1920s and early thirties, but there was a pause after the mid-forties which was followed by a new burst of energy after 1951. Collective enthusiasms—that is, creative acts—may come in spurts, for all we know, and this may apply to revolutionary movements as well as literary ones.

During the forties activity I was still in my early twenties, first getting out of college, then working haphazardly in the advertising agencies, scraping a living first as a free-lancer, then as a permanent employee. I married in 1944 and with my wife Stephanie moved to New York, for further study and a taste of bohemian life. My health unfitted me for enlistment in the war, so that I was able to leave Canada and register at Columbia University in New York. Up to that time I had not quite found my direction or voice as a poet, but now things began to take a turn.

I had of course published. Ryerson Press in Toronto had brought out the book *Unit of Five,* in which I was one of the young poets included. After this, while I was living in New York, the same Canadian firm brought out my first separate book, *East of the City.*

However, no book of mine appeared from First Statement Press, where other poets were being published who were my boon companions. I was perhaps already running my own race—a condition which became more marked as time went on.

I eventually entered the Ph.D. course at Columbia and graduated with a doctorate in English and Comparative Literature; but I was ill-prepared for this work, and at the beginning had no such serious intentions. I had no honours training in literature, which would have given me concentrated undergraduate study in the subject. In fact I had wandered all over the lot in the general course at McGill, with courses in political science, psychology, and philosophy, as well as English and French literature, since my notion of education, so far as I had any, was that of self-fulfillment in the broadest sense. I had no practical purposes, beyond poetry and seeing into life as far as possible. Why was I born? In order to know, Socrates had taught me.

As a result, when it came to graduate study for the Ph.D., I had a hard time of it, even though I was an older student than most (almost thirty). I learned by intensive reading what I should have packed away back home in my fresh youth, and this probably showed even later in my orals, where I was still a learner—and mainly a poet, not a concentrated scholar like the rest.

However, I did catch up to a certain extent. I started at Columbia with courses in article writing, poetry, and even journalism, since I was still an advertising writer and a journalist by trade. But I also took a course in medieval history; and this was so immensely exciting an experience for me that I decided to go solidly into history, and in 1946 I received a master's degree in that field. The subject which I pitched on in history, and which I continued in the department of English and Comparative Literature, was the history of the profession of letters, a question which interests me to this day and which provides the leading theme for the present autobiographical essay.

Being concerned with poetry, and with the importance of poetry in the past, it has struck me from the beginning of my career that in our time poetry, and in fact any writing with a view to permanence, which is what the arts must have as a first condition of their greater value, does not find a place in the existing culture. While billions of words are being poured out in printed form, in newspapers, magazines, and popular books, little or nothing of this has any lasting value. By definition, then, we are already in, or are entering into, a dark age. Looking over time, periods that have left no permanent record, or little of worth, are negligible; while great civilizations and celebrated moments in history are those which leave durable works of value. I wanted to know the history of this question—the reason why modern culture seems to prefer the journalistic and the ephemeral to the genuine and the durable, in the arts.

The most fascinating part of the curriculum at Columbia was a high-powered seminar with Lionel Trilling and Jacques Barzun; but extracurricular activities were even more engrossing. I met the burgeoning novelist Herbert Gold, as well as the psychologist Zygmunt Piotrowski, as personal friends. With Herb Gold I played some handball in nearby courts and aped the style of James Joyce on the typewriter. But I was a slow poet beside these flashing lights and never made much impression on them.

I wrote to Ezra Pound, who was then incarcerated in an asylum in Washington, D.C., having broadcast to American troops during the war in Italy—all about Usura, the Unwobbling Pivot of Confucius, and the writings of John Adams—so that he was accused of treason, but finally considered *non compos mentis,* unfit for trial. Pound wrote back, and a kind of correspondence followed which led to my higher education in the reality of modern poetry.

Through Pound I came to meet several writers and artists in New York and vicinity (he sent me addresses and telephone numbers which I sometimes followed up—please note that I was up to my ears in graduate work, and from 1947 on I was also teaching English at the City College of New York). I came to know Paul Blackburn the poet, as a friend; and Michael Lekakis the sculptor, whom I valued highly; and Cid Corman, the editor of Origin, as well as several other camp followers of Ezra Pound, some not so savoury as others. Frankly, I never could understand why I should go chasing after some disciple or other of Ezra's to add a cubit to my stature, so I did not follow up all his rec-

STUDIES IN CANADIAN LITERATURE

Louis Dudek & Raymond Souster

Frank Davey

ommendations. There was Marianne Moore whom he wanted me to visit with a parcel, but much as I admired MM I used the post instead. And of course William Carlos Williams, whose address I knew offhand—and occasionally exchanged a note with—but I never bothered to visit him. Also E.E. Cummings, whom I did not meet until he came to Montreal for a reading and I introduced him to the audience. I had a distrust of such personal contacts, since the real life is the life of the mind, and there we meet daily with our kind and carry on our conversations.

What Pound opened up for me was a great curiosity about contemporary poetry—and its engagement with the cause of civilization. I got out of New York in 1951; I returned to Montreal to teach at McGill University. The return began a new productive stage in my career. I was now in my thirty-third year of life and ready to work on poetry and teaching in earnest.

I came to McGill with a mission. It may be that the worst teachers, as well as the best, are teachers with a mission, but I came with the confidence that I had something very important to teach. There were in fact two things. The first was modern poetry and literature, which had evolved fully abroad but which had barely started in Canada with small groups of poets having a limited audience. The message of modernism was to be spread abroad, through students, lectures, and magazines. It was also to be directed at poetry in Canada, at new promising writers; and outlets had to be created for these new promising writers; and outlets had to be created for these new voices. Then the second program was the massive movement of European literature and thought since the eighteenth century, with its profound practical implications, which students' minds had still to experience, like buckets of cold water thrown at them from a high lectern.

It was a few years before I was able to teach everything I wanted to teach. But sudden changes in the department made this possible, and as one student (Ruth Wisse, now a prominent teacher herself) said a few years later, "You happen to be teaching all the most interesting courses in the department." I received enthusiastic support from students very often, as many teachers do in their best years, so that it is not entirely vain to record this one remark. Classes grew from twenty or thirty to nearly five hundred in those years before the student revolution, and I was extremely busy trying to keep up with my vast area of teaching.

The subject of my European literature survey was divided into a two-year course (four terms) which many students took in successive years: the period from eighteenth-century rationalism and enlightenment to romanticism and realism; and the period from naturalism to modernism. My six radio lectures, published under the title *The First Person in Literature,* give a fair outline of some of the leading ideas. Also, Emery Neff's *Revolution in European Poetry* provides a good view of the background for the first part; while a recent book like Allan Bloom's *Closing of the American Mind* deals with many of the central books and ideas that formed part of the entire two-year course. In fact, the substance of literature and thought to which American students are now said to be closed was precisely the subject matter which it was my mission at that time to open them.

This huge course—a study, really, of the subversive currents in modern thought—was virtually brought to an end by the student revolution in the early sixties. "What I have been teaching you, and warning you against," I said to my students, "has now arrived, right here in the classroom"—as radical students began to raid the lecture halls and harangue teachers. The course in question was familiarly known as "Journey to the End of the Night," after Céline's novel, which terminated the two-year course—and the night, it seemed, had closed in upon us.

Beyond the classroom, this activism of my teaching program led to magazine activity and literary publishing of various kinds. With Raymond Souster and Irving Layton we set up Contact Press, derived from Souster's magazine *Contact,* with perhaps a bow to Williams and McAlmon's earlier magazine with the same name. Through this press we published *Cerberus,* our own three-poet book, and after that some thirty of the most promising poets in Canada, a list which came to include most of the established poetry in the country: names like Al Purdy, Alden Nowlan, John Newlove, F.R. Scott, Phyllis Webb, Eli Mandel, D.G. Jones, W. W. E.

Ross, Gwendolyn MacEwen, R. G. Everson, George Bowering, Milton Acorn, Margaret Atwood, and others. At the university, I started the McGill Poetry Series, which published only ten books, but also launched some prominent names, Leonard Cohen, Daryl Hine, George Ellenbogen, Dave Solway, Pierre Coupey, and Seymour Mayne among the rest, all of whom are still active and writing. And then there was the magazine *CIV/n,* which lasted through seven numbers from 1953 to 1955.

CIV/n was edited by Aileen Collins, with the help of her coeditors Wanda and Stanley Rozynski; but advising these editors, in manuscript-reading sessions, were Layton and myself, and sometimes other people willing to help and assist. The title of the magazine came from a letter of Ezra Pound's which I had seen quoted: "CIV/n not a one-man job"—that is, *Civilization,* in order to have it, you must work together and in concert.

After *CIV/n* ceased publication I started the magazine Delta in 1957 and continued single-handed until 1966. ("Civilization" had become a one-man job.) Actually, I bought an old Chandler and Price printing press and installed it in my basement in Verdun, Montreal's working class-suburb. The press was not too noisy, I loved the smell of printer's ink, so that on this press I printed the early numbers of the magazine as well as my own satirical poetry *Laughing Stalks.* Eventually this work became too demanding and I went to a downtown printer for the job.

For publishing books, I started a small press in 1965, *Delta* Canada, with my friends Michael Gnarowski and Glen Siebrasse. Gnarowski was one of my earliest students at the university, then a young man from Shanghai, where his father had run a prosperous business. Through Delta Canada we published some thirty-two titles in the years between 1965 and 1971, a list of poets that includes R.G. Everson, F.R. Scott, Eldon Grier, Gerald Robitaille (who brought us in direct touch with Henry Miller), as well as John Robert Colombo, and Peter van Toorn. The press also brought out my *Collected Poetry* in 1971.

Following Delta Canada, I continued publishing through a small press called DC Books, partly because this name was descended from "Delta Canada" but more so because I had the assistance now of Aileen Collins and the stationery indicated "Dudek / Collins (editors)"; Aileen Collins and I were married in 1970. The press published a short list of interesting poets, new and old, in the next few years, among them Henry Beissel, Avi Boxer, and Laurence Hutchman. The method of publication that began with First Statement Press and Contact Press in Montreal has continued and has spread throughout Canada to such vigorous presses as The House of Anansi, Coach House Press (Toronto), Oberon Press, Quarry Press (Kingston), and many others scattered over the country. In my own view, small presses and magazines represent the effort of a literary minority, such as it is, to make a small separate place for itself and to survive in a commercial society.

My own poetry had continued throughout these years, despite the overwhelming amount of work I had taken on, in teaching, student poetry reading, editing, publishing, printing, as well as magazine and newspaper writing. I was writing regularly for the weekend newspapers, vide my collection of newspaper articles *In Defence of Art*, edited by Aileen Collins. I was also guest-lecturing at numerous conferences and universities; and broadcasting frequently over the CBC (it broadcast and published my heavy lectures *The First Person in Literature)*. Other books resulting from this Chautauqua activity are *Selected Essays and Criticism* and the six lectures in *Technology and Culture*.

The notion that a professorial job is an easy one, or is cut off from the real world, is a misconception among people who have never known a busy professor or have never been near a university. There may be some profs having an easy time of it, but in my local experience I have not seen any. Most of them are harried beyond words. Fortunately, I did not need a vacant mind and perfect leisure in order to write. I wrote when I could and when I had to, which was most of the time, in spare moments between one task and another, during a quiet lunch, or in the evening at home. There is a powerful great self underlying our paltry conscious self, which thinks unceasingly, untiringly, and gives us catar-

Louis Dudek, 1980s.

acts and clusters of words from time to time whether we want them or not. We have to edit this stuff, and dispose of most of it as unusable, but it is the source of our best thinking, and our life's plans, and our hope for the future. It is the source from which I have gotten most of my poetry—or rather, all of my poetry, since I have never written a poem consciously from a prepared plan.

There are two stages in the writing of a poem, as I know it: dumping it out, and then working on it. The first stage involves a certain amount of tension and holding one's breath, but one gets over it quickly, whether in a surge or in several short spurts; the second stage demands a good deal of time. My habit over the years was to write the first draft of a poem and to put it by, then to work on it a few days or a few weeks later. There was not always the free afternoon, or day, to work on a single poem; and in the early days I had often wasted much time laboring over a poem that turned out to be a misguided failure. Leaving a draft to cool for a while saved time, since I would know better after a pause whether the poem was worth laboring on or not.

The result of this two-stage method of writing, however, was that hundreds of poems in rough manuscript and in sketchy drafts collected in my desk drawers and files, or simply among the papers that crowded my desk. When I retired in 1984 I decided to spend some time cleaning up these unfinished poems, destroying some, putting some aside as unusable, and finishing others, no matter how short, as poems fit for publication. This exhausting work occupied me for several years, but I ended with some five hundred poems that could possibly be considered worth preserving. Gradually these poems were divided into three books, and eventually condensed further into two. First, Ken Norris, an energetic editor and poet in his own right, assisted Véhicule Press in selecting from the total a manageable book of 141 pages, which was published under the title *Zembla's Rocks*.

Writing is obviously a mimesis, or imitation, of someone thinking. When we read an essay, we are willing to assume—it is actually our pleasure to assume—that the essay is the thought process of the man writing. He asks a question, pauses, considers various sides of the issue, and perhaps reaches a conclusion. We think this is how he thought the matter through. But actually the essay is a construct; the author designed it carefully to give it that air of naturalness, or reflection—as in Emerson, or Stevenson—that we take to be his way of thinking.

This is also true of the poem, the novel, the prepared lecture, or even the play. It is a construct that conveys to us an intellectual form, that is, the mode of thought, fictive and conventionalized, of a particular individual. Even a depersonalized, self-annihilating, irrational work must do so.

The autobiography of a poet that matters has to do with the writing of poetry. And this can only be shown by citing actual poems to show the road travelled.

Aileen Collins & Louis Dudek, after Dudek received The Order of Canada, Ottawa, 1984.

Photo Courtesy of Aileen Collins

A LOUIS DUDEK BIBLIOGRAPHY

~ POETRY

Unit of Five [With Ronald Hambleton, P.K. Page, Raymond Souster, James Wreford]. Edited by Ronald Hambleton. Ryerson Press, Toronto, 1944.
East of the City. Ryerson Press, Toronto, 1946.
The Searching Image. Ryerson Press, 1952.
Cerberus. [Preface by Louis Dudek]. Contact Press, Toronto, 1952.
Twenty-Four Poems. Contact Press, 1952.
Europe. Laocoon (Contact) Press, 1956. [reprinted by The Porcupine's Quill, 1991]
The Transparent Sea. Contact Press, 1956.
En Mexico. Contact Press, 1958.
Laughing Stalks. Contact Press, 1958.
Atlantis. Delta Canada, Montreal, 1967.
Collected Poetry. Delta Canada, 1971.
Epigrams. Montreal: DC Books, Montreal, 1975.
Selected Poems. Ottawa: Golden Dog Press, Ottawa, 1975.
Cross-Section: Poems 1940-1980. Coach House Press, Toronto, 1980.
Continuation I. Véhicule Press, Montreal, 1981.
Poems From Atlantis. The Golden Dog Press, 1981.
Zembla's Rocks. Véhicule Press, 1986.
Continuation II. Véhicule Press, 1988.
Small Perfect Things. DC Books, 1991.
The Caged Tiger. Empyreal Press, Montreal, 1997.
The Poetry of Louis Dudek: Definitive Edition. Golden Dog Press, 1998.
The Surface of Time. [Includes the long poem "Continuation III"]. Montreal: Empyreal Press, 2000.

~ AUDIO

The Green Beyond: Poems. Phonodisc. CBC Publications, Toronto, 1973.

~ ESSAYS & NON-FICTION

Literature and the Press: A History of Printing, Printed Media, and Their Relation to Literature. Toronto: Ryerson/Contact Press, 1960.
The First Person in Literature: Six Talks for CBC Radio. CBC, 1967.
Autumn. Poetry Goes Public, Calgary1978.
Technology and Culture: Six Lectures. The Golden Dog Press, 1979.
Ideas for Poetry. Véhicule Press, 1983.
Infinite Worlds: The Poetry of Louis Dudek [Ed. Robin Blaser], Véhicule Press, 1988.
In Defense of Art [With an Introduction by Aileen Collins], Quarry Press, 1988.
Paradise: Essays on Myth, Art, and Reality. Montreal: Véhicule Press, 1992.
The Birth of Reason. DC Books, 1994.
1941 Diary. Empyreal Press, Montreal, 1996.
Reality Games. Empyreal Press, 1998.

~ EDITED BY

Canadian Poems (1850-1952) [Edited with Irving Layton]. Contact Press, Toronto, 1952.

The Selected Poems by Raymond Souster. Edited and chosen by Louis Dudek. Contact Press, 1956.

Montréal, Paris d'Amerique/Paris of America [With Michel Regnier]. Ryerson Press (Toronto) & Éditions du Jour (Montréal), 1961.

Poetry of Our Time: An Introduction to Twentieth-Century Poetry, Including Modern Canadian Poetry. The MacMillan Company of Canada Ltd., Toronto, 1966.

The Making of Modern Poetry in Canada [With Michael Gnarowski], Ryerson Press, Toronto, 1967.

Worlds of Poetry: All Kinds of Everything. Clarke, Irwin, Toronto/Vancouver, 1973.

Dk/Some Letters of Ezra Pound. Edited with Notes by Louis Dudek. DC Books, Montreal, 1974.

~ TRANSLATED BY

Graffiti: New Poems in Translation, by Pierre DesRuisseaux. DC Books, Montreal, 2002.

Some Poems of Jean Narrache: Translated and With an Introduction by Louis Dudek. Unpublished manuscript, Montreal, 1999.

~ IN TRANSLATION

Dudek, l'essential: Anthologie portative de Louis Dudek. Trans. and selected by Pierre DesRuisseaux. With an introduction by Michael Gnarowski. Les Éditions Triptyque, Montréal, Québec, 1997.

~ SOME BOOKS ABOUT

It Needs to Be Said [Louis Dudek issue], No. 4, Autumn 1974.

Louis Dudek & Raymond Souster, by Frank Davey. Douglas & McIntyre [Studies in Canadian Literature], Vancouver 1980.

"Louis Dudek: Texts and Essays," edited by B.P. Nichol and Frank Davey in *Open Letter,* Fourth Series, Nos. 8-9 [also known as "The Louis Dudek Issue"], Spring & Summer 1981.

Louis Dudek: A Biographical Introduction to his Poetry, by Susan Stromberg-Stein. The Golden Dog Press, Ottawa, 1983.

Louis Dudek: Essays on His Works. Edited by George Hildebrand. Guernica Editions [Writers Series], Toronto, 2001.

CONTRIBUTORS

JOHN ASFOUR Born in Lebanon in 1945, immigrated to Canada in 1968. Dr. Asfour holds a Ph.D. in English literature from McGill University. Dr. Asfour is a human rights activist and has served as the President of the Canadian Arab Federation (from 1995-2002). He is the author of several poetry collections, the latest of which is *The Fields of My Blood* (Empyreal Press, 1998).

BERNHARD BEUTLER Bernhard Beutler, publicist, born in 1936 in Hamburg. Dr. Phil (PhD) in Hamburg, 1978. Member of the I.F.J. (International Federation of journalists) and of the Académie des Sciences, Belles-Lettres et Arts de Lyon. Distinctions: Médaille d'Or, Académie des Sciences, Belles-Lettres et Arts de Lyon, 194; Chevalier de l'Ordre des Arts et des Lettres, 1994; Chevalier dans l'Ordre des Palmes Académiques, 1995.

MARIANNE BLUGER was born in Ottawa in 1945. She has a B.A. from McGill University and since 1975 has been Executive Secretary Treasurer of the Canadian Writers' Federation. She is a field-naturalist, birder, gardener, dart player, and avid devotee of modern Japanese forms. Her most recent poetry collection is *Scissor, Paper, Woman* (Penumbra Press, 2000).

AILEEN COLLINS Aileen Collins has worked in education for over thirty years as teacher, consultant and curriculum writer. She is currently part of an English Language Arts team that is writing the new curriculum for the elementary and secondary schools of Québec. She has also been known as "the *CIV/n* female" (See *Dk/Some Letters of Ezra Pound. Edited with Notes by Louis Dudek*. Montreal: DC Books, 1974. Letter dated 21/55 from EP to Dk, p. 61).

JOHN ROBERT COLOMBO, regarded as "Canada's Master Gatherer," is the author/editor of over 150 books largely devoted to the lore and literature of Canada, as well as a cultural commentator and communications consultant who has contributed to many of Canada's major newspapers, magazines, and journals. He served as General Editor of *The Canadian Global Almanac,* an 800-page annual of "Facts about Canada and the World" published by Macmillan Canada from 1990 to 1999. Andrei Voznesensky has referred to Colombo's books of poetry as "significant and profound."

ANTONIO D'ALFONSO was born in Montreal. Published his first book in 1973. Founded Guernica Editions in 1978. Founded *Vice Versa* in 1982 (with four other friends), made a few short films and moved to Toronto in 1992. He is the author of over ten books and anthologies, and he was a finalist for the Emile Nelligan Award, 1987, and for the Saint-Sulpice Award, 1999.

PIERRE DESRUISSEAUX is a poet, editor, translator and authority on Quebec popular culture. Born in Sherbrooke, Quebec in 1945, he is the author of numerous volumes of poetry, non-fiction and fiction. His poetry collection *Monème* won the 1989 Governor-General's Award. His 2000 poetry collection, *Graffites,* was translated into English and published by DC Books as *Graffiti: New Poems in Translation* (2002).

STEWART DONOVAN teaches Literature and Film at St. Thomas University in Fredericton, New Brunswick. Poet, novelist and biographer, he is the founding editor of *The Nashwaaak Review.* His biography of R.J. MacSween is forthcoming from McGill-Queen's University Press. At present he is completing a novel set in Cape Breton entitled *Down North With Laura.*

GREGORY DUDEK is an Associate Professor with the School of Computer Science and a member of the McGill Research Centre for Intelligent Machines (CIM). In 2002 he was named a William Dawson Scholar. He is the co-author (with Michael Jenkin) *Computational Principles of Mobile Robotics* (Cambridge University Press, 2000). He resides in Montreal with his wife Krys, and their two children.

STEPHANIE ZUPERKO DUDEK received her MA in Psychology at Columbia University, and her PhD in Psychology at New York University, and has had a long distinguished career in the teaching and practice of psychology. "Louis and I met/ At a McGill University social affair/ Fell in love,/ Were married and a week later left for New York City / With my father's blessings/ To become immersed in an/ Intellectual search via a post-grad education/ And the splendors of New York art/ And metropolitan life." (From Zuperko-Dudek's poem, "To Louis Dudek")

GEORGE ELLENBOGEN was born in Montreal; currently lives in the Boston area where he teaches poetry and directs the Forum for Creative Writing at Bentley College. He is former poetry editor of *Boston Today,* the author of several poetry collections, most recent of which is *The Rhino Gate Poems* (Véhicule Press, 1997), and is the subject of a documentary film, "George Ellenbogen: Canadian Poet in America."

RAYMOND FILIP teaches Music and Literature at John Abbott College. His latest book is entitled *Backscatter: New and Selected Poems* (Guernica Editions, 2001). His work has been selected for inclusion in *The Penguin Treasury of Canadian Popular Songs and Poems* (Penguin, 2003). He is working on an upcoming guitar-cum-poetry performance piece entitled "The Guitar Is Nervous." His golf story "Lonesome Onesome" recently appeared in *Lituanus,* a Baltic Studies publication put out by the University of Chicago.

MICHAEL GNAROWSKI, professor, poet, editor and critic was born in Shanghai, China in 1934. He studied at McGill University (B.A., 1956), Indiana University (1959), the Université de Montréal (M.A., 1960), and received his Ph.D. in English literature from the University of Ottawa in 1967. While an undergraduate at McGill, Gnarowski began to publish his poetry in the magazine, *Yes* (1956-1970) which he co-edited. Literary periodicals with which he was involved or edited include *Le Chien d'or/The Golden Dog* (1970-1972), *Delta,* Golden Dog Press (founded 1971), and Tecumseh Press. He was founding editor of Carleton University Press, and for many years was General Editor of The Carleton Library Series. He was Louis Dudek's friend and colleague for nearly fifty years.

BETTY GUSTAFSON, a retired professional nurse, lives in North Hatley. She is currently assisting Bruce Whiteman in the assembly of research for a biography of her husband, the distinguished Canadian poet Ralph Gustafson, who passed away in 1995.

GEORGE HILDEBRAND left the University of Saskatchewan with his B.A. in English in 1965. Impressed by Frank Scott's convocation address, he eventually ended up at McGill where he earned an M.A. and a Ph.D. Since 1976, he has taught English at Dawson College in Montreal. He also works as a translator and copy editor for the Féderation autonome du collègial; his most recent publication is *Louis Dudek: Essays on His Works* (Guernica, 2001).

LAURENCE HUTCHMAN Laurence Hutchman has published six books of poetry: *The Twilight Kingdom, Explorations, Blue Riders, Foreign National, Emery* and *Beyond Borders.* He has also co-edited with Anne Compton, Ross Leckie, and Robin McGrath Coastlines: *The Poetry of Atlantic Canada.* Louis Dudek published his second book *Explorations* in 1975. He teaches Canadian Literature at the Université de Moncton in Edmundston, New Brunswick.

LIONEL KEARNS makes his home on the West Coast. Over the last 40 years his poetry and stories have appeared in a variety of magazines, anthologies and books. In the early Sixties Kearns was involved with the Tish poets at UBC. From 1966 to 1986 he taught in the English Department at SFU, taking a year out in 1981-2 to be the Writer-in-Residence at Concordia University in Montreal. He was also the first Writer-in-Electronic-Residence (1988) in the Wired Writers (WIER) project in Canadian schools. Kearns latest work can be seen at http://www.lionelkearns.com/convergences.

STEVE LUXTON, Montreal poet, teacher and publisher, was born in Coventry, England. He is a founder of The Montreal Storytellers, as well as an original editor of *The Moosehead Review*. He edited the 1981 short story collection *Saturday Night at the Forum* (1981) and (with Janice LaDuke) the women's poetry anthology *Full Moon* (1983). Along with other volumes of poetry, he is the author of *The Hills that Pass By* (DC, 1987).

STEPHEN MORRISSEY, poet and college professor, is the author of seven books of poetry, including *Mapping the Soul, Selected Poems 1978-1998*. Morrissey was a student of Louis Dudek's at McGill University in the early 1970s. He is working on a new collection of poems, about growing up in Montreal.

KEN NORRIS teaches Canadian literature at the University of Maine. His most recent book is *Hotel Montreal: New And Selected Poems* (Talonbooks, 2001).

STANLEY ROZYNSKI was a cousin and very close friend of Louis Dudek. They grew up a few doors apart in the east end of Montreal and though some twelve years apart in age, remained good friends throughout Louis' life. "Remembering Louis" is also a biography of Stanley and of the influence of LD on his life. Stanley and his wife Wanda live in Way's Mills in the Eastern Townships of Quebec where he makes sculpture and his wife is a potter.

SONJA A. SKARSTEDT poet, painter, editor and publisher, is the author of three volumes of poetry, most recent of which is *Beautiful Chaos* (Empyreal Press, 2000), and a play, *Saint Francis of Esplanade* (Empyreal, 2001).

RAYMOND SOUSTER, Officer of the Order of Canada, a founding member and Life Member of the League of Canadian Poets, was born in Toronto on January 15, 1921. His work first appeared in *Unit of Five* from Ryerson Press in 1944. He is the author of over eighteen books of poetry and anthologies, and he won the Governor-General's Award for Poetry in 1964.

TOBIE STEINHOUSE was born in Montreal. She was a founding member of the Atelier libre de recherches graphiques de Montréal and of The Guilde Graphique. She has won many awards and is a member of the Royal Canadian Academy of Arts. "Poetry is a vital source of inspiration for me, a way of communicating inner visions and feelings. It creates a world of serenity, leaving my reveries free to roam while safeguarding my thoughts."

RONALD SUTHERLAND was born and raised in the largely French-speaking east end of Montreal. He taught at l'Université de Sherbrooke and founded the discipline of Comparative Canadian Literature. He has published numerous scholarly articles and books, humourous vignettes for newspapers and two novels, one of which, *Lark des Neiges (Snow Lark* in paperback) became the feature film *Suzanne*. His most recent novel is *How Elvis Saved Quebec* (Borealis, 2002).

TODD SWIFT was born in Montreal on Good Friday, 1966 and presently lives in Paris, France. He has written over sixty hours of TV, mainly with Thor Bishopric, for HBO and others. His writing has appeared in an international array of publications and he is the co-editor of several anthologies. In 2002, DC Books released his new poetry collection, *Café Alibi*. In 2003, he published *100 Poets Against the War* (Salt Publishing), which now holds the record for "the fastest poetry anthology ever assembled and disseminated."

MOHAMUD SIAD TOGANE is a Somali-born poet who has lived in Montreal for over thirty years. He is the author of *The Bottle and the Bushman* (The Muses' Company, 1986) and his second poetry collection, *This Devil's Concoction of Clans* is slated for the 2003 fall season.

COLLETT TRACEY Collett Tracey teaches Canadian Literature at Carleton University in Ottawa. She undertook her Ph.D. (2002) through the Université de Montréal, under the direction of Dr. Michael Gnarowski and Dr. Howard Roiter for which she researched First Statement Press, Contact Press and Delta Canada—three important little presses that spanned the rise and development of modernist poetry in Canada. It was through this work that she came to know Louis Dudek, with whom she frequently met for interviews, and who was extremely generous with his time and support.

TONY TREMBLAY is an Associate Professor of Canadian and Cultural Studies at St. Thomas University in Fredericton, NB. Some of his recent work on Louis Dudek includes "Exploring the Influence of Ezra Pound on the Cultural Production of Louis Dudek" *(ECW* 74); "Louis Dudek and the Question of Quebec" (forthcoming in *English Poetry in Quebec,* 1976-2001); and "Louis Dudek: Canada's 'Ideogram of Reality'" *(The Antigonish Review* 117).

BRUCE WHITEMAN was born near Toronto in 1952. He is currently the Head Librarian of the William Andrews Clark Memorial Library at UCLA. Published extensively as a poet, scholar, cultural historian and book reviewer, his recent books include *Visible Stars: New and Selected Poems* (1995) and *The Invisible World Is in Decline* (2000).

CAROLYN ZONAILO is a poet who was born in Vancouver, British Columbia, and has lived for the past dozen years in Montreal. Zonailo is of Doukhobor heritage; she has published nine books of poetry, her most recent *The Goddess in the Garden,* Ekstasis Editions, 2002.

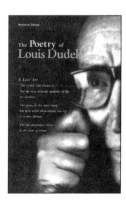

Lous Dudek receiving The Canadian Writers Award, at Ben's Delicatessen, Montreal, Friday March 2, 1990.

Like a streetcar, like a terrible tractor,

It is all rumbling and tumbling in me when you are gone.

from "At Parting" *(The Poetry of Louis Dudek: Definitive Edition)* p.1 "Night Scene"

Reading that is not edifying is [likely] wasteful.

Imagination is a cocktail we drink to be drained.

Deep sleep here

THE TWENTIETH SPEAKER

Putting it there may put on an extra ... count... gratis ...

What art is for — the ephemerals

[SHELFLIST / BORROWER NOTIFIED / LOST / STACK / UL / CAT / DEPT / OUT] ...

PS 1853

James R. Randall
26? Harvard Street
Cambridge, Mass. 02138

Reading
is thinking the thoughts of another man.
Given Gods can prove useful.
Aisai, the dissolution of the world.

Our final verdict is never in
In literature, the final verdict
is never in.

We are, some of us, fated in our
last years to defend the system
which in our youth we ~~set~~ ~~were out~~
to destroy.
(the Edith Wharton)

(I used to be concerned about my ~~body~~)
but the dissolution of the world!

All we have is
the actual up.
and the divine
is something we
see in it,

writing books is for, in a
sense, people to read them that [don't]
kills you.
Sept 16/79

600 billion a year
spent on armaments
in the world 1980

The [only] myself ~~just then~~
so qui me because the and thing found to
appear.
May 1980
There is what meets a thing or fact dripping.

Democracy
MEDIOCRITY
Mediocracy

Is the sun was shown
till glom
... when found th ...

Merci
Loris Smith